Locating Lost Family Members & Friends

Modern genealogical research
techniques for locating the people
of your past and present

Kathleen W. Hinckley

BETTERWAY BOOKS
CINCINNATI, OHIO

Locating Lost Family Members & Friends. Copyright © 1999 by Kathleen W. Hinckley. Manufactured in the United States of America. All rights reserved. No part of this book may be reproduced in any form or by any electronic or mechanical means including information storage and retrieval systems without permission in writing from the publisher, except by a reviewer, who may quote brief passages in a review. Published by Betterway Books, an imprint of F&W Publications, Inc., 1507 Dana Avenue, Cincinnati, Ohio 45207. (800) 289-0963. First edition.

Other fine Betterway Books are available from your local bookstore or direct from the publisher.

03 02 01 00 99   5 4 3 2 1

Library of Congress Cataloging-in-Publication Data

Hinckley, Kathleen W.
    Locating lost family members & friends / Kathleen W. Hinckley.
        p.   cm.
    Includes bibliographical references and index.
    ISBN 1-55870-503-1 (alk. paper)
    1. Genealogy. 2. United States—Genealogy Handbooks, manuals, etc. 3. Missing persons—Investigation—United States. I. Title. II. Title: Locating lost family members and friends.
CS14.H56 1999
929′.1′072073—dc21

99-27408
CIP

Associate editor: Christine Doyle
Interior designer: Sandy Kent
Cover designer: Stephanie Redman
Production coordinator: Erin Boggs
Cover illustration by Jeff Ernst

In memory of

MARY N. SPEAKMAN, CG
(1920-1996)

my friend and mentor

About the Author

Kathleen Hinckley, a Certified Genealogical Record Specialist, has located hundreds of living persons for attorneys, heir searchers, and adoptees for over fifteen years by combining her specialized skills as a genealogist and private investigator. She owns and operates a research business specializing in locating living persons throughout the United States.

A nationally known genealogist, she gives workshops and lectures on the subject of locating living persons. Hinckley is the author of "Tracking Twentieth-Century Ancestors" in *The Source: A Guidebook of American Genealogy*, Revised Edition, and has written several articles published in the *Association of Professional Genealogist Quarterly*, the *National Genealogical Society Quarterly* and the Family TreeMaker Web site. Hinckley is Executive Secretary of the Association of Professional Genealogists and a senior member of the Professional Private Investigators Association of Colorado.

Acknowledgments

This book would not have been possible without the clients who shared their personal stories and gave me the opportunity to learn from experience. Each case was unique, and every client taught me the value of friendships and family relationships. I know that the research results changed many lives, but the clients may not realize that their brief entry into my life affected me as well.

A special thank-you goes to William Brohaugh, Editorial Director of Betterway Books. He did not know that I'd been planning this book for ten years; when he approached me about writing for Betterway, his timing was perfect. He opened the door that I needed to reach my goal. Thank you, Bill.

I am a better researcher than a writer. The organized, smooth presentation of material in this book would not have been possible without the critique and comments from my friends and colleagues who read my manuscript. Sharon K. Boatwright, MA; Kay Germain Ingalls, CGRS; and Frank Ranieri read every word in every chapter. Others who read portions of my book include Sheila Benedict, CGRS; Jake Gehring; Birdie Holsclaw; James Jeffrey; Suzanne McVetty, CG; and Craig Scott, CGRS.

Thank you, too, to Vincent Ranieri and Glen Westberg for permitting the use of their WWII military discharge and WWII draft registration, respectively, as illustrations.

Icons Used in This Book

Brick Wall Buster
How to turn dead ends into opportunities

Printed Source
Directories, books, pamphlets and other paper archives

Case Study
Examples of this book's advice at work

Quotes
Useful words direct from the experts

CD Source
Databases and other information available on CD-ROM

Reminder
"Don't-Forget" items to keep in mind

\di'fin\ *vb*
Definitions
Terminology and jargon explained

Research Tip
Ways to make research more efficient

For More Info
Where to turn for more in-depth coverage

See Also
Where in this book to find related information

Idea Generator
Techniques and prods for further thinking

Sources
Where to go for information, supplies, etc.

Important
Information and tips you can't overlook

Supplies
Advice on day-to-day office tools

Internet Source
Where on the web to find what you need

Technique
How to conduct research, solve problems, and get answers

Library/Archive Source
Repositories that might have the information you need

Timesaver
Shaving minutes and hours off the clock

Microfilm Source
Information available on microfilm

Tip
Ways to make research more efficient

Money Saver
Getting the most out of research dollars

Warning
Stop before you make a mistake

Notes
Thoughts, ideas and related insights

Table of Contents At a Glance

Table of Contents

Introduction

Friends drift apart.
Families quarrel and separate.
Babies are adopted.

Years fly by, then loved ones want to find each other.

A re you looking for someone? If so, you are not alone. People want to reconnect in today's disconnected society. The reasons vary tremendously. A Vietnam veteran wanted to find a buddy from the war and repay the twenty dollars he had borrowed. A computer specialist's younger brother was a drug addict in the 1960s and left the family. He wanted to find him and see if he was OK. A thirty-year-old woman wanted to find her father, whom she had not seen since she was ten years old.

Your reasons for finding someone may be different, but the sources and techniques for locating them will be similar. This book will teach you how to be your own detective. You'll not only discover how to search for people on the Internet, but you'll learn how to access public records in courthouses and how to find information in libraries and archives.

There is a hidden bonus in this book. The sources and research methodology described throughout the book are used in traditional genealogical research; therefore, **Locating Lost Family Members & Friends is also a guide to getting started in genealogy**. When you start climbing your family tree, you begin with the present and work backward in time. The first one hundred years of your research will be in the twentieth century—the focus of this book.

Whether you are trying to locate a living person or climbing your family tree, *Locating Lost Family Members & Friends* will give you the confidence and skills to find people. I hope you enjoy the challenge and thrill of research, and I wish you success in finding your friends and family.

Important

ONE

Beginning the Search

Locating a living person can feel like looking for a needle in a haystack. You sift through records and databases that list hundreds, thousands, even millions of people, yet you do not find the person you seek. Sometimes you think it's the right person, but after contacting him, you learn he just has the same name. Your head begins to spin. The more you look, the more discouraged you become. By organizing your search, your efforts will be more focused and successful. This book will describe several avenues that your search can take. An organized search will point you down the proper roads.

BEGIN WITH HOMEWORK

Let's pretend you are searching for a man named John Foster who resided in Atlanta in 1976. You check the current telephone books on CD-ROM (or the Internet), but there are eighty-two John Fosters in the state of Georgia. You need more information. You need to do some homework.

Knowing John's middle name, the name of his wife (if he's married), his occupation, his approximate age or a previous address would help your search. Your homework is to examine Atlanta city directories, marriage records, real estate transactions and voter registrations.

The more resources you use to gather information, the more you learn about John Foster. The city directories and marriage, real estate and voter records provide **identifiers—that is, facts that separate one person from another.** John Foster now becomes John Robert Foster III, who married Ruth Marie Williams on 30 May 1978. The Atlanta voter registrations provide exact dates of birth for both John and Ruth. They purchased a home in 1980 and sold it in 1990. The power of attorney in the real estate records indicates John moved to Miami, Florida. Our search jumps from 1976 in Atlanta to 1990 in Miami.

You should be able to find John easily in Miami records, but you cannot find anyone that fits the profile. Your head begins to spin again, but the solution is

\di'fin\ *vb*

Definitions

to do more homework. In this case, you interview former neighbors.

One of the neighbors knows the reason John and Ruth sold their home—they were getting a divorce. The divorce records indicate Ruth legally changed her name back to Ruth Marie Williams. A search of the Atlanta marriage records reveals she was married in 1992 to Albert Schmachtenberg. Albert and Ruth are easy to find since their surname is unusual. They are listed in the telephone directory. An interview with Ruth reveals that John is behind in his child support payments. Ruth gives us his last known address in Denver.

The Denver address is an apartment building. John is no longer a resident, and the apartment manager will not disclose any information about him. You are so close, yet so far. Will you ever find John? You need to do more homework—visit the Department of Motor Vehicles.

John's driver's record and motor vehicle registration have different addresses. The driver's record shows the same address the ex-wife gave us, but the vehicle registration gives a new address. An interview with the apartment manager there confirms that John is a current resident. John Robert Foster III has finally been located!

ORGANIZE YOUR SEARCH

Researching records is a waste of time if you don't stay organized. It is critical to record in a central place the time period searched (for example, "searched marriage records 1965–1975"), the spelling variations examined (for example, "checked Wilson and Willson") and the results of every step. We all organize differently. It is more important that you *do* organize than *how* you organize. Below are a few examples of how to maintain order in the chaos that will result from complex searches.

Telephone Log For each call, record the date, the telephone number, to whom you spoke and the results of the interview.

Research Log Record the exact title and time period of the records searched and results of the search. For example: "Searched unpublished card index to obituaries in the *Rocky Mountain News*, 1945–1965, located at the Denver Public Library. Found one reference for a John Willson who died 10 December 1950; no references for John Wilson."

Correspondence Log Keep a list of when and why letters were written to libraries, archives, courthouses or families.

Chronological and Geographical History Prepare a chronological and geographical summary of the person being researched. The capsule may shed light on ideas for research or reveal time periods that need completion. For example,

1922 Born in Minneapolis, Minnesota
1930 Moved with family to Des Moines, Iowa
1940 Graduated from Des Moines High School
1942 Married in Sioux City, Iowa
1943 Son born in Sioux City, Iowa
1945 Joined the Army, WWII

PREPARE A WORK SHEET

Pulling together the facts about the targeted person is vital to successful research. A city directory will give you an address or the name of a spouse; a marriage record may provide the names of parents or siblings; and a voter registration may give an exact date of birth. When you begin to search for a driving record, you may need the date of birth. If you haven't prepared a summary for the individual, you may forget that you even have the date.

A simple work sheet can help organize the facts you've found, as well as highlight the holes that need researching. The work sheet also provides a tool to record incomplete or estimated information, such as names of family members, former addresses and dates of birth. An example of a filled-in work sheet appears on page 5. A blank sheet that you can photocopy and use appears in Appendix G on page 167.

The work sheet can be redesigned and individualized according to your style or type of search. Write *facts* in red ink on the work sheet; that will make it clear that the remaining information is not documented or confirmed. If a piece of information is speculative, put a question mark after the data.

The dates and places are the most important data on your work sheet. You will select types and dates of records based on this data. If a date is off by five years, it could seriously affect your research results. My experience suggests that most people are not very good at estimating dates. For example, they will say that a grandparent died "about five years ago," when, in fact, the grandparent died ten years ago. If you only search death records using the five-year estimate, you will not find the record. Accurate estimates are critical.

To prevent errors in your date estimates, try to correlate the date with an event that is more dateable. For example, the person you seek married Susan Smith in Columbus, Ohio, the same year your son graduated from high school. Perhaps you can relate the date to a sporting event (the Broncos won the Super Bowl that year), what car you were driving, where you were employed, or a news event (the O.J. Simpson trial).

The Information You'll Collect

Every tidbit of information you have about the person has the potential to be valuable in the research. Here's a list of items on the work sheet with explanations of why the information may be important:

- **Full Name** Some individuals reverse their first and middle name or are known only by a middle name, but are listed in public records with the full legal name. Some records may also be indexed by a nickname. Therefore, every possible variation of a person's name is important in a search.
- **Variants of Surname** Names can be misspelled and incorrectly indexed.
- **Social Security Number** The first three digits reveal the individual's state of residence when he obtained the Social Security number (see chapter seven). Some driver's records can only be accessed by a Social Security number.
- **Date of Birth** Driver's records, voter registrations, school records and many other records can be searched with more accuracy if a birth date is known.

A Useful Form You Can Reproduce

For a full-sized blank copy of the Research Worksheet form, see page 167. You are free to photocopy this form for personal use.

Research Tip

RESEARCH WORK SHEET

Full Name _Alfred John Green (Nicknames: Al and Jack)_
First, middle, last, nickname, maiden name

Spelling Variants of Surname _Greene_

Social Security Number _____

Date and Place of Birth _About 1945, Chicago (?)_
If exact date of birth is unknown; give approximate five-year range

Physical Description _6', brown eyes_

Marital Status _still single in 1975_
Name of spouse(s) or ex-spouse(s) and date of marriage(s) and divorce(s), if applicable

Occupation(s) _engineer_

Employers _____
Include dates and addresses if known

Last Known Address _1975—Seattle_

As many as possible. If exact address unknown, list city and/or state. Include dates of former addresses.

Prior Telephone Number(s) _____

Education _1964—attended Univ. of Colorado_
High school, occupational, college. Include years attended and whether graduated.

Military Service _Army, Vietnam_
Branch, rank, dates, place of discharge, serial number

Religion _Catholic_

Hobbies _Ski_

Financial Status _____

Children: Names, Birth Dates and Birthplaces _unknown_

_____

_____

Name/Address/Telephone of Friends _____

_____

_____

Family Information
   For each sibling: name, birth date, last known address, marital status (marriage[s], names of spouse[s], ex-spouse[s]), date and place of death.
   For parents/stepparents: names, birth dates, last known address(es), marriage(s), dates and places of death
   For children: marriages
older brother: George Green, Jr.
Father: George Green (Chicago?)

_____

Signature _____
(Photocopy from marriage record, deeds or court documents)

- **Place of Birth** If the research results in a dead end, it is sometimes beneficial to begin with the birth of the individual and research the parents and/or siblings.
- **Physical Description** A physical description may be useful when determining if the person on a record fits the correct profile.
- **Marital Status and Dates of Marriage/Divorce** Marriage and divorce records provide information that can advance a search, such as exact birth dates, dates and places of previous marriages, military information, names of parents, names of witnesses who may be family members and religious denomination.
- **Occupation** The type of occupation gives clues to memberships (e.g., in unions) or professional licenses.
- **Employers** Some employers will confirm if an individual is currently employed. They may also indicate why a person was terminated or if he was transferred to another division or location.
- **Last Known Addresses and Dates** Using this information, you can research real estate and tax assessor records or interview landlords and neighbors.
- **Prior Telephone Numbers** Researching the telephone number may reveal the number was listed in the name of a friend or relative. If the person did this in the past, she may repeat this behavior.
- **Education** Information on attendance at high school, trade school or college will lead to research in yearbooks, alumni association records, school archives and class reunion data.
- **Military Service** Military records are confidential for seventy-five years. The data may be helpful in using military locator services or finding buddies that attended any past military reunions.
- **Religion** Churches sometimes cooperate in searches. Baptisms, marriages and transfers of membership can provide clues or data important to the search.
- **Hobbies** A strong interest in a hobby may provide clues to memberships.
- **Financial Status** A strong or weak financial status will suggest research into liens, real estate holdings or bankruptcy records.
- **Names and Birth Dates of Children** If you cannot find the person, perhaps you can find the children, who will likely know the whereabouts of their parent.
- **Friends** Interview friends to gather more data, such as a current address.
- **Family Information** Researching the family will help gather data needed to locate a living person.
- **Signature** Comparing signatures can sometimes prove identity.

RECORD FAMILY INFORMATION AND RELATIONSHIPS

No one is an island. We have parents and grandparents, siblings, children, aunts, uncles and cousins. Sometimes your research will temporarily focus on other family members in order to locate the person you seek. For example, if you are locating an individual whose last known address dates from the 1950s, you may have better success by tracking the parents of the targeted person. In researching the parents, you discover the father died in 1965. His newspaper obituary will most likely give the residence (city and state) of the survivors. Your research then jumps from a last known address in 1950 to a different address in 1965.

Genealogists are excellent people finders because they research *whole families*. Some organize their ancestry data onto family group sheets that summarize the basic facts (birth date and place, marriage/divorce data, death date and place) of the parents and children. Although these forms were created to organize ancestral data, they can also help you organize facts when searching for the living. The arrangement of the data upon family group sheets may vary, but the different versions include the same data.

Family group sheets can be downloaded on the Internet at www.everton .com/charts/freeform.html and www.familytreemaker.com/fgs.html or can be purchased from genealogy supply vendors such as

Supplies

Ancestry
(800) ANCESTRY ([800] 262-3787)
www.ancestry.com

Everton Publishers
(800) 443-6325
www.everton.com

National Genealogical Society
(703) 525-0052
www.ngsgenealogy.org/

Family group sheets are also created by genealogy software. **The most common genealogy software programs include**

Sources

Family Tree Maker	www.familytreemaker.com
Ultimate Family Tree	www.uftree.com/uft/uft.html
The Master Genealogist	www.whollygenes.com
PAF	www.genealogy.org/~paf/
Reunion for MAC	www.leisterpro.com/
Generations	www.sierra.com/titles/genealogy/
(formerly Reunion for Windows)	bot.html

TIME TO DO THE RESEARCH

Now the fun begins. We've organized the information we know about the person and can begin collecting documents that give us more data.

The process of locating living people is not a strict formula. A series of steps might work for one search, but not the next one. You need flexibility and

Technique

TEN BASIC RESEARCH RULES

1. Stay organized.

2. Work with *facts*, not guesses.

3. Question the accuracy of every fact on every document. Errors do exist.

4. Never assume. Prove it instead.

5. Analyze the evidence again and again and again. When you reach a dead end, go back to what you know about a person and start over.

6. Do not rely solely on computer databases.

7. Do not rush the research or jump to hasty conclusions.

8. Do not work in a vacuum. Librarians, clerks, genealogists, archivists, family members and private investigators can assist you.

9. Keep an open mind.

10. Accept the fact that some people cannot be found.

---

creativity to pull information from records and put it together in a logical order.

The balance of this book will provide information on sources to help in your search. You are putting a puzzle together piece by piece. Sometimes the smallest piece of information is what makes the picture complete. Keep your eyes open; you never know what you might find!

TWO

The Telephone Directory

Sometimes a search can be simple, but we skip the obvious and immediately launch into a complex research strategy. Why make the search difficult? The person you are seeking just might be listed in the local telephone directory. The availability of nationwide telephone directories on CD-ROM and the Internet makes this a particularly valuable first step when looking for someone.

If you do not find the person listed in a telephone directory, but you have a former address, try calling a neighbor. Some directories, particularly those available on CD-ROM, allow address searches. An interview with a neighbor may advance your research if she knows why, when or where the individual moved.

Research Tip

The telephone book is particularly useful when researching unusual surnames.

TYPES OF TELEPHONE DIRECTORIES

Gone are the days of one official telephone book published by the local telephone company. Today we have the official directory created by the telephone company and unofficial directories created by commercial firms (using mailing lists and public records). They are published on paper, CD-ROM, microfiche and the Internet.

U.S. Telephone Directories on the Internet

Because the databases supporting Internet directories vary, a thorough search should include as many databases as possible. A test search for me and for my parents, two brothers and nephew, who all live in the same city, proved the point. As you will see in the table on page 10, I was not listed in Lookup USA, and the Four11 directory listed me as K. (rather than Kathleen) Hinckley. The search for my parents, brothers and nephew (the Westbergs) revealed that

Directory	Information Vendor	URL	Hinckley Search	Westbergs Searches
AnyWho		http://www.anywho.com/	Standard Listing	Standard Listings
Bigfoot		http://www.bigfoot.com/	Standard Listing	Standard Listings
Four11	Metromail	http://four11.com/	Listed as K. Hinckley	Standard Listings
InfoSpace		http://www.infospace.com/	Standard Listing	Standard Listings
Lookup USA		http://www.lookupusa.com/	NOT LISTED	Standard Listings
pc411		http://pc411.com/	Standard Listing	Gave first name of mother and sister-in-law; other directories did not.
Switchboard	Database America	http://www.switchboard.com/	Standard Listing	One brother not listed
WhoWhere		http://whowhere.com/	Standard Listing	Standard Listings

Internet Source

Switchboard did not list one brother and pc411 gave names of wives not found in any of the other directories.

A current list of telephone directories on the Internet can be found on the Web site "Telephone Directories on the Web," at http://contractjobs.com/tel/. This site identifies white pages and yellow pages in the U.S., as well as nearly fifty foreign countries.

Most Internet directories are searchable by name only. There are a few, however, that provide search capabilities for address or telephone number. This is important when compiling a list of neighbors or when you only have an individual's telephone number.

Telephone searches are becoming more and more sophisticated, particularly using the Internet. But beware of claims made by software developers. One shareware program claimed it could search up to twenty different directories concurrently on the Internet. The program, however, did not produce the same results as my directory-by-directory search. One brother was listed in seven directories in the individual directory search, but was not even found in the shareware program's search.

U.S. Telephone Directories on CD-ROM

CD Source

Some of the telephone directories on the Web are also available on CD-ROM. The advantages of having telephone databases on CD-ROM are convenience and the ability to archive outdated versions (see page 11). A CD-ROM directory also allows more search capabilities, such as sorting by county or business type. CD-ROM directories can be purchased at their publishers' Web sites or at stores that sell software. **The two best-known CD-ROM phone directories** are InfoUSA (http://infousa.com) and PhoneDisk Powerfinder (http://www.hallogr am.com/mailers/fonedisc/pro.html). These directories are updated at least twice a year; be certain you purchase the latest version.

Searching for my own listing on a CD-ROM directory uncovered a problem that may occur often. I was listed twice at my street address (once as Kathleen Hinckley and again as my business name); however, one of the addresses listed my city as Broomfield rather than Arvada and had an incorrect zip code. When I did a "neighbor search," some of my neighbors were listed, but not all were because of the error in name of city. This proves the point that you must examine directories slowly and carefully and try a variety of search methods.

OUTDATED TELEPHONE DIRECTORIES

Although a current telephone directory identifies the whereabouts of an individual, you will also need to conduct historical research. As explained in chapter one, the more data you can collect about an individual, the better your chances for a successful search. For example, if you begin with a last known address from 1960, it can be difficult to leap forward nearly forty years without some knowledge of residence history. By examining each telephone directory from 1960 to the present, you may be able to identify address changes. This information will assist in searching other public records. City directories (see chapter three) are a better tool for this type of research, but many communities are not represented with a city directory. Telephone directories, on the other hand, are published for every town or city, regardless of size.

Finding outdated telephone directories is not easy. Directories are printed on low-quality paper and are intended for short-term use. Most libraries only maintain an inventory of current directories. The directories can, however, be located with some persistence. Logical places to inquire would be the local public libraries, local and state historical societies and genealogical society libraries. Some university libraries also have outdated Phonefiche or directory collections.

The Library of Congress has some old telephone directories for the U.S. and more than one hundred foreign countries, but the collection is extremely erratic. For example, according to their catalog on the Internet (http://lcweb.loc.gov/catalog/), they have telephone directories for Fort Wayne, Indiana, for 1933 and Gary, Indiana, for 1930 to 1942, but no other years and no other Indiana cities.

Noncurrent paper telephone directories at the Library of Congress can be accessed in the Local History and Genealogy Reading Room by filling out a call slip using "Telephone Directory" as the call number, the town and state as the title, and the years needed as the volume numbers. Pre-1976 telephone directories for Alabama, Alaska, Arizona, Arkansas and California have been microfilmed and can only be accessed in the Microform Reading Room. Directories for New York City and the surrounding area published from 1878 to 1959 are also in the Microform Reading Room. The goal of the microfilming project by the Library of Congress is to film all directories published before 1976, which was when Phonefiche began.

Americana Unlimited (P.O. Box 50447, 1701 N. Eleventh Ave., Tucson, AZ 85703; (520) 792-3453) **sells 16mm microfilm copies of the following telephone directories:**

Case Study

ADOPTION CASE SOLVED WITH THE TELEPHONE DIRECTORY

An adoptee, born in Colorado, knew his birth mother's name and approximate age. He did not know where the birth mother was born, nor did he have any other information about her family. An advantage in this case was that the surname was very unusual. Checking the Social Security Death Index (see chapter seven), we discovered that at least 80 percent of people with that surname had died in Michigan. A nationwide search of a telephone database gave similar statistics. Therefore, we concentrated our search in Michigan. After two hours of telephoning families in Michigan, we interviewed relatives of the birth mother and identified and located her. She was a widow residing in Colorado, had not given birth to any other children, and attended the same church as the adoptee. Mother and son were reunited the next day.

Microfilm Source

California	Los Angeles Exchange	1934
	Los Angeles Extended Area	1934, 1937–1938, 1940–1942
	Los Angeles and Los Angeles County	1926, 1929–1931
	Los Angeles County	1933–1934, 1936–1941
Illinois	Chicago	1907–1942
New York City	Bronx and Manhattan	1913, 1915, 1921–1922, 1924–1928
	Bronx	1929–1937
	Brooklyn and Queens	1913, 1915, 1921–1922, 1924–1925
	Brooklyn	1929, 1933-1941
	Manhattan	1929–1942
	Queens	1929–1930, 1932–1941
	Staten Island	1913, 1915, 1921–1922, 1924–1925, 1929, 1933–1938

Some inventories of telephone directories are beginning to appear on the Internet. For example, on the Kansas State Historical Society's Web site (http://history.cc.ukans.edu/heritage/kshs/library/tele-a.htm), the inventory lists hundreds of telephone directories for Kansas towns. The directories do not circulate through interlibrary loan, however; you need to visit the library or hire a professional genealogist.

Telephone companies usually archive outdated telephone directories, but even this practice is being discontinued. In 1990, the Telecommunications History Group, Inc. (1005 Seventeenth St., or P.O. Box 8719, Denver, CO 80201-8719; [303] 296-1221) was created to preserve the history of the telecommunications industry. **Their collection includes nearly eleven thousand telephone directories published from 1890 to 1992** by Bell Companies in Arizona, Colorado, Idaho, Montana, New Mexico, Oregon, Utah, Washington and Wyoming. In addition, they are actively procuring directories from the former Northwestern Bell states of Iowa, Minnesota, Nebraska, North Dakota and South Dakota. The facility is open to individuals doing research.

Printed Source

RESEARCHING TELEPHONE DIRECTORIES

When researching telephone directories, it is important to record the name, address *and* the telephone number, because when an individual moves, he does not always change his telephone number. This can be particularly important when researching a common surname. If you find a listing is not exactly as it was the year before, the telephone number can verify that the person listed at the two different addresses is actually the same.

The format of the listing may also change occasionally, which also makes the telephone number an important element. Widows often change their telephone listing to their husband's initials or their own initials. For example:

Year	Name Listed	Address Listed	Telephone Number Listed
1960	Smith, Robert L	3125 Lawrence	555-1234
1961	Smith, Robert L	3125 Lawrence	555-1234
1962	Smith, RL (Robert L Smith died in 1961, and his widow, Beatrice, changed the listing to "RL Smith.")	3125 Lawrence	555-1234
1963	Smith, B (Beatrice changed her listing to "B Smith.")	3125 Lawrence	555-1234
1964	Smith, B (Beatrice moved to 2905 Fairfax, but her telephone number remained the same; therefore, you know you are tracking the correct individual.)	2905 Fairfax	555-1234

Another advantage of searching outdated telephone directories is the possibility of obtaining unlisted telephone numbers. In other words, an individual may have a listed telephone number for a few years, then decide to change to a nonpublished or nonlisted status.

NONLISTED AND NONPUBLISHED TELEPHONE NUMBERS

About 35 percent of Americans have nonlisted or nonpublished telephone numbers. A nonlisted number is omitted from the official telephone directory, but is available from directory assistance. A nonpublished number is not published in the directory and not available from directory assistance.

When you don't find a listing for the individual you seek, call directory assistance. If the number is nonlisted, the operator will give you the information; however, if the number is nonpublished, the operator will play a recorded message that says, "At the customer's request, the number is nonpublished and not listed in our records."

Even if you hear this message, at least you have verification that the person is living and residing in that particular city. If he owns real estate, you can obtain his address from the tax assessor's office (see chapter ten) and write a letter. If the individual is renting, you may be able to obtain an address from a voter registration (see chapter fourteen) or a driver's record (see chapter fifteen).

TELEPHONE DIRECTORY RESEARCH TIPS

- Search *both* the official telephone directories (published by the telephone company) and the various directories published by commercial firms on CD-ROM or the Internet. Compare and analyze the results.
- Check all spelling variations of the surname. Example:

Kaiser
Kayser
Keiser
Kiser
Kizer

- **Check all variations of the person's name, including nicknames and a middle name.** Example:
  Parker, William
  Parker, William A.
  Parker, W.
  Parker, W. A.
  Parker, Will
  Parker, Bill
  Parker, Billy
  Parker, Andrew (first name dropped; middle name used)
  Parker, Andy
  Parker, A.

  Refer to Christine Rose's *Nicknames: Past and Present*, 3d edition (see appendix E) to help identify possible origins of a nickname. As Christine Rose cautions, "If the record shows 'Willie,' is it really William? What about Wilfred or Willard or Willis or Wilmer or Wilton or Wiley, or even a female called Wilhelmina?"

- Use the advanced search technique found in some CD-ROM telephone directories to search by county. You can create a list of all families with a surname who reside in the same county and increase the odds of finding persons related to each other.

- Scan the listings for typographical errors, particularly in directories not prepared by the telephone company.

- If you do not find a listing in the husband's name, check for a listing in the wife's name. (A trick used by someone avoiding bill collectors is to register the telephone in the wife's name, the wife's maiden name or the wife's hyphenated name to make it more difficult to find him.)

- Study all listings under the surname, just in case there is an unusual twist to the style of listing. For example, the listing may be "Parker, Jane and William" rather than "Parker, William." The person may have a listing under an unusual nickname, such as Blue. One case was solved upon discovering that the targeted individual had a listing under the name of her cat. People can be creative in covering their tracks.

- Search for the listing in both the residential white pages and the business white pages. Many self-employed individuals (or their spouses) are listed by name in the business white pages, but not in the residential white pages.

- Check the yellow pages when searching for a professional such as an attorney, doctor, dentist, realtor, insurance agent or accountant. A business telephone number may be listed under the person's name, but not a residential number.

- More than fifty-six million Americans own cell phones, contributing to the 900 percent increase in telephone numbers since 1986. Telephone numbers for cell phones, faxes, modems and pagers are not in the white pages. Therefore, tracking a person via a telephone number obtained from a source other than a directory can often lead to dead ends. These numbers might be listed in CD-ROM or Internet directories, thus providing a clue to the whereabouts of the individual.

- When you find a telephone listing, dial the directory assistance operator to confirm that the listing is current. The Internet and CD-ROM telephone directories are notoriously outdated.

THREE

City Directories and Householder Directories

Case Study

MISSING HEIR SEARCH: CITY DIRECTORY CRACKS THE CASE

Our search for Jacob and Janice Smith (surname fictitious) was not progressing. Marriage, death and divorce searches produced nothing. When the city directory was consulted, we discovered we had been using the *middle* names of the targeted couple. Their full names were Edgar Jacob Smith and Estelle Janice Smith. Using this new information, we were able to learn of their deaths and subsequently locate their heirs.

T he city directory is *the* most valuable source used to locate people. It can provide such information as full name, exact address, name of spouse, employment data and names of relatives residing at the same address. In other words, city directories provide many important identifiers about individuals, and the more you know about the person you are tracking, the higher your success rate.

WHAT IS A CITY DIRECTORY?

City directories have been published for more than 150 years in nearly all cities in the U.S. They are similar to telephone directories, but contain much more. City directories list the name, address and place of employment for every adult within a household, as well as the name of the spouse, home ownership and marital status (for women). City directories also list names and addresses of cemeteries, churches, fraternal organizations, hospitals, insurance companies, newspapers and schools.

For cities, these directories are issued annually; smaller communities may go three to five years between publications. Chicago, New York City and Los Angeles discontinued publication of city directories in 1928–29, 1933–34 and 1942, respectively, because of population size. Other metropolitan cities have stopped publication due to various circumstances.

City directories can hide research treasures because they are unpredictable in content. For example, the 1948 directory for Summit, Milburn, and Springfield, New Jersey, gives the following information:

> Karpenski Juliana E
> married Robert F Bradfield
> Kasparian Karton (wid Abraham)
> died June 27, 1947, age 71

Kastner Gordon C (Gertrude A)
rem to Kentucky [removed/moved to Kentucky]

Classified Business Section

The classified business section in city directories (similar to today's yellow pages) lists names and addresses of schools, churches, cemeteries, hospitals, orphanages and organizations. A page from the business section of a city directory appears on page 19.

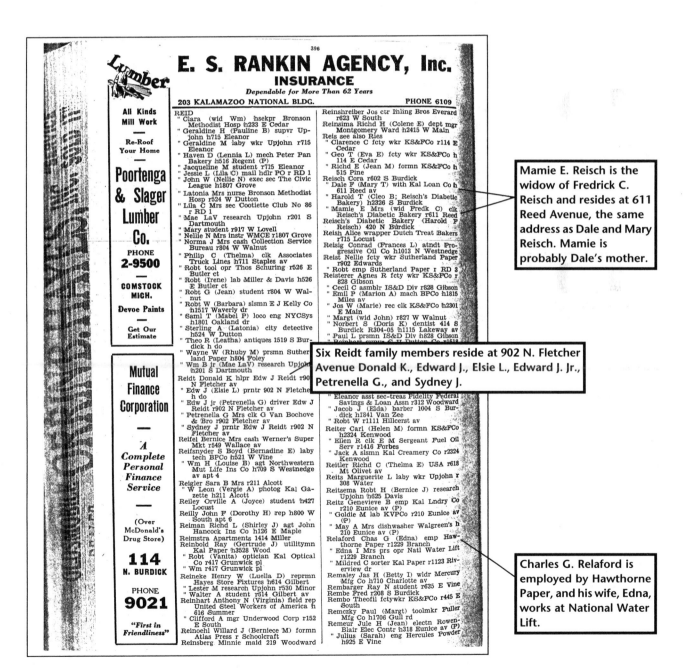

This 1947 city directory for Kalamazoo, Michigan, is a typical example of information found in such directories.

STEWART TITLE OF GREELEY
Security Abstract Co.

916 10TH ST.

DENVER M. WIGGINS · RES. PHONE 352-2973
CLEONA M. NELSON · RES. PHONE 352-7846
JUDITH A. KLEIN · RES. PHONE 353-0004

TITLE INSURANCE ABSTRACTS
352-4571

JOHNSON'S GREELEY DIRECTORY — 321

FIRST UNITED METHODIST CHURCH THE -REV. MARVIN H ADAMS MINISTER, REV. D M BLEYLE ASSOC. MINISTER, REV. LEON MILLER ASSOC. MINISTER, DR CHARLES W MC LAIN COUNSELOR, REV. ROBERT INGLIS CAMPUS MINISTER, JOHN A BERRY & RUBY G BERRY WKRS. WITH CHILDREN, FRANK L WEAVER LAY STAFF WORKER & LAURA FEHR SECY. 917-10TH AV 353-5522
FIRST UNITED PRESBYTERIAN CHURCH Rev Thomas A Ewing pastor 1321-9th Av 352-3030
FISCH Forest N (Phyllis A admv asst Dept of Business & Finance UNC) prof UNC 18 Levis Rd 352-4460
FISCHER Allan student 2011-5th Av (#6) 352-0970
FISCHER Bruce 2029 5th St 356-2283
FISCHER Dennis (Darlene) dist mgr Northern Colo Industrial Laundry 2280 1st Av ®
FISCHER Dennis (Sherri meat cutter Monfort's) meat cutter Monfort's 3004 Lakeside Dr Evans (#6) 356-1412
FISCHER Dennis C (Darlene computer opr Geriatrics Inc) student UNC 2280 1st Av (#47) 352-2767
FISCHER Helen B 1931-14th Av 352-5213
FISCHER Linda student 2205 10th Av Ct 353-6829
FISCUS Warren E (Genevieve V) emp Heath Constn Co 815-36th Av ® 353-0382
FISH John (Carolyn Gatewood) student 1227-9th Av ® 352-8978
FISH TANK THE -TROPICAL FISH, AQUARIUMS & SUPPLIES- GARY D BRYAN & RUSSELL C LONG PTNRS. 1533-2ND AV '16TH ST & 85 BY-PASS' 352-3160
FISHBACK CAMERA film processing 826 9th St 353-9596
FISHER Albert J Jr 1418-27th Av 356-0687
FISHER Carol A student 3320- W 7th St (#11) 353-9381
FISHER Dennis tchr Heath Jr HS 2100 27th Av Ct (#3) 356-0853
FISHER Eddie student 2017½ -8th Av ....
FISHER Erma L 3409- W 7th St (#B) 352-7067
FISHER Florence Mrs checker Safeway 1008 18th Av 352-5501
FISHER Frank R (Teresa) emp Flatiron 1434-6th St 356-3260
FISHER George A Jr (Karen) opr ofcr Colo Air Natl Guard 1 Aspen Dr Loveland (#J-8) ....
FISHER Geraldine 1418-27th Av ® 356-0687
FISHER Harry L (Alice C) ownr Harry L Fisher Gun Shop 2539 10th Av Ct ® 352-7314
FISHER HARRY L GUN SHOP Harry L Fisher ownr 2539 10th Av Ct ® 352-7314
FISHER Jack A (Charlene) ptnr Fisher Moore Contrs 400 37th Av Ct Ch James '61 Jerry '63 356-2205
FISHER James T (Kathy S opr Mtn Bell) grad student CSU 1200-26th Av (#D) Ch Todd '65 Derek '69 Jeremy '71 352-0070
FISHER Jane tchrs aide Scot Sch 2100 27th Av Ct (#3) 356-0853
FISHER Joanna 2412 Reservoir Rd (#301-A) ....
FISHER Larry R (Linda R) mach Harsh Hoist 3912 Glacier Dr ® Ch Lynette '72 352-2843
FISHER Louise tchr Maplewood sch 1521-11th Av (#8) 352-3232
FISHER Mary 1418-27th Av 356-0687
FISHER Nellie 708-22nd St (#401) 352-2421
FISHER Norman R (Esther) electn Canyon Valley Elec 1310 16th Av ® Ch Stephen '56 Martha '58 Tim '61 Jeff '62 Jody '64 Scott '67 Charlene '69 John '70 ....
FISHER Stanley (Lucille assembler Hewlett Packard) trk drvr Cowan Concrete 414 37th Av ® Ch Debra Sue '57 Robin Lynn 353-3911
FISHER Sue emp Flood & Peterson Inc 406 W Union Av LaSalle ....
FISHER Terry D (Susan J) ins agt Flood & Peterson 2133 BuenaVista Dr ® Ch Jeffrey '72 353-7806
FISHMAN Jeff student UNC 2056 30th St 356-2954
FISK George J (Pauline) retired 1728 15th Av ® 352-8188
FISK James W (B J rep World Book Encyclopedia & Childcraft) emp Home L & P 1820 Reservoir Rd ® Ch Jane '59 352-9366
FISK Kenn 1820 Reservoir Rd 352-9366
FITCH Barry 725 27th Av 356-1427
FITCH Charles meat dept asst mgr King Soopers ....
FITCH Constance ofc clk JC Penney 2515 12th Av Ct ....
FITCH John (Theresa) announcer KFKA Radio 3280 65th Av ....
FITCH Lloyd L (Geraldine G) dir Boys World Inc 725 27th Av ® Ch Constance '57 356-1427
FITCH M R Rev retired 1006-14th Av (#C) 353-0974

FITHIAN Betty M tchr Madison Sch #6 1010 18th St ® Ch Virginia '57 David '60 352-2945
FITHIAN Jerry (Carol clk Hallmark Gift Shop) student 604-23rd St 353-9553
FITZGERALD James P (Judith) emp Nelson Haley Patterson & Quirk 2440 14th Av ....
FITZPATRICK Charles P (Rhonda public health nurse Weld Cty) 433-27th Av 356-7796
FITZPATRICK Frank J (Alice M) dist mgr Mtn Bell 1771 28th Av ® 353-7773
FITZPATRICK Gerald M (Elizabeth) pro golfer Greeley Country Club 133 N 21st Av (#77) Ch Gerald '72 356-2135
FITZPATRICK Patsy 1518-9th Av 353-8118
FITZPATRICK S L emp Joslins 3103 17th Av (#55) ® Ch Sean '67 Shannon '69 356-4721
FIX J 2430-14th Av Ct 356-6670
FIX James J (Sandra L) emp King Soopers 101 E 20th St (#68) 352-1134
FLACK Carroll E (Lu deputy clk Weld Cty) secy Greeley Loveland Irrgn Co E of Greeley 352-1824
FLACK Duane E Dr (Colleen) mgr Monfort Feedlot 5225 65th Av ® Ch Cindy '59 Laurie '61 Susan '62 352-2751
FLAGG Archie L watchmaker Graybeal Inc 818½ 8th St ....
FLAGLE W H (Nonna secy Madison Sch) slsmn A&N Glass & Paint Co 2535-16th Av ® Ch Teresa '61 Russell '62 353-3231
FLAHERTY Michael (Betty Jane) slsmn Panel-IT 3335 W 19th St ® 356-2625
FLAHERTY Wm (Martha) mech-shop foreman Colo Kenworth Inc 293 N 15th Av Brighton ....
FLAMMING Joan 1628 9th Av (#23) 352-4230
FLANNELLY Arthur W (Betty Sue) ins agt Lott Agcy 1650 27th Av ® Ch Jane '58 356-7146
FLANNIGAN Michael W (Patricia D) psychology conslr UNC 2412 25th St Rd ® Ch Corin '71 353-7789
FLASCHE Jack (Lois chkr K-Mart) drywlr 4113 Yosemite Dr ® Ch Kimla '62 Dale '65 356-1195
FLAT Reuben 2700 'C' St (#168) ....
FLATELAND Kenneth J (Edith dep cty clk Weld Cty) slsmn Randalls Shoes 2642 12th Av ® 352-1930
FLATELAND Steven inhalation therapist WCGH 2629 23rd Av Bldg B (#16) 353-7349
FLATIRON MATERIALS CO concrete Jack Verser mgr 190 N 25th Av 356-3366
FLATIRON PAVING CO paving contr, excavation, sand & gravel, slurry seal Ted McMurren pres PO Bx 1137 353-2777
FLAUGHER Donald W appr hvy equipt opr Pink Willson Co Elms Hotel LaSalle ....
FLAUGHER James R (Susan K) cement finisher 120 21st Av Ch Anna '73 353-4976
FLAUGHER Rose Mary secy Will-Helen Trkg 124 21st Av Ch Nancy '57 353-2149
FLEA FLICKER THE 721 26th St 356-2275
FLECK Karen student 3315 W 6th St Rd ® 353-3861
FLECK Robert R (Loretta J self emp bkpg) emp Monforts 3315 W 6th St Rd Ch Howard '58 Susan '61 Lori '62 353-3861
FLEENOR Emma 1902-7th Av 352-7043
FLEENOR Orville (Joyce piano tchr) emp Farmhand 1621 22nd Av 352-8236
FLEER Cindy student UNC 1900-11th Av (#108) 352-0660
FLEER Steven M (REbecca) student UNC 508 17th St (#207) 356-3594
FLEISCHMANN Ottilie F F 610-22nd St (#18) 352-1257
FLEMING Robert R (Jean) agt Mutual of Omaha Ins 1023 22nd Av Ch Robin '59 356-0547
FLESCH Clifford R (Nancy J clk-typt Weld Cty Lbry) underwriter State Farm Ins 1724 29th Av Pl ® Ch Julie '63 Carol '68 353-5778
FLESHER Mike farm dir KFKA Radio ....
FLESHER R L (Helen L) emp State Farm Ins 2158 27th Av ® Ch Debra '57 Doug '59 353-3552
FLESNER William T (Evelyn F) emp MacKenzie Cabinet Co 1005 31st St Evans ® Ch Thomas '68 352-4926
FLETCHER Charles (Deborah emp Greeley Pub Schs) student UNC 2617 23rd Av (#23) 356-6354
FLETCHER ELECTRIC -ELECTRICAL CONTRACTORS- SAMUEL L FLETCHER OWNER 1821-4TH AV 353-1396
FLETCHER Harley 'Skip' student 1821 15th Av 353-1604

Go to the Church ... of your choice....

PROFESSIONAL FINANCE CO.
COLLECTION SPECIALISTS
PHONE 352-5000
1428 · 7TH AVE.   No Collection - No Charge - We make collections anywhere

SERVICES OFFERED
COMPLETE COLLECTION SERVICE
CREDIT CONSULTATION SERVICE
SHORT CHECK COLLECTION SERVICE
REPOSSESSIONS OF ALL KINDS
PRE-COLLECTION SERVICE

Norman R. and Esther Fisher list eight children: Stephen, '56; Martha, '58; Tim, '61; Jeff, '62; Jody, '64; Scott, '67; Charlene, '69; and John, '70.

Directories for smaller communities—such as this 1975 Greeley, Colorado, (population 54,000) directory—sometimes list the given name and birth year for children.

Householder or Crisscross Directories

The householder directory, sometimes called a crisscross, cross-index or reverse directory, indexes streets alphabetically and numerically, with a family head or business named for each address. This index is sometimes a section within the city directory, but more often it is a separate volume. A page from a cross-index directory appears on page 20.

Suburban Directories

As the population increased within metropolitan areas, publishers began separating the cities from their suburbs. They would issue the usual city directory,

This 1950 Denver City Directory's classified section lists nurses. This could be extremely helpful in adoption cases when you have only a given name, but do know that the birth mother was a nurse. The list of nurses could narrow the search to one or two nurses with that name. This 1950 directory includes occupational groupings not likely to be found in today's yellow pages, such as artists, clergymen (in an alphabetical list separate from names of churches), dressmakers, geologists, inventors, music teachers, shoe repairers, stenographers and tailors.

but also print a suburban directory. For example, R.L. Polk and Company published three directories for Miami, Florida, in 1972: (1) the Miami Directory; (2) the Miami North Suburban Directory that includes Biscayne Park, El Portal, Hialeah, Medley, Miami Beach, Miami Shores, Miami Springs, North Miami, North Miami Beach, Opa-Locka and Virginia Gardens; and (3) the Miami South Suburban Directory that includes Coral Cables, South Miami and

The 1967–68 *Bresser's Cross-Index Directory* for Denver, Colorado, lists streets alphabetically with house numbers in ascending order. This type of directory helps identify current and former neighbors. It also reveals whether the resident is a tenant or homeowner. In the latter case, real estate records (chapter ten) will be a follow-up source.

West Miami. Pay attention to this possibility when searching directories for a large metropolitan area. If you don't find the person you seek in the city directory, check the suburban directory.

County Directories

County directories are published in rural areas, with listings for each community within the county boundaries. A page from a county directory appears on page 21.

283

LARIMER COUNTY
ALPHABETICAL LIST OF NAMES

A

A & W ROOT BEER DRIVE INN Vivian Hamann mgr & ownr
802 Mountain Av (Ber) 532-9983
A B C REALTY -FARMS & RANCHES, ALL TYPES OF REAL ESTATE-
212 E MOUNTAIN FT COLLINS 482-0345
A DREAM HOME DECORATING CONTRACTOR interior decorators
W of Ft Collins 482-5102
A T S EMPLOYMENT SERVICE Frank W Kirschner Jr ownr
1st Natl Tower Bldg Ft C (#702) 493-4220
A-1 ANSWERING SERVICE Rocky Mtn Bldg Ft C 482-6817
A-1 TRASH SERVICE -RUBBISH REMOVAL, SANITATION SERVICE-
436 N ROOSEVELT FT COLLINS 484-9044
ESTES PARK 586-3724
ABCO SALES & SERVICE -MOBILE HOME SALES & SERVICE-
400 N COLLEGE AV FT COLLINS 484-2448
ABRAM Richard Marys Lake Rd (EP) 586-2582
ABRAMS Gus G (Helen H) farmer
620 E Cty Rd #12 Rt 1 Box 203 '2 mi N½ mi E of Ber' (Ber) Ⓗ ... 532-2961
ACKELSON Dennis W (Wendy opr Mtn Bell Tel) emp Eastman Kodak
4610 Loma Linda Ln Ft C (#2) 493-1317
ACKELSON Ernest B Jr (Dixie emp Kodak) 2808 Tharp LaPorte 482-2847
ACOTT Richard D (Connie) broker Acott & Assoc Inc
4033 Buckskin Tr LaPorte Ⓗ Ch Stephen '59 Lorri Ann '61 Garret '63 ... 484-9960
ADAIR Donald L 3216 W Cty Rd 50 Ft C 484-9556
ADAMS Don R (Barbara L) slsmn Longmont Realty
1036 S Cty Rd #21 (Ber) Ⓗ Ch Angie '61 Scott '64 532-2463
ADAMS Herbert D 3408 Rawhide Dr Ft C 484-8517
ADAMS Robert P (Janice W) prof CSU 6416 Fossil Crest Ft C Ⓗ Ch
Jessica '65 Mark '67 493-0168
ADKISSON William L (Altie) retired 235-2nd St (#28) (Ber) Ⓗ ... 532-3541
ADLER Irvin E (L Darlene) farmer
Cty Rd #5 Rt 1 Box 95 'SE of Ber' (Ber) Ch Karen '64 Gregg '68
Kevin '72 532-3510
ADLER Reinhardt F (Kathryn) retired 1119-4th St Rt 1 Box 257 (Ber) ... 532-2535
ADLER Robert D constn wkr Colo-Wyoming Constn 1006-4th St (Ber) ... 532-2176
ADLER Robert L (Kathlyn) constn welding-Colo-Wyoming Constn
1006-4th St (Ber) Ⓗ Ch Judy '59 532-2176
ADMINISTRATION BUILDING Oval Dr CSU Campus Ft C 491-1101
ADRIEL HILLS 1601 Weber Ft C 493-1810
AGLAND INC -GRAIN ELEVATOR, PETROLEUM PRODUCTS- GARY
BRAGDON FEED MGR. & CAL CLAIBOURNE PETROLEUM MGR.
280 FACTORY RD 'PO BOX 338' EATON 454-2791
AGRICULTURAL SCIENCES CSU Campus Ft C 491-6274
AGRONOMY FARM 3028 S Cty Rd 11 Ft C 482-2507
AGRONOMY RESEARCH CENTER SE of Ft C 484-9272
AGRONOMY RESEARCH CENTER SE of Ft C 484-9861
AGUIRRE Frank 5317 S County Rd 3-F Ft C 482-1089
AHLBRANDT Theodore J (Eva Anna) farmer & feeder
4625 S Cty Rd 9 Ft C 482-5948
AHRENS Charles A (Gertrude) hay farmer
1510 N Shields Rd '3/4 mi W on Willox Ln' Ⓗ 484-8391
AIRWAYS APPLIANCE CENTER -COMPLETE LINE OF HOTPOINT
APPLIANCES, DAY OR NIGHT SERVICE ON ALL MAKES &
MODELS, RETAIL & CONTRACTOR SALES- 806 N COLLEGE AV FT
COLLINS 493-5891
AFTER 6:00 484-1773
AKERS V M 1853 Kedron Cir Ft C 482-7055

AL'S CUSTOM BUILDERS bld contrs 813 N US Hwy 287 Ft C ... 493-3155
AL'S SERVICE serv sta Al Burr ownr 817 Mountain Av (Ber) 532-3130
ALBER Tom E (Loretta pt tm emp Charco Broiler) mgr Charco Broiler
1101 Buttonwood Ft C 'on 3 Silos Rd' Ⓗ Ch Thomas '58 Letha '62
Donnie '66 484-2960
ALBERSCHARDT William L (Violet R) retired
1909 North US 287 Ft C 482-8682
ALBIN Don C 1939 Kedron Dr Ft C 493-5706
ALBRECHT CONSTRUCTION CO INC genl contrs S of Ft Collins ... 493-5084
ALBRECHT Duane E (Janette E) brick mason
Rt 2 Box 95 'W of Ber' (Ber) Ch Duane Jr '68 Valarie '73 532-3450
ALBRECHT Guenther (Hildegard emp CSU) emp Woodward Gov
Rt 2 Bx 210 Ft C Ⓗ 482-9645
ALBRIGHT Alice C Mrs 829 Sunrise Av Ft C 482-0028
ALCOHOLICS ANONYMOUS assn-org Ft Collins 493-0012
ALDEN Evelyn nurses aide Eventide Nursing Home-Longmont
845-3rd St (Ber) 532-2130
ALDEN Harvey W (Margie) stone mason 845-3rd St (Ber) Ⓗ 532-2130
ALDEN Howard (Elza) prof CSU 800 E Cty Rd #58 'N of Ft C' Ch
Carole '60 Susan '63 Stuart '67 David '71 482-0983
ALDEN James H stone mason 845-3rd St (Ber) 532-2130
ALDRICH Dennis W 2714 Park Lake Ct Ft C 484-5702
ALDRICH John W (Joanne) emp PV REA
2907 Green Tree Cir Ft C Ⓗ Ch Shannon '69 484-2410
ALEXANDER Donald C (Margaret) rancher & emp Mtn Bell Tel
1120 S Cty Rd #27E (Ber) Ⓗ Ch Mike '59 532-2515
ALEXANDER Harriet slsldy Continental West Rlty Inc
3201 E Cty Rd 36 Ft C 493-4730
ALEXANDER Herb (Eather) emp water dept 2630 Ferndale Ft C Ⓗ ... 482-8948
ALEXANDER Patty 1120 S Cty Rd #27E (Ber) 532-2515
ALEXANDER William C (Stephanie M) asst prof CSU
1701 E Cty Rd 58 Ft C Ch Sabina '62 Jordan '64 484-3866
ALFANO Didj 928 E Douglas Rd Ft C 493-9290
ALFORD Raleigh N (Jeanine) vice pres The Berthoud Natl Bank
1812 Glenwood Dr (Ber) Ch Nicole '60 Burke '63 532-2380
ALL SEASONS HEATING & COOLING Kenneth Brock ownr
235-2nd St (Ber) 532-2076
ALLARD A WAYNE DR vet & owner Allard Animal Hospital
714 Taft Av Loveland (ofc) 667-9230
ALLARD ANIMAL HOSPITAL 714 Taft Av Loveland 667-9230
ALLARDICE David R (Jean) student CSU 300 E Harmony Rd Ft C Ch
Suzanne '70 493-4289
ALLEN Barbara Rural Rt Ft C 482-1588
ALLEN Guy Rev (Ruth N) retired 308 Lake Av (Ber) Ⓗ 532-2955
ALLEN H Brett (Donna G RN) v pres Ricks Furn 3408 Shiloh Ft C Ⓗ
Ch Dynnee '69 Spotty '71 482-0368
ALLEN James P (Donna LPN PV Meml Hosp) student CSU
Cloverleaf Mobile Pk 'E of Ft C' (#54) Ch Karen '69 484-8814

ALLEN PLUMBING AND HEATING INC -PLUMBING, HEATING, HOT
WATER HEATING, WATER HEATERS, GARBAGE DISPOSALS-
101 LINK LANE FT COLLINS 484-4841

ALLEN Melben 1812 Indian Meadows Ln Ft C 493-2648
ALLEN Steven Rural Rt Ft C 482-1588
ALLEN William atty Allen Mitchell & Rogers Rural Rt Ft C (res) Ch
Bradford '57 482-1588
ALLIED MUTUAL INSURANCE AGENCY Robert E Whalen agent
549-3rd St (Ber) 532-3131

Larimer County, Colorado's 1975 county directory combines residents from Bellvue, Berthoud, Estes Park, Drake, Fort Collins, LaPorte, Loveland, Masonville, Timnath, Virginia Dale and Wellington into one alphabetical index. Given names and birth years are given for children, and homeowners are marked with a circled *H*.

HOW TO USE CITY DIRECTORIES

City directory research is more complex than it may appear, requiring slower and more methodical research to uncover important data. The directories vary in content from year to year. One year might give the middle name of an individual; another year might list a nickname. One year may list the name of the twenty-year-old son who is attending school; the next year he will not be listed. It is therefore imperative to search *every possible year* and to examine *every listing* for the surname.

Important

Examples of Data From a City Directory

Following are some listings from the 1979 Denver City Directory:

Combs	Anthony M retd h 3100 Cherry Creek Dr S Apt 207
"	Brenda J tchr D P S r 14911 Randolph Pl
"	Cameron studt r 491 Magnolia St
"	Clyde & Rose Marie; truck driver h 1733 Vine St
"	Cynthia h 2359 Race St
"	Debbie r 1733 Vine St
"	Donald E & Awyn J; archt Moore Combs & Birch h 3264 S Grape St
"	Ellsworth retd h 1390 High St Apt 202
"	Frances M Mrs aide D P S h 3616 Quitman St
"	Fred A & Colleen K (Combs Automotive) h 4725 Highline Pl
"	Fred J & Edith H; electn Gates h 264 S Washington St
"	Freightair Inc Terry Combs 8100 E 32d Av
"	Gates Denver Inc Robert Cloughley Pres 8100 E 43d Av
"	Grant & Rosalee M; emp D G H h 730 E Center Av
"	Harold B h 460 S Marion Pkwy Apt 1354
"	Harry B Jr & Joan C; emp Combs Airways h 5701 Montview Blvd
"	Jennifer L tchr D P S r Arvada
"	Jim A & Sally N; driver B F Walker-Noble h 1488 S Mariposa St
"	Joan h 491 Magnolia St
"	John W & Brenda; ship clk Nationwide Paper h 14911 Randolph Pl
"	Keith emp Van Schaak h 2030 Kearney St
"	Keith h 9725 E Harvard Av Apt B435
"	Malcolm & Deahn; ofc mgr Boyd Realty & Invest Co h 2709 S Harrison St
"	Marion clk h 4390 E Mississippi Av Apt 404
"	Mark A h 5240 Highline Pl
"	Mary M Mrs retd h 1820 S Wyandot St

Anthony M. Combs Anthony M. Combs is retired and residing in apartment 207 at 3100 Cherry Creek Drive South. There are no other Combs listings at this address. By researching this address in the householder (or crisscross) portion of the directory, we learn that 3100 Cherry Creek Drive South is the Cherry Creek Towers Apartments. This information may be useful if we want to interview the manager of the apartment complex.

Cameron Combs and Joan Combs Cameron and Joan both reside at 491 Magnolia Street. The *r* (placed before the address for Cameron) is an abbreviation for *resident* or *roomer*, and the *h* (prior to the address for Joan) means

HOUSEHOLDER DIRECTORY HELPS LOCATE BIRTH MOTHER

We were tracing a birth mother and grandmother who had lived together in a home owned by the grandmother. The two women were listed in city directories for ten years, but then seemingly disappeared. They could not be found in city directories, telephone directories or marriage records. It appeared they moved out of the city or state.

Since the grandmother owned her home, there should have been a real estate transaction when she sold the house. We searched grantor indexes (see chapter ten) for ten years following the last city directory entry, but we could not find the sale of her property.

We decided the index of grantees (buyers of property) might help us find the sale, but we needed the name of the buyer to search the real estate records.

Using the householder directories we found that the grandmother had rented out her home for the five years before she sold it. The directory gave the name of the new owner.

Using the name of the new property owner, the deed was located. The reason we were unable to find the deed using the grandmother's name was because the two women had moved out of state, the grandmother had died, the daughter had married (which changed her name), and the trustee for the grandmother's estate was the grantor in the deed record.

With the information on the death of the grandmother and the married name of the daughter, we were able to locate the birth mother quickly.

householder. Joan Combs, therefore, is the householder or head of the house, and probably the mother of Cameron Combs.

Using the householder section of this directory, we can identify Joan's neighbors:

Magnolia Street

471	Morris Milton	• 377-8132
480★	Farrell David M	• 377-7907
491★	Combs Joan	
496	Cohen Abraham R	• 322-8434

The circle (•) in the Morris, Farrell and Cohen listings indicate they are homeowners, and listings with a star (★) are new. David M. Farrell, therefore, is a new homeowner; the Morris and Cohen listings are not new. Joan Combs is a new listing and rents her home, since she is not listed as a homeowner. **In researching Joan Combs, this 1979 city directory tells you** that she has a son named Cameron. Since persons are not listed in the directory until they are eighteen years old, you can estimate Cameron's date of birth between 1959 and 1961. You know that Joan is renting her home; lived somewhere else prior to 1979; and her neighbors are Milton Morris, David Farrell and Abraham Cohen. An interview with these neighbors may produce more information about Cameron or Joan.

Keith Combs There are two listings for the name Keith Combs. This serves as an excellent example of how you must always be aware of the possibility that there can be two (or more) persons with the same name residing in the same area—even when the name is unusual. The city directory can give information to help separate the persons with the same names to avoid confusion when searching other records. In this case, one Keith Combs is employed by Van Schaak, a realty company (you can learn this by looking up Van Schaak in the directory). In subsequent directories, this information may be invaluable in determining which Keith is the one you seek.

Comparing City Directory Research Results

On page 25 is a study of the Hunter family from 1913 through 1945, which illustrates the value of searching every year and comparing data. The purpose of this search was to locate living descendants of Pauline Hunter. (The years not listed gave duplicate information and are therefore not included in the table.)

The city directories provided the following information in the search of Pauline Hunter's descendants:

- Pauline Hunter is the widow of Henry Hunter who probably died prior to 1913.
- Pauline has at least three children: Celestine L., David R. and Frank R.
- Pauline Hunter died after 1933.
- Frank R. Hunter married Estelle Katherine (maiden name unknown) prior to 1923.
- Frank R. Hunter died about 1944.
- Frank R. and Estelle Hunter had at least two children: Dorothy B. and Marjorie J.

With this information you can search marriage, probate, cemetery and death records to locate the living descendants.

LOCATING DIRECTORIES

The only way to currently access city directories is to locate a library that contains the cities and years you are interested in or to borrow microfiche from AGLL (http://www.heritagequest.com/genealogy/microfilm/). In the near future, however, city directories will begin appearing on-line with full facsimile images and full text searching. Primary Source Media has entered the on-line database library market with a new product called City Directories Online. It will be based on the *Bibliography of American Directories Through 1860* and

Year	
1913	Hunter David R, lineman Phone Co, r 17 W 3rd Ave Hunter Frank R, installer Phone Co, r 17 W 3rd Ave Hunter Pauline Mrs., r 17 W 3rd Ave These three individuals are related to each other since they have the same surname and reside at the same address.
1915	Hunter Celestine L Miss, phone opr, r 17 W 3rd Ave This is the only year that Celestine is listed in the directories. If every year had not been examined, this information would have been missed. Hunter Pauline Mrs., r 17 W 3rd Ave No listing for Frank R or David R
1917	Hunter David R, lineman Phone Co, r 49 S Sherman Hunter Frank R, installer Phone Co, r 710 W 1st Ave Hunter Pauline Mrs., r 49 S Sherman
1918	No listings
1919	No listings
1920	No listings
1921	No listings
1922	No listings When a family is not listed in a directory for five or more years, it usually means they moved or are deceased. But it can also mean they were missed in the door-to-door gathering of information.
1923	Hunter Frank R (Estelle K), slsman h 627 W 1st Ave It is unknown if this Frank R Hunter is the same individual as the Frank R Hunter listed in 1913 and 1917 since the occupation is different and the address is slightly different. Estelle K is the wife of this Frank R Hunter.
1928	Hunter Frank R (Estelle Katherine) h 421 Ellsworth This year's directory is the only directory that gave the middle name of Estelle. Hunter Pauline Mrs. r 421 Ellsworth We now have Pauline Hunter residing with Frank R Hunter, suggesting that this is the same family listed in the 1913–1917 directories. It is unknown why Pauline did not appear in directories from 1918–1927.
1933	Hunter Pauline (wid Henry), r 421 Ellsworth This is the first time that the name of Pauline's deceased husband was given.
1938	Hunter Frank R (Estelle K), slsman, h 552 Marion Hunter Dorothy B, r 552 Marion Hunter Marjorie J, r 552 Marion Dorothy and Marjorie are daughters of Frank and Estelle Hunter. Children are listed when they are students or employed.
1945	Hunter Estelle K (wid Frank R), h 552 Marion We now have an approximate date of death for Frank R Hunter.

the collections of the Library of Congress and the American Antiquarian Society. The initial phase will include directories from ninety-nine cities prior to 1859. The database will eventually include material up to 1960, and individuals may eventually be invited to subscribe. For additional information and pricing, write sales@psmedia.com or call (800) 444-0799.

Major repositories that hold city directory collections are:
- Allen County Public Library, Fort Wayne, Indiana

Sources

http://www.acpl.lib.in.us/genealogy/genealogy.html
A collection of thirty thousand R.L. Polk directories dated 1964 to the present, with significant earlier holdings for some cities. The library also holds many directories produced by other publishers for smaller cities and rural areas.

- American Antiquarian Society, 185 Salisbury St., Worcester, MA 01605; (508) 755-5221. The American Antiquarian Society (AAS) was founded in 1812 in Worcester, Massachusetts. AAS is the third-oldest historical society in this country and the first to be national rather than regional in its purpose and in the scope of its collections. They have more than 6,500 directories published before 1877 and hold one of the largest collections of city directories in the U.S. Directories published 1821 or later are not cataloged, but are listed alphabetically by name of town and city in a continually updated checklist.

- Library of Congress, Washington, DC
  Directories for nearly seven hundred U.S. cities are on microfilm at the Library of Congress. A list organized alphabetically by state and city is at http://www.kinquest.com/genealogy/citydir.html.
  Also, see James C. Neagles's *The Library of Congress: A Guide to Genealogical and Historical Research* (Salt Lake City: Ancestry Pub., 1990). City directories are inventoried for each state and Australia, Canada, England, Ireland and Scotland.

- Newberry Library, Chicago, Illinois
  http://www.newberry.org/
  The Newberry Library directory holdings cover all parts of the U.S., large cities, small towns, counties and rural areas. They do not, however, collect directories after 1930.

- New England Historic Genealogical Society, Boston, Massachusetts
  http://www.nehgs.org/
  This collection emphasizes the New England states.

The Family History Library (FHL) in Salt Lake City (see sidebar at left) has an outstanding collection of city directories in microform and books. Listed below are cities that are available for 1902 to 1935 on microfilm. There are a few cities that have missing volumes or may begin later or end sooner, but generally speaking most of these cities are filmed through 1935.

Library/Archive Source

THE FAMILY HISTORY LIBRARY

The Family History Library in Salt Lake City, Utah, is the largest genealogical library in the world. Much of the information housed there can also be accessed at any of its 3,200 Family History Centers located around the country. To find the one nearest you, check your local yellow pages under Churches—Church of Jesus Christ of Latter-day Saints (or your local business white pages under Church of Jesus Christ of Latter-day Saints) and look for the term *Family History Center.*

ALABAMA	CALIFORNIA	Stockton
Birmingham	Bakersfield	COLORADO
Mobile	Fresno	Colorado Springs
Montgomery	Long Beach	Denver
ARIZONA	Los Angeles	Grand Junction
Phoenix	Oakland	CONNECTICUT
Tucson	Sacramento	Ansonia
ARKANSAS	San Diego	Bridgeport
Texarkana	San Francisco	Bristol

Danbury
Hartford
Middletown
New Haven
Norwich
Southington
Stamford

DISTRICT OF COLUMBIA
Washington

FLORIDA
Jacksonville
Miami
Pensacola
St. Petersburg
Tampa

GEORGIA
Atlanta
Columbus
Savannah

HAWAII
Honolulu

IDAHO
Boise
Pocatello

ILLINOIS
Belleville
Chicago (ends 1929)
Evanston
Joliet
Moline
Peoria
Rock Island
Rockford
Springfield

INDIANA
Evansville
Fort Wayne
Gary
Indianapolis
Lafayette
New Albany
Richmond

IOWA
Burlington
Des Moines
Iowa City

KANSAS
Emporia
Leavenworth
Ottawa
Topeka

KENTUCKY
Covington
Lexington
Louisville

LOUISIANA
New Orleans

MAINE
Augusta
Biddeford/Saco
Portland
Westbrook

MARYLAND
Baltimore

MASSACHUSETTS
Boston
Brockton
Cambridge
Chelsea
Clinton
Fall River
Gloucester
Haverhill
Holyoke
Leominster
Lowell
Lynn
Medford
Milford
New Bedford
Newburyport
Salem
Taunton
Worcester

MICHIGAN
Ann Arbor
Battle Creek
Coldwater
Detroit
Grand Rapids
Kalamazoo
Petoskey

MINNESOTA
Duluth
Minneapolis
St. Paul

MISSOURI
Kansas City
St. Joseph
St. Louis

MONTANA
Billings
Butte
Great Falls
Livingston

NEBRASKA
Hastings
Omaha

NEW HAMPSHIRE
Concord
Dover
Keene
Manchester
Nashua
Portsmouth

NEW JERSEY
Atlantic City
Camden
Elizabeth
Newark
Paterson
Trenton

NEW MEXICO
Albuquerque

NEW YORK
Albany
Auburn
Binghamton
Brooklyn
Buffalo
Cortland
ElmiraGeneva
Hudson
Ithaca
Kingston
Middletown
Newburgh
New York

Oswego
Poughkeepsie
Rochester
Rome
Schenectady
Syracuse
Troy
Utica
Yonkers
NORTH CAROLINA
Asheville
Greensboro
Raleigh
NORTH DAKOTA
Fargo
OHIO
Chillicothe
Cincinnati
Cleveland
Columbus
Dayton
Mansfield
Marietta
Portsmouth
Sandusky
Springfield
Steubenville
Toledo
Zanesville
OKLAHOMA
Enid
Tulsa
OREGON
Astoria

Portland
PENNSYLVANIA
Carnegie
Chester
Erie
Harrisburg
Lancaster
Norristown
Philadelphia
Pittsburgh
Reading
Scranton
Williamsport
RHODE ISLAND
East Providence
Providence
SOUTH CAROLINA
Charleston
Columbia
SOUTH DAKOTA
Sioux Falls
TENNESSEE
Chattanooga
Knoxville
Memphis
Nashville
TEXAS
Amarillo
Austin
Beaumont
Dallas
Fort Worth
Galveston
Houston

San Antonio
Waco
UTAH
Logan
Ogden
Salt Lake City
VERMONT
Barre
Brattleboro
VIRGINIA
Norfolk
Petersburg
Richmond
WASHINGTON
Bellingham
Everett
Seattle
WEST VIRGINIA
Clarksburg
Wheeling
WISCONSIN
Appleton
Fond du Lac
Green Bay
Kenosha
Madison
Milwaukee
Oshkosh
Racine
Watertown
WYOMING
Laramie

To locate city directories in the Family History Library catalog, do a locality search and enter the name of the city and state. Searching the catalog by county name will *not* produce information on city directories.

In addition to its microfilm holdings, the Family History Library in Salt Lake City has hundreds of city directories in book form that can only be searched at the library. None of the cities are 100 percent complete. (For Boulder, Colorado, for instance, FHL has only the volumes from 1916, 1936, 1940, 1962, 1965, 1971, 1975, 1978, 1983 and 1988–89. Sioux City, Iowa, directories date from 1939, 1942, 1959, 1961, 1965, 1973, 1974 and 1988, while only the 1990 volume from Red Wing, Minnesota, is available.) To determine if your city of interest is in their collection, do a locality search in the catalog.

CITY DIRECTORY RESEARCH TIPS

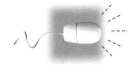

- **Refer to Cyndi's List on the Internet (http://www.cyndilist.com/finding .htm) for links to city directory inventories at various libraries.**
- Remember that the data in city directories is usually at least one year old by the time of publication.
- When requesting photocopies of city directory entries from a public library, request that all pages with the surname of interest be copied. You need all those pages so you can study the entries line by line and compare addresses and occupations.
- If you do not find the person or family in the city directory, check the suburban directory, if appropriate.
- Use surname spelling variants (as discussed in chapter two).
- Beware of confusing individuals who have the same name.
- Search every year possible.
- Examine each line (surname) and match addresses.
- Examine the changes, additions and deletions section.
- Use the classified business section to obtain names of churches, cemeteries, etc., that may help in the research.
- Supplement city directory research results with telephone book results.
- Use the city directory to estimate divorce and death dates. By tracking an individual in every year, the separation from a spouse due to divorce or death will be revealed in the directory.

FOUR

Birth Certificates

P rivacy laws in nearly all states mandate that birth records are only available to the individual named on the birth record (registrant), the parents or legal guardian of the registrant, or a legal representative. Some birth records are available to anyone if the record was created at least seventy-five to one hundred years ago or if the person is deceased.

If birth records were more accessible, most searches could be completed easily. Sometimes knowing an exact birth date or the person's full name will narrow a search to just a few individuals, rather than hundreds. Knowing the names of the parents of the individual also might be valuable in the search.

This information is found in most birth records:
- full name
- exact date of birth
- place of birth (sometimes includes name of hospital)
- number of birth for mother (clue to number of siblings)
- names of the father and mother
- ages of the father and mother at the time of the child's birth
- occupations of the father and mother
- mother's maiden name
- address of the father and mother
- birthplaces of the father and mother

TYPES OF BIRTH CERTIFICATES

\di'fin\ *vb*

Definitions

There are three types of birth certificates:

Original An original birth certificate is the record created and filed at birth. The certificates are issued by county or state governments in short form and long form. Original birth certificates are sealed (closed) for adopted children when the amended certificate is issued.

Amended or Corrected This is a revised birth record with additional or corrected information (e.g., the names of birth parents are changed to the names of the adoptive parents; or the name of birth father is added; or corrections regarding the spelling of names are made). An amended birth certificate for adopted children is usually not labeled as amended; therefore, some adopted children do not know they are adopted unless the parents tell them or they find other documents within personal papers. Birth certificates amended for other reasons usually have *Amended* stamped upon the face of the document. Affidavits with supporting documentation are submitted to the health department that issues the certificate and kept on file.

Amended birth certificates created for adopted children often have the same certificate number as the original certificate. Therefore, when a birth index (that is, a list of birth certificates on file) is available for the time period needed, a search for the matching number can be made, although it takes considerable research time.

Delayed A delayed certificate is issued several years after a birth, usually because an original record was not filed. Many delayed certificates were issued in the early 1940s as proof of age for Social Security applicants or to prove age for military service. Applicants proved their age by attaching documents such as baptism, family Bible, school or census records. Sometimes they would include an affidavit by an individual who was present at the birth or baptism.

Birth Registration

Birth certificates were not issued by most states until 1910 or later, and full participation in birth registration was not immediate. Sometimes it took as long as twenty years for doctors, hospitals and individuals to comply with the law. For this reason, some birth records do not exist even though a state law requiring registration was in effect when the child was born. Delayed certificates were issued when the individual needed to prove age for Social Security, military service or to obtain a passport.

OBTAINING BIRTH CERTIFICATES

Birth certificates are issued by the state health department or county health department where the birth occurred. VitalChek Network, Inc. ([800] 255-4214; http://www.vitalchek.com/) will provide the correct telephone or fax number to place your order with state and county health departments. Most states will accept credit cards, although they charge an extra fee for this service. The cost of birth certificates varies from five to twenty-five dollars each.

Many states are posting information and forms on the Internet. Use the words *vital records* plus the name of the state in search engines to find these Web sites.

The chart below lists by state the year statewide birth registration began and information on public availability of records or indexes. This list will change occasionally as states release indexes or modify their policies.

Brick Wall Buster

"LONG-FORM" BIRTH CERTIFICATE HELPS SOLVE ADOPTION CASE

An adoptee in his mid sixties knew he was born in Illinois, but did not know where in Illinois. His amended birth certificate was a short form and only gave the state of birth. He requested the long-form birth certificate, which named the hospital in Chicago where he was born. With this information, we were able to match his birth certificate number with Chicago births and determine the name of his birth mother. We could not have accomplished this without obtaining the long-form birth certificate.

Technique

State	Year Statewide Registration Began	Location and Date of Public Indexes (FHL = Family History Library, Salt Lake City NEHGS = New England Historic Genealogical Society, Boston)
Alabama	1908	FHL: Statewide index 1917-1919
Alaska	1913; however complete records were not kept until after WWII	
Arizona	1909	
Arkansas	1914	FHL: Some county records.
California	1905	FHL: Many county records (see Los Angeles example at page 34).
Colorado	1907	FHL: Transcripts for some counties.
Connecticut	1897	
Delaware	1881	FHL: Statewide index 1861-1913.
District of Columbia	1871	
Florida	1899	FHL: Delayed birth certificates for a few counties 1870s–1940s.
Georgia	1919	FHL: Index to delayed birth certificates available for a few counties; various years are covered.
Hawaii	1842; adhered to by 1929	FHL: Birth records and transcripts 1896–1903; indexes 1896–1909. Birth index 1909–1949 and birth records 1901–1916. Delayed birth registrations 1859–1903; delayed birth records 1904–1907.
Idaho	1911	FHL: Some county records have been microfilmed. Indexed abstracts available for some counties.
Illinois	1916	FHL: Many delayed birth registrations have been filmed. Cook County (Chicago) birth index 1871–1916. Chicago birth records 1878–1922.
Indiana	1907	FHL: WPA transcripts of records and indexes for twenty-five counties, 1882–1920. Some delayed birth records have been microfilmed.
Iowa	1880	FHL: Statewide index 1880–1934.
Kansas	1911	
Kentucky	1911	FHL: Statewide index 1911–1954.
Louisiana	1914	
Maine	1892	FHL: Statewide index 1892–1922.
Maryland	1898; Baltimore began in 1875	
Massachusetts	As early as 1639	FHL: Statewide indexes through 1971; delayed and corrected, 1893–1970. NEHGS: Holland, Massachusetts 1891–1955. NEHGS: Plainfield, Massachusetts 1785–1983. NEHGS: Seekonk, Massachusetts 1850–1954.
Michigan	1867	FHL: Delayed birth records for about twenty counties.
Minnesota	1900	
Mississippi	1912	
Missouri	1909	
Montana	1907	

Nebraska	1905	
Nevada	1911	
New Hampshire	1883	
New Jersey	1848	New Jersey State Archives: Index 1901--1923.
New Mexico	1920	
New York	1881	FHL: Manhattan index 1881–1965. FHL: Brooklyn index 1881–1965. FHL: Bronx index 1898–1965 (missing 1911). FHL: Queens index 1847–1965 (missing 1911). FHL: Staten Island index 1847–1965 (missing 1911).
North Carolina	1913	
North Dakota	1907	
Ohio	1867	FHL: Corrected and delayed registrations 1941–1960s for some counties. Cincinnati birth index 1846–1908.
Oklahoma	1908	
Oregon	1903	
Pennsylvania	1906	FHL: Delayed birth registrations for many counties. Allegheny County 1875–1905. Allegheny City 1878–1907. McKeesport 1892–1906. Pittsburgh 1870–1912. Philadelphia 1904–1915; corrections 1872–1915 and 1967–1981. York 1888–1905.
Rhode Island	1853; adhered to by about 1915	FHL: Index 1853–1878; records 1852–1900. FHL: East Providence birth index 1862–1946.
South Carolina	1915	FHL: Index 1877–1901.
South Dakota	1905	
Tennessee	1908	FHL: Indexes 1908–1925 for a few counties. Chattanooga 1881–1913. Knoxville 1911–1915.
Texas	1903	FHL: Statewide index 1900–1945, plus delayed birth registrations index.
Utah	1905	FHL: Salt Lake City births 1890–1950.
Vermont	1955	FHL: Statewide index to town records 1760–1908.
Virginia	1912	FHL: Birth index 1853–1896. Birth records 1853–1941. A few counties have been microfilmed into the 1960s.
Washington	1968	FHL: 1907–1959; delayed 1936–1953.
West Virginia	1917	FHL: Birth certificates and delayed certificates 1852–1930. Some counties have been microfilmed into the 1960s.
Wisconsin	1907	FHL: 1850s–1907; delayed birth registrations filed 1937–1942.
Wyoming	1909	

The Works Progress Administration (WPA) transcripts of birth, marriage and death indexes for twenty-five Indiana counties, 1882–1920, are also searchable at Family Tree Maker's subscription library, http://www.genealogylibrary.com.

Sources

OBTAINING VITAL RECORDS

Thomas Jay Kemp's *International Vital Records Handbook*, 3d edition (see appendix E) includes copies of application forms that you may photocopy and use to order records. Many public libraries have this book in the reference or genealogy department. The handbook is current as of the date of publication only; it is advisable to telephone the health department to verify fees and addresses.

The National Center for Health Statistics publishes information for requesting vital certificates, titled *Where to Write for Vital Records*. It is available on the Internet at http://www.cdc.gov/nchswww/howto/w2w/w2welcom.htm.

BIRTH RECORDS AT THE FAMILY HISTORY LIBRARY, SALT LAKE CITY

As the previous chart indicates, the Family History Library has microfilm copies of many birth indexes and certificates. One example is the index to births in Los Angeles, California, 1905–1923. They also have microfilm copies of Los Angeles original birth certificates for 1905 to 1919 plus delayed certificates of birth filed from 1943 to 1964.

A certificate of birth of a female born 8 October 1919, in Los Angeles and amended in 1928, was found in the birth records named above. An "Affidavit for Correction of a Record," signed by the mother and father of the child, was filed with the birth certificate. The parents were residing in Broome County, New York, in 1928, thus providing important information if anyone was trying to locate this family. The affidavit stated that the original certificate omitted the name of the child (it was blank on the original), that the name of the father was wrong (it was a completely different name), that the original certificate incorrectly stated the father was deceased (he was indeed alive), and that the maiden name of the mother was incorrect (Morton; not Norton). A new birth certificate was issued, using the same certificate number, and stamped "Amended 1-21-28; see attached affidavit."

NONTRADITIONAL BIRTH RECORDS
Persons Born in Foreign Countries Who Are U.S. Citizens at Birth

Births of children born to U.S. citizens residing in foreign countries are reported to the nearest American consular office and to the U.S. Department of State in Washington, DC. To obtain a copy of a report of this type of birth, write to Passport Services, Correspondence Branch, U.S. Department of State, Washington, DC 20524. State the full name of the child at birth, date of birth, place of birth and names of parents. Also include any information about the U.S. passport on which the child's name was first included. Sign the request, and state your relationship to the person whose record is being requested and the reason for the request. To determine the current fee, consult *Where to Write for Vital Records* by the National Center for Health Statistics. This publication can be found at most public libraries and on the Internet (at http://www.cdc.gov/nchs www/howto/w2w/w2welcom.htm).

Alien Children Adopted by U.S. Citizens

Birth certifications for alien children adopted by U.S. citizens and lawfully admitted to the U.S. are filed in the state of adoption, but they may also be on file with the Immigration and Naturalization Service (INS), U.S. Department of Justice, Washington, DC 20536. Requests must be submitted on INS Form G-641, which can be obtained from any INS office.

A NOTE ABOUT ACCESSING VITAL RECORDS

Access to vital records (birth, marriage and death certificates) is extremely unpredictable. The state laws and access policies continually change throughout the U.S.; therefore, the Federation of Genealogical Societies (FGS) and the National Genealogical Society (NGS) have established a Records Preservation and Access Committee. This joint committee seeks to identify areas of concern and provide help to organizations attempting to change access or preservation policies. In addition, the committee seeks to develop a national network of experts, advisors and organizations to be of assistance when critical records are in danger of being destroyed or when access to important documents is unreasonably restricted.

If you feel you are unlawfully denied access to a vital record, contact FGS or NGS. They may have an update on the state in question and be able to advise if any bills have been drafted to change the law.

Federation of Genealogical Societies
Records Preservation and Access Committee
P.O. Box 200940
Austin, TX 78720-0940
Phone: (512) 336-2731
Fax: (512) 336-2732
E-mail: fgs-office@fgs.org
http://www.fgs.org/

National Genealogical Society
4527 Seventeenth St. North
Arlington, VA 22207-2399
Phone: (703) 525-0050 or (800) 473-0060
http://www.ngsgenealogy.org/

Births in International Territory on Aircraft or Seagoing Vessels

When a birth occurs in international territory, whether on an aircraft or a seagoing vessel, the record is filed based on the direction in which the mode of transportation was moving when the event occurred.

- If the vessel or aircraft was *outbound* or had docked or landed at a foreign destination, requests for copies of the record should be made to the U.S. Department of State, Washington, DC 20522-1705.
- If the vessel or aircraft was *inbound* and the first port of entry was in the U.S., write to the registration authority in the city where the vessel or aircraft docked or landed in the U.S.
- If a vessel was of U.S. registry, contact the U.S. Coast Guard facility at

BIRTH INDEX IDENTIFIES BIRTH FATHER

An adoptee, born in 1939, was searching for her birth parents. The adoption file named the father and said he was born in 1904 in Pittsburgh, Pennsylvania. A search of the Pittsburgh Birth Register, 1870–1905, located at the Family History Library, indicated there was only one male with the name being searched, and he was born in 1895, not 1904. Using the name of the individual and the 1895 birth date, the Social Security Death Benefits Index (see chapter seven) was searched and a match made. This case could not have been solved without using the birth register. The Social Security Death Benefits Index had several entries for the name being searched, but with an exact birth date, we could identify an entry worth pursuing.

the port of entry and/or search the vessel logs at the U.S. Coast Guard facility at the vessel's final port of call for that voyage.

Births That Occur on Airplanes or Trains Crossing the Continental U.S.

If a birth occurs on an airplane or train crossing the continental U.S., the record is filed in the county where the mother and child disembark from the plane or train, even when several stops are made along the way.

BIRTH CERTIFICATE RESEARCH TIPS

- When ordering a birth certificate via U.S. Mail, send a check or money order. Do not send cash.
- Send a self-addressed stamped envelope (SASE) with mail requests to speed the process. Enclosing an overnight postmarked envelope with a birth certificate request will further speed the process.
- Always request the long-form birth certificate. The extra information may be helpful in other research.
- When a birth certificate does not include the signature of the doctor, the certificate may not be the original. In other words, it may be an amended birth certificate for an adopted child. There are exceptions, of course. Some forms do not provide a space for name of doctor.
- When ordering a birth certificate of a deceased person, enclose a copy of the death certificate. Many states will issue the birth certificate if you prove the person is deceased. They usually stamp *Deceased* across the face of the certificate so it cannot be used for other purposes.

FIVE

Marriage and Divorce Records

Research Tip

Marriage and divorce records contain a wealth of information that is useful in locating a living person. These records provide names, dates, places, addresses and other clues that can be important to the research process. For example, a woman's maiden name, obtained from a marriage record, may be essential information in a search. A divorce file may include Social Security numbers for both parties or exact birth dates of the children. As mentioned in chapter one, every piece of information about an individual helps create a profile needed for a successful search.

MARRIAGE LICENSE AND CERTIFICATE

Two documents are created when a couple marries: a marriage license and a marriage certificate. **When ordering copies of a marriage record, be sure to request the license *and* the certificate.** The contents of these documents will vary from one state to another and even between counties within a state. Colorado marriage records, for example, do not name the parents of the bride and groom, but many other states' documents do. Below is a list of the possible contents in a marriage license and/or certificate.

- Full names of bride and groom
- Ages or birth dates of bride and groom
- Birthplaces of bride and groom
- Address(es) of bride and groom
- Occupations of bride and groom
- Names of parents of bride and groom
- Previous marriage status (married, never married, widowed)
- How last marriage ended (death, divorce or annulment)
- Number of previous marriages
- If divorced, where divorced
- Name of person performing the ceremony (clue to religious affiliation)

Tip

- Names of witnesses (may be relatives)
- Signatures of bride and groom

Women are more difficult to track than men because of their name changes. A woman who marries often changes her surname to that of her husband. If they divorce, she may return to her maiden name, marry again and assume the name of her new husband. Some women hyphenate their maiden and married names, and some change their name completely for privacy. For example:

- Jane Brown (maiden name) marries Michael Porter and changes her name to Jane Porter.
- Jane and Michael Porter divorce.
- Jane Porter marries Henry Smith and changes her name to Jane Smith.
- Jane and Henry Smith divorce.
- Jane Smith legally changes her name to Jane Booth (surname of her great-grandfather) to prevent her ex-husband from finding her.
- Jane Booth marries Robert Fulton and does not change her name, but begins using Christy Booth, based on her middle name.

The names in the above scenario were changed for privacy, but the events are true. The marriage and divorce records would reveal the name changes until Jane changed her surname to Booth. At that point you would need to search county court records for the name change. Name changes are public record; therefore, Jane may have fooled her ex-husband, but a good researcher would eventually find the paper trail.

Case Study

DIVORCE FILE ASSISTANCE

We were trying to locate a man who had married and divorced three times. The divorce file from his first marriage turned out to be a wealth of information needed to locate him. The file was at least two inches thick with ten years' worth of documents filed by his ex-wife. She was attempting to collect child support and reported his whereabouts and employment to the court every few months. The information contained in this file helped locate him, enabling the third wife (who had no knowledge of the first wife) to collect child support.

DIVORCE RECORDS

Divorce records can be rich in data. Contents can include

- full names of husband and wife
- addresses and changes of address
- ages or birth dates of husband and wife
- Social Security numbers of husband and wife
- date and place of marriage of husband and wife
- maiden name of wife
- full names and birth dates of children
- name and address of employer(s)
- financial affidavits
- military service information
- inventory of assets, including vehicles and real estate

FINDING MARRIAGE AND DIVORCE RECORDS

Finding marriage and divorce records is often a challenge. Someone can marry or divorce in their hometown, in Las Vegas, in Mexico or anywhere else depending upon residency requirements. If you do not have a solid residential history of the person you are researching, it may be nearly impossible to know where he married or divorced.

Marriages and divorces are recorded with the county or district clerks, so **the most logical place to begin a search is in the couple's county of residence.** If that does not work, search neighboring counties.

If you are fortunate, your search will lead to a state that maintains an index to all marriages or divorces. Otherwise, you will have to search bride and groom indexes at the county courthouse. Many of these indexes, depending upon time period, are handwritten and indexed by only the first letter of the surname.

Beginning on page 40 is a list of states with statewide indexes. You may note that some states (California and Oregon, for example) discontinued indexing marriage records on a statewide basis. If the index, or a portion of the index, is held by the Family History Library or the New England Historic Genealogical Society, this is also noted. Although many states have an index to marriages, the original record is usually held by the county court.

Marriage and Divorce Indexes by County at the Family History Library

The Family History Library has hundreds of additional marriage and divorce records for the twentieth century, but they are for individual counties or cities. For example, the library has the Anderson County, Tennessee, marriage index 1838–1987, plus the marriage records from 1919 to 1974. The index to marriages in East Providence, Rhode Island, 1862–1946, is another example. Explore the Family History Library catalog—you'll find many others.

Marriage and Divorce Indexes on the Internet

Three states have placed these indexes on the Internet. Their addresses are

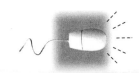

Colorado Marriages and Divorces, marriages 1975–1997, divorces 1975–July 1998
http://www.quickinfo.net/madi/comadi.html

Kentucky Marriages and Divorces, 1973–1993
http://ukcc.uky.edu/~vitalrec/

Maine Marriages, 1892–1966
http://www.state.me.us/sos/arc/archives/genealogy/marriage.htm

OBTAINING A COPY OF A MARRIAGE OR DIVORCE RECORD

Marriage records are more available to the public than any other type of vital record. For this reason you can usually obtain a photocopy of a marriage license or certificate by simply writing to the county clerk of court and paying a fee for the record.

Divorce records are not as easy to obtain. Some states consider them open to the public, but some states also seal the files for seventy-five or one hundred

STATE WEB SITES

To determine if the state you are researching has vital record indexes on-line, explore the state's Web site. All state Web sites have the address www.state .xx.us, where *xx* is the two-letter abbreviation of the state. For example, North Carolina's is www.state.nc. us, and Colorado's is www .state.co.us.

MARRIAGE AND DIVORCE STATEWIDE INDEXES BY
STATE HEALTH DEPARTMENTS
Public Availability of Indexes Reported for Family History Library (FHL) and
New England Historic Genealogical Society (NEHGS)

State	Marriage	Divorce
Alabama	1936–1959 (FHL) Certificates 1936–1992 (FHL)	1908–1937 (FHL) 1950–1959 (FHL) Certificates 1938–1992 (FHL)
Alaska		1950–
Arkansas	1917–	1923–
California	1949–1985 (FHL has indexes 1960–1985; NEHGS has indexes 1960–1985)	1962–
Colorado	Groom only index 1900–1939 (FHL) Bride and groom index 1975–1992 (FHL)	1900–1939; 1975–1992 (FHL)
Connecticut		1947–
District of Columbia	1811–1921	
Florida	1927–1969 (FHL) (NEHGS has indexes 1927–1991)	1927–1991 (NEHGS)
Georgia	1964–1992 (FHL)	1965–1992 (FHL)
Hawaii	1909–1949 (FHL)	1951–
Idaho	1947–	1947–
Illinois	1962–	1962–
Indiana	1958–	
Kansas	1913–	1951–
Kentucky	1958– 1972–1990 (FHL)	1958–
Maine	Brides 1892– (FHL 1895–1953) Grooms 1956–	
Maryland	June 1951–	
Massachusetts	1841–1971 (FHL) (NEHGS has Holland, MA 1891–1955; Plainfield, MA 1785–1983; Williamsburg, MA marriage intentions 1900–1930)	1952– (FHL 1952–1970)
Michigan	1872–1921	
Minnesota	1958–	1970–
Mississippi	Grooms only index Pre-1926 (FHL)	
Missouri		July 1948–
Montana		July 1943–
Nevada	1968– (Clark County [Las Vegas] has index 1907–1968; FHL has index 1968–1991)	1968–
New Hampshire		Prior to 1938 (FHL) Prior to 1938 (NEHGS)

New York	1881–1917 (excludes New York City; FHL has New York City index 1888–1937)	
North Carolina	1962–	
North Dakota	1925–	1949–
Ohio	1949–	
Oregon	1906–1924, 1946–1959, 1966–1989	1946–1960, 1966–1989
Rhode Island		1962–
South Dakota	1905–	1905–
Tennessee	1945–	1945–
Texas	1966–	1968–
Vermont	1871–1908 (FHL), 1909–1941, 1942–1954	1861–1968
Washington	1968–	1968–
West Virginia	1921–	
Wisconsin	1852–1907 (FHL), 1973–1984	1965–1984 (FHL)
Wyoming	1941–	1941–

years. Some courts even destroy divorce files. For example, Jackson County, Missouri, destroys divorce files after twenty-five years. Divorce files are generally found in civil court or domestic relations court.

Check these sources (see appendix E) for addresses and telephone numbers for county courthouses:

- *Ancestry's Red Book: American State, County and Town Sources*, revised edition, edited by Alice Eichholz, Ph.D., CG
- *The Handybook for Genealogists*, 9th edition.
- *The Sourcebook of County Court Records*, 4th edition.

MARRIAGE AND DIVORCE RECORDS RESEARCH TIPS

- When ordering by mail, include a SASE with your request.
- When examining indexes yourself, check spelling variations (see "Telephone Directory Research Tips," chapter two).
- Remember to ask for the marriage license *and* the marriage certificate.
- A divorce decree is merely the order to dissolve the marriage. Request the entire file, which contains additional information.
- Check indexes to name changes at the county court. Many women change their surname immediately following a divorce; others, a few years later.

Microfilm Source

SOURCE OF THE MICHIGAN INDEX

The microfilmed Michigan index (in chart on page 40) is available at the Library of Michigan; State Archives of Michigan; the Burton Historical Collection of the Detroit Public Library; and the Allen County Public Library in Fort Wayne, Indiana.

SIX

Death Certificates; Obituaries; Cemetery, Funeral Home and Probate Records

G athering information about a deceased person can sometimes help find a living person. Stepping backward one or two generations will develop a broader profile of the person within a family unit and give you more clues to follow. For example, if you lose track of someone, you may uncover a new path by focusing your research on that person's deceased parents, grandparents, siblings or other relatives.

USING DEATH-RELATED RECORDS TO LOCATE THE LIVING

When someone dies, a chain of events begins:

(1) A death certificate is issued;

(2) A funeral notice or obituary is published in the newspaper;

(3) A funeral home or mortuary arranges for the cremation or burial of the body;

(4) A cemetery headstone is sometimes erected; and

(5) The estate is probated.

These records are full of information you can use to locate a living person. Suppose you track a person to the year 1959 and have no further clues to advance the research, but you do know the names of your target person's parents.

You refocus your research and begin tracking your target's parents. You find them in the city directories from 1955 through 1970. In 1970, the directory listing changes from naming both parents to naming the wife as a widow. You now have an estimated date of death for the father.

Using the newspaper index at the public library, you find the father's obituary. It names his survivors, including the name and address of the son whom

Brick Wall Buster

you are trying to locate. Your research just jumped from 1959 to 1970, and your odds of success have greatly improved.

If you cannot locate the son with the 1970 address, refocus your research on the mother and determine her date of death. Repeat the steps, and hopefully you'll obtain more recent information on the son.

DEATH CERTIFICATES
Death Certificate Contents
Death certificates are similar in content from state to state, although the forms are not exactly alike. The information will also vary by time period; e.g., a death certificate from the 1940s may name the birthplaces of the deceased person's parents, whereas a present-day certificate may not.

This information is found in most death certificates:
- full name of deceased
- Social Security number
- regular address of deceased
- length of residence at place of death
- date and place of death
- cause of death (this is marked out by some states)
- date and place of birth of deceased
- names and birthplaces of parents of deceased
- military service
- name of funeral home
- date of burial or cremation
- name and address of informant (often a relative)
- signature of doctor or coroner

Warning

Death certificates are well known for errors. The informant (that is, the person supplying the information) is often a surviving spouse or child and this person is mourning the loss of a loved one; the information they give may be inadvertently incorrect. For this reason, you must question the data as you use it for further research.

How to Obtain a Death Certificate
Death certificates are issued by the state (or county) health department where the death occurred. VitalChek Network, Inc. ([800] 255-4214; http://www.vital chek.com/) will provide the correct telephone or fax number to place your order with state and county health departments. The cost of death certificates varies from five dollars to twenty-five dollars each. Most states will accept credit cards, although they charge an extra fee for this service. If you do not have the exact date of death, some states will search their index, but will also charge an extra fee for this service.

State health departments are beginning to post request forms on the Internet, along with information on fees and addresses. To determine if the state you are researching has done this, go to the state's Web site (see page 39). You can

See Also

For more information on applying for vital records, see the sources listed on page 137.

also use the search engines to find other Web sites that provide vital record information by using the words *Vital Records* plus the name of the state.

Types of Death Certificates

There are two types of death certificates: abstracts and the original documents. Always request a "full" copy of a death record, as every item of information can be important in your search. Following are two death certificates for the same individual: Henry C. Hinckley, who died in 1937. The certificate issued by Wood County, West Virginia, (below) is an abstract of the actual death record, whereas the one issued by the State of West Virginia (page 45) is a photocopy of the original document.

DEATH INDEXES
Social Security Death Index

The Social Security Death Index (sometimes called the Social Security Death Benefits Index or the National Death Index) is a database of information that lists the name, birth date, death date, Social Security number and place of death for more than sixty million people. It is, by far, the most important and useful source for obtaining information for persons who died after 1962. For all its listings, however, it is not a complete index to all people who died in the United States. See chapter seven for more information.

Twentieth Century Death Indexes at Family History Library

You can search some indexes yourself. The Family History Library has the statewide death indexes listed in the chart on page 46; these can be searched in Salt Lake City or ordered through a local Family History Center.

Certificate STATE OF WEST VIRGINIA **of Death**

STATE OF WEST VIRGINIA
WOOD COUNTY COURT CLERK'S OFFICE

I, L. W. BURDETTE, Clerk of the County Court aforesaid, and as such, custodian of the records of Births and Deaths, hereby certify that_____ HENRY C. HINCKLEY

died in Wood County and State of West Virginia on the ___25th___ day of ___DECEMBER___, 19_37_, as reference to Death Record No. ___4___ Page ___96___, of my office aforesaid, will show.

Date of Birth_____ Place of Birth ___WEST VIRGINIA___

Parents' Names_____

Cause of Death___ACUTE BRONCHITIS_____

Place of Death___WOOD COUNTY, WEST VIRGINIA_____

IN TESTIMONY WHEREOF, I have hereunto affixed my signature and the Official Seal this ___16th___ day of___SEPTEMBER___, 19_76_, at Parkersburg, County and State aforesaid.

Death Recorded ___YEAR 1937___

By _____ *L W Burdette*
        DEPUTY   CLERK WOOD COUNTY COURT

A. V. S. Form

PARKERSBURG

STANDARD CERTIFICATE OF DEATH
West Virginia State Department of Health

D Price

PLACE OF DEATH *Home 610 Kenner St*

Registered No. *18704*

County *Wood*

District *Parkersburg* (Dist. No. *543*)

Town or City *Parkersburg*

No. *610 Kenner* Street
(If death occurred in a hospital or institution, give its name instead of street and number)

PLACE OF RESIDENCE: STATE _____ Length of residence where death occurred ___ yrs. ___ mos. ___ ds.
(If not same as place of death)

County *Wood*

District *Parkersburg* (Dist. No. *543*)

Town or City *Parkersburg.*

No. *610 Kenner* Street

2 FULL NAME *Henry C Hinckley*

(Local Registrar's Serial No. *534*)

PERSONAL AND STATISTICAL PARTICULARS

MEDICAL CERTIFICATE OF DEATH

3. SEX	4. COLOR OR RACE	5. Single Married, Widowed, or Divorced (write the word)
Male	*White*	*Widowed*

6. IF MARRIED, WIDOWED, OR DIVORCED
Husband of
(or) Wife of

7. DATE OF BIRTH
(month, day, and year) *Nov 5 1861*

8. AGE	Years	Months	Days	IF LESS than 1 day, ___ hrs. or ___ min.
	76	*1*		

9. TRADE PROFESSION or particular kind of work done, as spinner, sawyer, bookkeeper, etc.

10. INDUSTRY OR BUSINESS, in which work was done, as silk mill, bank, etc.

11. DATE DECEASED LAST WORKED at this occupation (month and year)

11. TOTAL TIME (years) spent in this occupation

12. BIRTHPLACE (city or town) (State or Country) *WVa*

13. NAME *Henry Hinckley*

14. BIRTHPLACE (city or town) (State or Country) *WVa*

15. MAIDEN NAME *Fannie Coe*

16. BIRTHPLACE (City or Town) (State or Country) *WVa.*

17. INFORMANT *C J Warne*
(Address)

18. BURIAL, CREMATION, OR REMOVAL
Place *Davisville* Date *Dec 26*, 19 *37*

19. FUNERAL DIRECTOR (Signature)
Warne Funeral Home
Fr. Dir. License No. *430* Embalmers No. *987*

20. FILED *12/25*, 19 *37* *S R Knight* Registrar.

---

21. DATE OF DEATH
(month, day and year) *Dec 25 1230* 19 *37*

22. I HEREBY CERTIFY, That I attended deceased from *Dec 23*
19 *37*, to *Dec 25th*, 19 *37*. I last saw him alive
on *Dec 24th*, 19 *37*, death is said to have occurred on the
date stated above, at *12 34 a.m.* m.
The principal cause of death and related causes of importance
were as follows:

Date of onset

Acute Bronchitis

General Debility

Other contributory causes of importance :

Name of operation *—* Date of _____

What test confirmed diagnosis _____ Was there any autopsy? _____

23. If death was due to external causes (violence) fill in also the following :

Accident, suicide, or homicide? _____ Date of injury _____, 19 ___

Where did injury occur? _____
(Specify City or Town, County, and State)

Specify whether injury occurred in industry, in home, or in public place.

Manner of injury _____

Nature of injury _____

24. Was disease or injury in any way related to occupation of deceased?
_____ If so, specify _____

(Signed) *Horace H. Price* M. D.

(Address) *907 Market St*

I hereby certify that the above is a true photo-static (photographic) copy of a record filed with the Division of Vital Statistics, West Virginia State Department of Health, Charleston, West Virginia.

Witness my hand and seal this twenty-eighth day of September , 1976 .

N H Dyer

N. H. Dyer, M. D., M. P. H., State Registrar

This full death certificate contains information not found in the abstract, including the address, birth date, sex, race and marital status of deceased; names and birthplaces of parents; place of burial; and name of funeral home—all valuable information when researching someone.

STATEWIDE DEATH INDEXES AVAILABLE THROUGH THE FAMILY HISTORY LIBRARY

State	Years	State	Years
Alabama	1908–1969	New Jersey	1901–1940 (not in FHL; located New Jersey State Archives)
California	1905–1988 and 1940–1990	New Mexico	1889–1940
Delaware	1855–1910	New York	1868–1965 (for New York City; actual death certificates through 1948 available at New York City Municipal Archives)
Florida (by year)	1877–1969	North Carolina	1901–1967 (certificates 1906–1994)
Georgia	1919–1993	Ohio	1913–1932 1941–1964 (veterans) (death records from 20 Dec 1908 through 31 Dec 1936 [and respective indexes] are located at the State Archives of Ohio, Ohio Historical Society)
Hawaii	1909–1949	Oregon	1903–1970 (deaths 1903–1989 available at Oregon State Archives, Oregon State Library, and Oregon Historical Society)
Idaho	1911–1932	Pennsylvania	1904–1915 (Philadelphia only)
Illinois Cook County Clerk Index Cook County Board Health Cook County Out-of-town	1916–1938 (certificates 1916–1945 excluding Chicago) 1871–1916 1871–1933 1909–1915	Rhode Island	1901–1943
Indiana	Some county death indexes available through 1920	Tennessee	1914–1942 (by county)
Kentucky	1911–1986	Texas	1900–1945
Maine	1892–1922 (NEHGS has Maine death index through 1970)	Vermont	1871–1908
Massachusetts	1844–1971	Washington	1907–1979
Michigan	1867–1914 (not in FHL; index available at Library of Michigan, State Archives of Michigan, Burton Historical Collection of the Detroit Public Library, and the Allen County Public Library in Fort Wayne, Indiana)	West Virginia	1925–1991 (index) 1917–1994 (certificates)
Minnesota	c1866–1915	Wisconsin	1852–1907 and 1959–1984

The Family History Library also has death indexes by county or city for some areas. For example, they filmed the index to deaths for East Providence, Rhode Island, 1862–1946.

There are also twentieth-century death indexes located at the New England Historic Genealogical Society. They include

California	1940–1987
Florida	1877–1991
Holland, Massachusetts	1891–1955
Plainfield, Massachusetts	1785–1983
Seekonk, Massachusetts	1850–1954

Twentieth-Century Death Indexes on the Internet

Some death indexes are on the Internet; more will probably be added in the future.

Internet Source

- http://www.ancestry.com (fee charged)

Connecticut	1949–1996
Kansas (Leavenworth County)	1870–1920 and 1923–1930
Kentucky	1911–1996
Louisiana: New Orleans (Newspaper Index)	1840–1970
Michigan	1971–1996
Missouri (Newspaper Death Index)	
Callaway County	1846–1926
Cole County	1884–1907
Montgomery County	1875–1994
North Carolina	1968–1997
Ohio	1958–1969 and 1989–1992
Vermont	1989–1996

- http://ukcc.uky.edu/~vitalrec/

Kentucky	1911–1992

- http://kadima.com/ (Ameridex; fee charged)

California	1965–1996
Ohio	1994–1996
Florida	Limited

- http://www.ohiohistory.org/textonly/resource/archlib/brthdth1.html

Ohio	1913–1937
	(eventually will span 1908–1944)

- http://www.state.tn.us/sos/statelib/pubsvs/death.htm

Tennessee	1914-1925 (partial index)

- http://www.rootsweb.com/~mnwadena/deathpage.htm

Wadena County, Minnesota	1880–1993

(Work-in-progress site. There are probably more county indexes such as this one on the Internet. Use the search engines to see if your county may be one of them.)

OBITUARIES AND FUNERAL NOTICES

A newspaper obituary and a funeral notice are not exactly the same. An obituary is a summary of the person's life, typically giving information on the deceased's education, career and family (funeral information may be included, as well). A funeral notice, on the other hand, announces the time and place of the funeral and usually lists names and addresses of survivors. Note the difference in the following obituary and funeral notice:

Obituary for Morris Dryfoos
Funeral services for Morris Dryfoos, retired Colorado cattleman, will be at 2 P.M. Friday in Fairmount Cemetery. Entombment will be in Fairmount. Mr. Dryfoos, who lived at 1580 St. Paul St., died Thursday in General Rose Hospital. He was 81. Born Sept. 13, 1879, in Mannheim, Germany, Mr. Dryfoos was brought to the United States in 1884. He lived in Chicago for many years and in 1906 married Miss Olga Goldstein in Chicago. The couple moved to Denver in 1923. Mr. Dryfoos was a member of Temple Emanuel. Surviving in addition to his wife are a son, Irving of Denver; a daughter, Mrs. Frances D. Baer of New York City; and four grandchildren.

Funeral Notice for Morris Dryfoos
Morris Dryfoos of 1580 St. Paul St. Husband of Olga Dryfoos; father of Irving S. Dryfoos, Denver; and Mrs. Frances D. Baer, Merrick, New York; also survived by four grandchildren. Services Fairmount Mausoleum Chapel, today at 2 P.M. Friends who wish may contribute to the charity of their choice.

The above obituary and funeral notice were both published by the *Denver Post* on Friday, 4 November 1960, but in different sections of the newspaper. When obituaries are not published on the same page as the funeral notices, they are easy to miss. To complicate this type of research, it is common to find obituaries published a week or two after the death. As you can see, it is important to be thorough in newspaper research.

Only about 10 percent of deaths are reported in both obituary and funeral notice format. The majority appear as brief funeral notices. The exception would be in small communities where nearly all deaths are reported in the obituary style.

RESEARCHING OUT-OF-TOWN DEATHS

When searching for an obituary outside your city of residence, you have five options:

1) Determine if a newspaper from that city is available through interlibrary loan for you to search.
2) Write or telephone the public library in the community of the deceased, and ask if they have an obituary index (sometimes called a "necrology file") and what services they offer to research and/or photocopy obituaries.
3) Study the Family History Library catalog to determine if they have microfilmed an index to obituaries in the area of your research.

4) Explore the Internet to determine if obituaries (or an index) are available on-line for the area and time period needed.

5) Hire a professional researcher (see chapter seventeen) to search the newspaper for you.

Obituary Indexes at Public Libraries

Public libraries often maintain obituary collections or indexes to their local newspaper. **An inquiry with the library may save you hours of research.** Some libraries are exceptionally helpful and will check the index, photocopy the obituary and fax or mail it to you. Some libraries require payment in advance, whereas others will bill you or provide the service free. Occasionally, library staff will refuse to give service over the telephone.

Timesaver

Obituary Indexes at the Family History Library

The Family History Library is famous for its microfilm collection of such original records as deeds, court records, vital certificates and church records. It is a little-known fact that the library also microfilms twentieth-century indexes to newspapers and collections of obituaries.

The Family History Library catalog cannot be searched by record type. In other words, you cannot obtain a list of all newspapers (for the entire U.S.) that are in the library's collection. Instead, you must search geographically, then by subject. If you are searching for newspapers or obituary indexes for Tennessee, for instance, you need to search by city, by county or by state, then search under the subheading of "newspapers" or "vital records" or "obituaries." The obituary references are sometimes cataloged under "vital records" since they are references to deaths. Here is a sample list of twentieth-century obituaries available at the Family History Library:

California: Index to San Francisco newspapers, 1904–1949
California: Obituaries in *San Francisco Chronicle*, 1978–1984
Florida: Death Notices, 1982, *The Miami Herald*
Illinois: Index to obituaries, 1906–July 1993, *Chicago Heights Star*
Kansas: Obituary card file, Jefferson County, Kansas, 1887–1989
Louisiana: Death notices, 1859–1961, Thibodaux, Louisiana and vicinity
Minnesota: Obituary index, 1888–1982, Mankato *Free Press*
Minnesota: Obituaries (prominent persons only), 1958–1970, Minneapolis *Star Tribune*
Nebraska: Mortuary notices and obituaries, 1986–1993, *Omaha World-Herald*
New York: Obituary index, 1980–1989, *Ithaca Journal*
South Dakota: Index to obituaries, 1975–1995, *Rapid City Journal*
Texas: Deaths and funerals, June 1955–Dec 1958, *The Dallas Morning News*

Obituaries on the Internet

There are several sites on the Internet that allow you access to obituaries:

• http://www.usgenweb.com/

The USGenWeb project is a volunteer program wherein genealogists "adopt" a state and create a Web site for that state under the USGenWeb project banner. Other volunteers adopt a county, then create a Web site for that county under the state project banner. Modern obituaries are often posted within these Web sites. They can be accessed by clicking on a state and then viewing the state's project archives or the county listings.

- http://www.cyndislist.com/obits.htm/

  Cyndi's List of Genealogy Sites on the Internet lists Web sites that index obituaries.

- http://www.ancestry.com (fee charged)

  Following is a sample list, many others are available.

California: *Los Angeles Daily News*	1990–1998
Louisiana: *The Advocate* (Baton Rouge)	1990–1998
Michigan: *The Grand Rapids Press*	1990–1998
Pennsylvania: *The Patriot-News* (Harrisburg)	1990–1998
Tennessee: *The Knoxville News-Sentinel*	1990–1998
Texas: *Ft. Worth Star-Telegram*	1990–1998
UMI Company Obituaries (85 newspapers)	1990–1997

- http://www.polaris.net/~legend/gateway5.htm

  This Web site links to more than three hundred obituary sites. For example, http://www.pconline.com/~mnobits/ indexes nearly 100,000 Minnesota obituaries from selected Minnesota newspapers beginning in September 1995. The search for the surname Westberg produced the following list:

WESTBERG# Barbara Ann, 57, Bloomington MN, Minneapolis Star Tribune, 06/29/97

WESTBERG# Barbara Ann, 57, Bloomington MN, Minneapolis Star Tribune, 06/28/97

WESTBERG# Bessie, 84, Cannon Falls MN, Minneapolis Star Tribune, 04/01/97

WESTBERG# Hilmer J, 90, Long Lake MN, Minneapolis Star Tribune, 05/03/96

WESTBERG# Lyle J, 72, MN, Sun City West AZ, Minneapolis Star Tribune, 08/07/96

WESTBERG# Lyle J, 72, MN, Sun City West AZ, Minneapolis Star Tribune, 08/08/96

WESTBERG# Victor D, 63, Cambridge MN, Minneapolis Star Tribune, 10/18/95

Notice that two different dates for the same newspaper are given for Barbara Westberg and Lyle Westberg. This is when an obituary or funeral notice is repeated by the newspaper. Sometimes these repeats are *not* exactly alike; therefore, thorough research demands that you examine all references.

Also note that Lyle Westberg died in Sun City, Arizona, but his death was reported in Minneapolis. In this case, Lyle may have retired to Sun City, or perhaps maintained summer and winter residences. His death was probably reported in both cities.

Obituaries of Nationally Prominent Individuals

The New York Times Obituaries Index, 1858–1968 (New York: New York Times, 1970) and *The New York Times Obituary Index II, 1969–1978* (New York: New York Times, 1980) are excellent sources to consult if researching a nationally prominent individual. The first volume covers September 1858 through December 1968 and includes more than 353,000 names. The second volume added more than 36,000 names.

The annual indexes to the *New York Times* can be searched for deaths after 1978. The names of persons with obituaries are indexed under the subheading "deaths." The *Personal Name Index to The New York Times 1851–1993*, edited by B.A. Falk Jr. and Valerie R. Falk, is also an excellent source for news items and obituaries of prominent individuals.

Published collections of obituaries for persons from specific professions or careers are also available. For example,

Printed Source

> Perry, Jeb H. *Variety Obits: An Index to Obituaries in Variety, 1905–1978.* Metuchen, New Jersey: Scarecrow Press, 1980.

> Vazzana, Eugene Michael. *Silent Film Necrology: Births and Deaths of Over 9000 Performers, Directors, Producers, and Other Filmmakers of the Silent Era, Through 1993.* Jefferson, North Carolina: McFarland, c1995.

> Yoder Brovont, Rosa L. *Old German Baptist Brethren: Obituary Summaries From the Vindicater, 1870–1994.* Camden, Indiana: R.L.Y. Brovont, c1995.

CEMETERY RECORDS

Cemetery records and tombstone inscriptions can provide information when you are locating a living person. The availability of this data will depend upon the records kept by the cemetery offices and their record-retention policies. Below is a list of information that can be obtained from cemetery records:

- Full name of deceased
- Date and place of birth of deceased
- Date and place of death of deceased
- Date of burial and/or cremation
- Name/address of owner of cemetery plot
- Name/address of person who took possession of cremated remains
- Name/address of survivors
- Location (lot/block) of burial within cemetery
- Whether burial is in a single grave or family plot
- If family plot, names of other persons buried within plot

- Inscription on tombstone (sometimes includes fraternal emblems)

The location of cemetery records will depend upon who owns the cemetery. For example, burials in a church cemetery will be documented by the individual church. Records from a city cemetery may be located at the city hall. Many large public and private cemeteries maintain an office on-site where you will find their records. (National cemeteries for veterans are discussed in chapter nine.)

Inventories of Cemeteries and Tombstone Inscriptions

Many genealogical and historical societies inventory the location of cemeteries within a county or state, as well as publish individual tombstone inscriptions. You might expect genealogical societies to concentrate on pre-twentieth-century tombstone inscriptions since genealogists concentrate on their ancestors. Fortunately, this is not true. When they extract the information from tombstones and other sources, they often provide information up to the date of publication. Therefore, you will find some published cemetery extractions into the 1980s and 1990s. The best way to find out if your geographical area of interest has been inventoried or published is to call the public library and ask.

Internet Source

The Internet is also an excellent place to search for cemetery inventories and inscriptions. The best place to start your search is **Cyndi's List of Genealogy Sites on the Internet** at http://www.cyndislist.com/. Cyndi presently provides links to more than thirty thousand genealogical Web sites organized into ninety research categories. She updates the list constantly with new sites and monitors Web site addresses.

FUNERAL HOME RECORDS

Research Tip

Funeral home research is extremely unpredictable. A particular funeral home might or might not still be in business today. The records might exist; they might not. The owner of the funeral home might answer your questions or tell you the information is confidential. You might obtain information critical to your research or find nothing helpful. **As unpredictable and frustrating as this can be, researching funeral home records is usually worth the time and effort required.**

Funeral directors collect information about deceased persons for the death certificate and obituary. But they have other information, too. They have names of pallbearers (who could be relatives) and information on who paid for the funeral. Sometimes they have complete addresses for survivors, rather than just the city and state reported in the obituary.

Whether or not you can obtain personal information from a funeral home depends upon their rules and policies. Funeral homes are privately owned and not subject to privacy laws.

If a funeral home is no longer in business, then finding its records can be difficult. The records may have been destroyed when the owner died. The children or grandchildren of a prior owner may have the records in their attic.

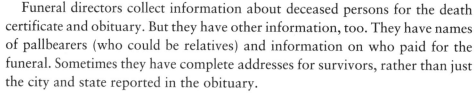

Some families donate the records to a public library or historical society.

It's also possible that the funeral home might have been sold to a competitor, who then merged the two businesses into one. To determine if this is the case, try telephoning a funeral home that is currently in business and ask if they know what happened to the funeral home you are interested in. Or check the index to the local newspaper for the name of the funeral home. Sometimes it is necessary to compile a "genealogy" of a funeral home to determine the current name of the business.

Funeral Home Records at the Family History Library

The Family History Library microfilms funeral home records whenever possible. The format of the Family History Library catalog requires that you search by name of city or county and then under the subheading "funeral home." Sometimes you'll find funeral home records within the listings for vital records. Below is a sampling of funeral home records that have been microfilmed:

California:	Los Angeles, Godeau & Martinoni, 1936–1984
California:	Los Angeles, Pierce Bros. & Co., 1898–1991
Idaho:	Boise, Summers Mortuary, 1910–1948
Illinois:	Chicago, Carlson Funeral Home, 1938–1974
Illinois:	Chicago, Otto Funeral Home,1912–1949
Illinois:	Chicago, Phillips-Peterson Funeral Home, 1937–1973
Michigan:	Grand Rapids, Latzek Funeral Home Index, 1903–1962
North Dakota:	Fargo, Hanson-Runsvold Funeral Home Index, 1921–1957
Ohio:	Cincinnati, Jacob Fuldner Funeral Home, 1885–1936
Ohio:	Cincinnati, Radel Funeral Home, 1909–1950
Ohio:	Cincinnati, Barrere Funeral Home, 1927–1953
Ohio:	Cincinnati, Weil Funeral Home, 1963–1986
Ohio:	Cincinnati, Wiltsee Funeral Home, 1870–1968
Pennsylvania:	Brookville, Galbraith Funeral Home, 1925–1978

PROBATE RECORDS

Probate is a court procedure by which a will is proved to be valid or invalid. In current usage, probate has been expanded to include all matters and proceedings pertaining to the administration of estates and guardianships. **There are two types of probate cases: (1) a testate probate, when the decedent (the deceased person) leaves a will; and (2) an intestate probate, when the decedent dies without a will.**

Probate records are public. Theoretically, you can walk into a courthouse and ask to see a probate file on anyone. There are exceptions, of course—when a file has been sealed for confidentiality, for instance—but very few probate files are closed.

It is not always as easy as it sounds. Probate courts have rules and policies that can affect your research. If the file is in the basement, you may have to wait twenty-four hours for retrieval. If the file is in off-site storage, you may

\di'fin\ *vb*

Definitions

have to wait a week or more. Also, the index may not be available to the public. The court will request a fee to search the index for you.

Should you telephone the probate court, the clerk may insist that the request be in writing. Sometimes the clerk will make photocopies of the file and mail it to you with a billing statement; other times they will refuse to do anything. You may need to hire a professional researcher to visit the courthouse on your behalf.

A very few twentieth-century probate records are held at the Family History Library. This may change, of course, and it is always worth the time and effort to check their library catalog for the county you are researching.

Information Found in Probate Files

Documents within a probate file will list the names and addresses of devisees (persons named in the will) and surviving family members. Creditors of the deceased will request payment from the court. These can include a credit card company, the funeral home or relatives who were owed money, for example. Some probate files cross-reference another court case when the decedent was in litigation with someone. The inventory of the estate may give clues to help in your research, such as information about real estate owned in another state.

The document titled "Final Distribution" will report each person's inheritance amount, as well as their name and address. Sometimes the address in the final distribution is different from when the case was opened, particularly when several months elapsed since the filing. Always be alert to this possibility—it may make a tremendous difference in locating someone.

DEATH RECORDS RESEARCH TIPS

- When requesting death certificates, if you do not have the exact date of death, remember that most states will search a range of years for an extra fee.
- Examine *every* obituary and funeral notice for the deceased person since they can vary in content from day to day, and may vary between newspapers, too.
- Records of cremations may be in a separate index than burials at the cemetery. Check both indexes.
- Cemetery and funeral home records may be indexed by year or cumulatively, such as 1900–1970. **If the clerk is checking the index, ask what type of index they have.** For example, if you tell the clerk that the person died "about 1955," it makes a difference if an annual index for 1955 was examined or a 1900–1970 cumulative index.
- Telephone operators at courthouses often confuse a request for probate court as one for probation court. To save time and frustration clarify your request when calling.

Research Tip

SEVEN

Social Security Administration

T he Social Security Administration (SSA) maintains a larger collection of data on individuals than does any other U.S. government agency. Most records at the SSA are confidential—the Privacy Act of 1974 prevents the SSA from releasing information about a living person without their written authorization—but there are three ways to use or access SSA information:

- The SSA's letter-forwarding service
- The Social Security Death Index
- Applications for Social Security numbers (deceased persons only)

LETTER-FORWARDING SERVICE

The SSA will attempt to forward letters to missing persons for compelling humanitarian or financial reasons. Typical humanitarian reasons include

- a serious illness or death of an immediate family member
- a parent wishing to locate a son or daughter
- a minor child is left without parental guardianship
- consent is needed in an adoption proceeding for the person's child
- a defendant in a felony case seeks a defense witness

Typical financial reasons include locating a person

- who is an heir or beneficiary of an estate
- to whom insurance proceeds are due
- for whom an important document is being held

To use this service, write two letters:

(1) Write a letter to the missing person and place it in an unsealed, unstamped envelope.
(2) Write a letter to the SSA and request their letter-forwarding service.

SSA HELPS SISTER FIND BROTHER

Bob had a serious dispute with his family. He moved out and cut off communication with all family members. About twenty-five years later, his mother was dying and wanted to see her son. Bob's sister wrote a letter to him, sent the letter to the SSA and asked them to forward it to his last known address. A few weeks later, Bob received the forwarded letter from the SSA, telephoned his sister and agreed to visit his mother. The letter-forwarding service by the SSA may seem like a long shot, but it does work.

Tip

**MORE LETTER-
FORWARDING SERVICES**

The Internal Revenue Service (IRS) has a letter-forwarding service similar to SSA's, although you must provide the Social Security number of the missing person. Letters regarding debt collection will not be forwarded. Send to:
  Internal Revenue Service
  Center
  Kansas City, MO 64999
  The Veterans Administration and most schools or universities will also forward letters. See chapter nine (Military Records) and chapter eleven (High School and College).

Research Tip

Explain that all other attempts have failed in locating the person. Provide as much information as possible about the person you are writing, such as his or her full name, maiden name (if applicable), name of parents, birth date and birthplace, Social Security number (if known) and last known address.

Both letters are read by the agency prior to forwarding. If SSA determines the letter meets their criteria, they will forward it in care of the employer who most recently reported earnings for the missing person. The SSA only has current addresses for persons receiving benefits. There is no charge if the letter is for humanitarian reasons; however, a three-dollar fee is charged to inform a missing person about money or property. (Make a personal check, cashier's check or money order payable to the Social Security Administration.) Send to:
  Social Security Administration
  Office of Public Inquiries
  6401 Security Blvd.
  Room 4-C-5 Annex
  Baltimore, MD 21235
  Phone: (800) 772-1213
  http://www.ssa.gov/faq_services.html

THE SOCIAL SECURITY NUMBER (SSN)

The Social Security number is the best identifier you can use to locate someone. Private investigators or researchers who have access to subscription databases (see chapter seventeen) can conduct Social Security traces with the number and usually obtain a current address. **Private researchers can sometimes find Social Security numbers in divorce files, bankruptcy cases, real estate records, voter registrations, military discharges and driving records.**

Over 390 million Social Security numbers have been issued since 1936. The nine-digit numbering system (explained below) allows about one billion possible combinations. This means about two-thirds of the numbers have not been assigned. The SSA does not reissue or recycle the numbers of deceased persons.

The nine-digit SSN is composed of three parts: area number, group number and serial number.

Social Security Number

XXX - XX - XXXX

Area Number - Group Number - Serial Number

Area Number

The area number is assigned by the geographical region. If a person applied for a Social Security number before 1972, the number indicates the location of the

Social Security office where the card was issued. This does not always match a person's state of residence. For example, a person residing in New Jersey may have applied for her SSN at an office in New York. For those persons who received their SSN after 1972, the area number represents the state in the applicant's mailing address.

The area number does *not* represent the applicant's state of birth, although many persons were born in the same state where they resided or applied for their SSN. The chart on page 58 is a numerical index to SSN area numbers.

Group Number

The middle two digits (the group number) are assigned more or less sequentially within a given area number. Because the SSA announces when new group numbers are assigned, these two digits are used as a code to identify fraudulent numbers.

Serial Number

The remaining four digits are randomly assigned. Numbers 2001–2999 and 7001–7999 are assigned to every fifth person receiving a SSN. Persons with these numbers are part of a sample group of workers and beneficiaries whose records are used for statistical research into economic and demographic conditions.

SOCIAL SECURITY DEATH INDEX (SSDI)

As emphasized in chapter six, successfully locating a living person sometimes involves researching deceased family members. The SSDI is the best resource to survey deaths. Some researchers have labeled the SSDI as the most important twentieth-century source because of the size and availability of the index.

What is the Social Security Death Index?

The SSA maintains a death master file (DMF), available on magnetic tape, cartridges or CD-ROM, with 59.7 million names of deceased people (current through June 1998). SSA will not search the file for the public. Instead, the file is available to the public for sale through the U.S. Department of Commerce's National Technical Information Service. Prices range from $1,500 for a onetime order of the entire DMF to $6,000 for the entire file with quarterly updates. The DMF is available to the public through the Freedom of Information Act. Rights of privacy do not apply because the data is about deceased people.

Genealogical and investigative services companies purchase the DMF and create indexes on CD-ROM or the Internet. Cambridge Statistical Research Associates, now known as Ameridex Information Systems (http://kadima.com/), was the first company to make this index available to the public, in 1992. The Family History Library in Salt Lake City quickly followed with their version of the index. Shortly afterwards, several genealogical or software companies created similar indexes. Many genealogical software companies now include the index in their software packages, and offer free searches of the index on the Internet.

Notes

MILITARY USE OF SSN

The U.S. Army and U.S. Air Force began using the SSN as the military service number on 1 July 1969. The U.S. Navy and U.S. Marine Corps initiated the same policy on 1 July 1972; the U.S. Coast Guard, on 1 October 1974. The Department of Veterans Affairs uses a patient's SSN as a hospital admission number. (See chapter nine for more information on veterans.)

Sources

SOCIAL SECURITY AREA NUMBERS BY GEOGRAPHIC REGION

001–003 New Hampshire	408–415 Tennessee	540–544 Oregon
004–007 Maine	416–424 Alabama	545–573 California
008–009 Vermont	425–428 Mississippi	574 Alaska
010–034 Massachusetts	429–432 Arkansas	574E Asian refugees between April 1975 and November 1979
035–039 Rhode Island	433–439 Louisiana	575–576 Hawaii
040–049 Connecticut	440–448 Oklahoma	577–579 District of Columbia
050–134 New York	449–467 Texas	580 Virgin Islands
135–158 New Jersey	468–477 Minnesota	580–584 Puerto Rico
159–211 Pennsylvania	478–485 Iowa	585 New Mexico
212–220 Maryland	486–500 Missouri	586 Guam, American Samoa, Philippine Islands, Northern Mariana Islands
221–222 Delaware	501–502 North Dakota	586SE Asian refugees between April 1975 and November 1979
223–231 Virginia	503–504 South Dakota	587–588 Mississippi
232–236 West Virginia	505–508 Nebraska	589–595 Florida
232, 237–246 North Carolina	509–515 Kansas	596–599 Puerto Rico
247–251 South Carolina	516–517 Montana	600–601 Arizona
252–260 Georgia	518–519 Idaho	602–626 California
261–267 Florida	520 Wyoming	627–645 Texas
268–302 Ohio	521–524 Colorado	646–647 Utah
303–317 Indiana	525 New Mexico	648–649 New Mexico
318–361 Illinois	526–527 Arizona	650–653 Wisconsin
362–386 Michigan	528–529 Utah	700–728 Railroad Retirement Board; used through June 1963, then discontinued
387–399 Wisconsin	530 Nevada	750–751 Hawaii
400–407 Kentucky	531–539 Washington	752–755 Mississippi 756–763 Tennessee

The numbers 900-999 are not valid area numbers. They were used for program purposes when state aid to the aged, blind and disabled was converted to a federal program administered by the SSA.

Some numbers are shown more than once because they have either been transferred from one state to another or divided for use among certain geographic locations.

Important

The index created from the DMF by the various genealogical or investigative companies is usually called the Social Security Death Index (although it is also referred to as the Social Security Death Benefits Index, Social Security Death Master File, Social Security Master Death Index, National Death Index, and SSDI). Nearly sixty million names of people who have died since 1962, plus a few pre-1962 deaths, are in this index. **But it does *not* list all deaths.**

	Family Search at Family History Library, Salt Lake City. Also available at Family History Centers throughout the U.S. and some public libraries. Not available on the Internet.	Ancestry, Inc. (http://www.ancestry.com)	Kindred Konnections (http://www.kindredkonnections.com)	Family Tree Maker (http://www.familytreemaker.com)	Ultimate Family Tree (http://www.uftree.com)
Scroll/browse multiple surnames	Yes	No	No	No	No
Soundex Search	Yes	Yes	No	Yes	No
Search by surname name only, i.e., given name is not required	Yes	Yes	Yes	Yes	No
Search by given name only, i.e., surname is not required	No	Yes	No	Yes	No
Search results sorted chronologically	Yes	No	Yes	Yes	No
Search results sorted alphabetically	Yes	Yes	Yes	Yes	Yes
Search results report foreign country place of death	Yes	No	No	No	No
Search by SSN only	No	Yes	No	Yes	No
Filter search by state of issuance of SSN	Yes	Yes	No	No	No
Filter search by death residence	Yes	Yes	Yes	Yes	Yes
Wild card searches allowed in name fields, e.g., for Hin*, search results will list all names that begin with *Hin* such as Hinckley, Hinkle, and Hines.	No	No	No	Yes	Yes

Information in the SSDI includes
- given name and surname (no middle names or initials)
- exact birth date
- Social Security number
- state of issuance of Social Security number
- death date (usually month and year only)
- death residence localities
- death benefit localities

The available indexes vary in their search abilities, as the table above shows. Keep in mind that these indexes evolve quickly and features may change. The ending date of the data may also vary. For example, one index may be complete through December 1997; another, through March 1999.

The shaded boxes above indicate desirable or ideal search features. As you can see, none of the indexes include all of the features; therefore, it may be necessary to use more than one index for thorough research.

To illustrate how you can access the SSDI, **I used the FamilySearch version of the SSDI to search for the death of movie star John Wayne.**

The search begins by entering the given and surname of the individual. You

Case Study

```
                    U.S. Social Security Death Index 1.30              01 JUL 1998
          Esc=Exit   F1=Help   F2=Print/Holding File   F4=Search   F5=Record Offices

    INDEX      Use      PgDn PgUp and press Enter for details.

    (-Name Group-) Name              Birth   Issuance Place   Death   Residence

     -WINES-
     John WINES ................   1885   Michigan         1976   Michigan
     John WEIN .................   1885   Ohio             1968   Ohio
     John WEIN .................   1885   Pennsylvania     1966
     John WEIN .................   1886   Michigan         1967   Michigan
     John WEIN .................   1887   New York         1966   New York
     John WEIN .................   1887   Pennsylvania     1976   Pennsylvania
     John WION .................   1888   Iowa             1965
     John WEINS ................   1888   Wisconsin        1970   Wisconsin
     John WINE .................   1889   California       1995   California
     John WION .................   1889   Pennsylvania     1988   Pennsylvania
     John WINE .................   1889   Virginia         1967   Virginia
     John WAYNE ................   1890   New York         1965
     John WINES ................   1891   Maryland         1979   Maryland
     John WAIN .................   1891   Ohio             1968   Ohio
     John WINE .................   1891   Pennsylvania     1962
     John WAYNE ................   1891   Not Identified   1979   Pennsylvania
     John WINES ................   1892   Illinois         1978   Illinois
     John WINES ................   1892   Indiana          1974   Indiana
     John WIENS ................   1892   Minnesota        1977   California
     John WINE .................   1892   Iowa             1981   Iowa
     John MCWAIN ...............   1893   Ohio             1975   Ohio
     John WAYNE ................   1893   Tennessee        1963
     John WAYNE ................   1893   Wisconsin        1968   Wisconsin
     John WIENS ................   1894   Oregon           1965   Oregon
     John WIENS ................   1894   Minnesota        1970   California
     John WION .................   1894   Michigan         1966   Michigan
     John WAYNE ................   1894   Missouri         1975   Missouri
     John WEYEN ................   1894   Washington       1971   Washington
     John WEAN .................   1895   Indiana          1969   Indiana
     John WEYN .................   1896   Illinois         1976   Illinois
     John WAYNE ................   1896   Arkansas         1973   Arkansas
     John WAYNE ................   1896   Missouri         1972   Missouri
     John WAYNE ................   1896   Iowa             1975   Iowa
     John WAINE ................   1896   New Jersey       1981   Florida
     John MCWAIN ...............   1897   Michigan         1962
     John WAYNE ................   1897   Michigan         1967   Louisiana
     John WIENS ................   1897   Minnesota        1981   Minnesota
     John WAYNE ................   1897   Oregon           1979   Oregon
     John WENE .................   1897   Arizona          1968   Missouri
     John MCWAYNE ..............   1897   Vermont          1970   Florida
     John WEINTZ ...............   1898   Wyoming          1979   Wyoming
     John WIENS ................   1898   Kansas           1984   Oklahoma
     John WIENS ................   1899   California       1980   California
     John WAINE ................   1899   New York         1973   New York
     John WEIN .................   1900   Indiana          1981   Indiana
     John WIENS ................   1900   Nebraska         1994   Oregon
     John WEINS ................   1900   New York         1965   New York
     John WAYNE ................   1900   New York         1976   Florida
     John WAIN .................   1900   New York         1981   Ireland
     John WHAYNE ...............   1900   Oklahoma         1967   Oklahoma
     John WEYEN ................   1900   Washington       1981   Washington
     John MCWAINE ..............   1901   Alabama          1949
     John WIEN .................   1901   Indiana          1988
     John WIENS ................   1901   Kansas           1982   Kansas
     John WIENS ................   1902   Colorado         1976   California
     John WYNES ................   1903   Georgia          1979   Georgia
     John WEIN .................   1903   Illinois         1979   Indiana
     John WIENS ................   1903   Indiana          1984   Indiana
     John WINES ................   1903   New York         1968   New York
     John WAIN .................   1903   New York         1979   Louisiana
     John WYNE .................   1903   West Virginia    1968
     John WEIN .................   1903   Ohio             1982   Ohio
     John MCWAYNE ..............   1903   Pennsylvania     1975   Pennsylvania
     John WEAN .................   1903   Pennsylvania     1981   Pennsylvania
     John WAYNE ................   1904   California       1988   California
     John WAYNE ................   1904   California       1992   California
     John WINES ................   1904   Pennsylvania     1976   Ohio
     John WEINS ................   1904   South Dakota     1972   California
     John WHAYNE ...............   1905   Oklahoma         1982   Arkansas
     John WAINE ................   1905   Pennsylvania     1970   Pennsylvania
     John WEIN .................   1905   Pennsylvania     1995   Pennsylvania
```

can specify the year of birth, but in this case you are going to retrieve all deaths for anyone named John Wayne. FamilySearch uses a proprietary phonetic equivalency search system (this is similar to the Soundex system that is explained in chapter eight, Census Records); therefore, surnames that are phonetically similar to Wayne will be in the list (such as Wines, Wein, Weins, Wain and Waine).

```
                U.S. Social Security Death Index 1.30        29 JUN 1998
     Esc=Exit  F1=Help  F2=Print/Holding File  F4=Search  F5=Record Offices

     INDEX    Use     PgDn PgUp and press Enter for details.

       (-Name Group-) Name          Birth  Issuance Place  Death  Residence

      -WINES-
       John WAYNE ................   1878   Illinois        1969   Texas
       John WAYNE ................   1882   Kentucky        1966   Ohio
       John WAYNE ................   1883   California       1962
       John WAYNE ................   1885   Kentucky        1968   Indiana
       John WAYNE ................   1890   New York        1965
       John WAYNE ................   1891   Not Identified  1979   Pennsylvania
       John WAYNE ................   1893   Tennessee       1963
       John WAYNE ................   1893   Wisconsin       1968   Wisconsin
       John WAYNE ................   1894   Missouri        1975   Missouri
       John WAYNE ................   1896   Arkansas        1973   Arkansas
       John WAYNE ................   1896   Missouri        1972   Missouri
       John WAYNE ................   1896   Iowa            1975   Iowa
       John WAYNE ................   1897   Michigan        1967   Louisiana
       John WAYNE ................   1897   Oregon          1979   Oregon
       John WAYNE ................   1900   New York        1976   Florida
       John WAYNE ................   1902   Georgia         1974   Georgia
       John WAYNE ................   1902   Kansas          1970   Kansas
       John WAYNE ................   1904   California       1988   California
       John WAYNE ................   1904   California       1992   California
       John WAYNE ................   1907   California       1979   California
       John WAYNE ................   1907   Texas           1970
       John WAYNE ................   1908   Connecticut     1989
       John WAYNE ................   1908   Missouri        1991
       John WAYNE ................   1908   Utah            1971   Utah
       John WAYNE ................   1912   WVa/N Caro      1978   West Virginia
       John WAYNE ................   1913   New Mexico      1995
       John WAYNE ................   1913   Georgia         1996   Georgia
       John WAYNE ................   1914   North Carolina  1995   North Carolina
       John WAYNE ................   1916   Ohio            1985   Ohio
       John WAYNE ................   1916   Washington      1981   Washington
       John WAYNE ................   1917   Michigan        1993   Florida
       John WAYNE ................   1917   North Carolina  1976
       John WAYNE ................   1917   West Virginia   1978
       John WAYNE ................   1919   New York        1980
       John WAYNE ................   1920   Ohio            1991
       John WAYNE ................   1920   Pennsylvania    1992
       John WAYNE ................   1922   New York        1988
       John WAYNE ................   1923   Illinois        1962
       John WAYNE ................   1923   Ohio            1991
       John WAYNE ................   1924   Illinois        1978   Illinois
       John WAYNE ................   1924   Ohio            1994   Ohio
       John WAYNE ................   1925   West Virginia   1986   West Virginia
       John WAYNE ................   1926   Pennsylvania    1978
       John WAYNE ................   1927   Arkansas        1991
       John WAYNE ................   1927   California      1994   California
       John WAYNE ................   1927   Missouri        1983   Missouri
       John WAYNE ................   1927   Wisconsin       1989   Wisconsin
       John WAYNE ................   1933   New Jersey      1987
       John WAYNE ................   1943   West Virginia   1993   Maryland
       John WAYNE ................   1944   Pennsylvania    1991
       Johnnie WAYNE ............   1927   Tennessee       1992   Tennessee
       Johnny WAYNE .............   1957   North Carolina  1980
       Johnny WAYNE .............   1981   New Mexico      1983   New Mexico
       Jon WAYNE ................   1965   Florida         1991
       Joseph WAYNE .............   1884   California      1973   California
       Joseph WAYNE .............   1886   California      1969   California
       Joseph WAYNE .............   1887   Kentucky        1965
       Joseph WAYNE .............   1888   Ohio            1967   Ohio
       Joseph WAYNE .............   1890   Illinois        1964
       Joseph WAYNE .............   1890   New Jersey      1969   New Jersey
       Joseph WAYNE .............   1891   Michigan        1981   Michigan
```

The information on this printout is from the United States government records
and is in the public domain. No claim to copyright is expressed or implied.

The graphic on page 60 is a partial list; there were 177 entries for the name John Wayne, plus 22 entries for J. Wayne, for a total of 199 possibilities. The names are listed in chronological order by year of birth from 1885 through 1950.

The graphic above shows a list shortened to fifty entries, created by searching for John Wayne entries with an exact surname spelling (W-A-Y-N-E). Note the listings for Johnnie, Johnny and Jon. This is an excellent example of variations of given names. When you do not find the person you seek using the traditional spelling, check for variations such as this.

A search can be filtered by state of issuance of the SSN or by state of residence at death. In the graphic below, the search was narrowed to any John Wayne (exact spelling) who died in California. Sometimes the death residence is not listed in the index, but the search results include those listings, as they might be California. The search engine does not allow the user to eliminate entries without a death residence.

```
                    U.S. Social Security Death Index 1.30              29 JUN 1998
        Esc=Exit  F1=Help  F2=Print/Holding File  F4=Search  F5=Record Offices

        INDEX     Use     PgDn PgUp and press Enter for details.

        (-Name Group-) Name          Birth  Issuance Place  Death  Residence

          -WINES-
          John WAYNE .............   1883   California       1962
          John WAYNE .............   1890   New York        1965
          John WAYNE .............   1893   Tennessee       1963
          John WAYNE .............   1904   California       1988   California
          John WAYNE .............   1904   California       1992   California
          John WAYNE .............   1907   California       1979   California
          John WAYNE .............   1907   Texas           1970
          John WAYNE .............   1908   Connecticut     1989
          John WAYNE .............   1908   Missouri        1991
          John WAYNE .............   1913   New Mexico      1995
          John WAYNE .............   1917   North Carolina  1976
          John WAYNE .............   1917   West Virginia   1978
          John WAYNE .............   1919   New York        1980
          John WAYNE .............   1920   Ohio            1991
          John WAYNE .............   1920   Pennsylvania    1992
          John WAYNE .............   1922   New York        1988
          John WAYNE .............   1923   Illinois        1962
          John WAYNE .............   1923   Ohio            1991
          John WAYNE .............   1926   Pennsylvania    1978
          John WAYNE .............   1927   Arkansas        1991
          John WAYNE .............   1927   California       1994   California
          John WAYNE .............   1933   New Jersey      1987
          John WAYNE .............   1944   Pennsylvania    1991
          Johnny WAYNE ...........   1957   North Carolina  1980
          Jon WAYNE ..............   1965   Florida         1991
          Joseph WAYNE ...........   1884   California       1973   California
          Joseph WAYNE ...........   1886   California       1969   California
          Joseph WAYNE ...........   1887   Kentucky        1965
          Joseph WAYNE ...........   1890   Illinois        1964
          Joseph WAYNE ...........   1896   Illinois        1965
          Joseph WAYNE ...........   1907   California       1975   California
```

The information on this printout is from the United States government records and is in the public domain. No claim to copyright is expressed or implied.

```
Social Security Death Index - 1996 Edition - Version 1.30

                            INDIVIDUAL RECORD

   29 JUN 1998                                                   Page 1

   ================================================================
   NAME: WAYNE, John
   ----------------------------------------------------------------
   Birth Date              Social Security Number
   26 May 1907             561-01-2534

   State of Issuance of Social Security Number
   California

   Death Date
   Jun 1979

   Death Residence Localities
   92660
   Newport Beach, Orange, California

   ================================================================

   The information on this printout is from the United States government records
   and is in the public domain. No claim to copyright is expressed or implied.
```

More detail is available for each entry. By clicking on the name John Wayne, born in 1907 and died in 1979 in California, we receive the individual record on page 62. An exact birth date, the SSN, month of death (some entries provide exact date of death) and additional information on death residence (generated from the zip code) are listed as shown.

The next research step would be to obtain an obituary and a death certificate. Of course, an exact date of death or burial makes newspaper research less time consuming. The SSDI usually only gives the month and year of death. When that occurs, there are several options to obtain the exact death date or to find an obituary:

Technique

- Obtain a copy of the death certificate. The month and year are usually enough data for the health departments, and the certificate will report the exact date of death.
- Telephone the cemetery office if you have a general idea of where the person may be buried. The cemetery record will report the exact date of death or interment.
- Telephone the local library and determine if there is a necrology or obituary index.
- Search the newspapers. A method that often saves time is to search every third or fourth day (since most funeral notices run for three or four days). Using this method, you can usually find the death notice or obituary in less than ten minutes.

To find John Wayne's obituary or report of death, the 1979 index to *The New York Times* was examined. There were several articles, including the one on page 64 published on June 12, 1979's front page.

ORIGINAL SOCIAL SECURITY APPLICATION (Form SS-5)

The original social security application (Form SS-5) gives the complete name, address, birth date, birthplace and physical description of the applicant. Sometimes the name and address of the person's employer are included. It also gives the full name of the father and maiden name of the mother—important information in some searches.

A copy of the application can be ordered from the Freedom of Information Officer, 4-H-8 Annex Bldg., 6401 Security Blvd., Baltimore, MD 21235. The fee is $7.00 if you supply the Social Security number or $16.50 if the Social Security number is unknown.

John Wayne completed his Social Security application (see page 64) in 1937, using his birth name of Marion Mitchell Morrison. He was born 26 May 1907, in Winterset, Iowa, to Clyde Leonard Morrison and Mary Alberta Brown. He signed the social security application as M.M. Morrison, but added that he was also known as John Wayne, his stage name. Immigrants who change their name may have reported the original variation of their name on the SS-5. This is another reason to gather every possible document about an individual.

Case Study

SS-5 HELPS LOCATE HEIR

A man had been estranged from his parents for several years. When he died, the court could not determine his heirs since no one knew the names of his parents. An heir researcher obtained a copy of the SS-5, which provided the complete names of the parents. The father's death was listed in the SSDI, which led to information to locate the mother. She was easy to find—she was listed in the telephone directory.

rs Continue to Arrive

By HENRY KAMM
Special to The New York Times

e 11 — of the Cambodian border from the area of
refugees Aranyaprathet northeast to the spot
to their where the temple of Preah Vihear domi-
orities in nates the landscape on the Cambodian
more will side.

on as pos-   The buses were crammed with Cambo-
ent and dians who had been told they were being
s in Thai- moved to another refugee camp. They as-
sembled at a spot near the border until
going to darkness had fallen over the deserted re-
ell-placed gion, which is flat and rocky on the Thai
ated that
had been
und Ara-

are being
nbodians
e heavily
Minister
ai side of
thet. The
ns, which
hment of
e border
ot forces
own, tak-
ans with

g column
Thai side

3egins
ther the
held an-
gs until
A12.

Debate
wn says
led now.
in Eu-

handicapped. It is a setback for both the
Federal Government and for the recently
organized groups of handicapped individuals whose efforts culminated in passage
of the Rehabilitation Act of 1973.

In another case the Court agreed today
to decide if New York State's latest attempt to provide state aid to parochial
schools is constitutional. [Page B1.]

The Justices unanimously overturned
the obscenity conviction of an adult book
store owner in New Hampton, Orange
County, N.Y., because of an "open-
ended" warrant that the High Court said
led to an unconstitutional search of the
store. [Page D19.]

The decision on the handicapped stu-

Continued on Page A6, Column 3

Continued on Page A13, Column 1

in the country's history when it was
signed in 1972. As reported yesterday in
The New York Times, two former Pull-

New York Planning

By RONALD SULLIVAN

The Koch administration said yesterday that it planned to close four municipal hospitals, including Metropolitan on
the upper East Side and Sydenham in
West Harlem, in an effort to reduce by $40
million the city's projected budget gap in
the fiscal year 1981.

Haskell G. Ward, Deputy Mayor for
Human Services, told a news conference

John Wayne Dead of Cancer on Coast at 72

By The Associated Press

LOS ANGELES, June 11 (AP) — John
Wayne, the veteran Hollywood actor,
died today at 5:23 P.M., Pacific daylight
time, at U.C.L.A. Medical Center, a hospital spokesman said. The cause of death
was given as complications from cancer.

Mr. Wayne, 72 years old, had been hos-
pitalized for treatment of cancer of the
lower abdomen since May 2, when he was
admitted for his second cancer operation
of the year. His lower intestine was partly
removed in the operation.

Mr. Wayne's second bout with cancer
began earlier this year with what was officially described as a routine gall blad-
der operation. He had entered the Medical Center Jan. 10 and two days later his
stomach was removed in a 9½-hour
operation when a low-grade cancerous
tumor was discovered.

'Duke,' an American Hero

By RICHARD F. SHEPARD

In more than 200 films made over 50
years, John Wayne saddled up to become
the greatest figure of one of America's
greatest native art forms, the western.

The movies he starred in rode the
range from out-of-the-money sagebrush
quickies to such classics as "Stagecoach"
and "Red River." He won an Oscar as
best actor for another western, "True
Grit," in 1969. Yet some of the best films
he made told stories far from the wilds of
the West, such as "The Quiet Man" and
"The Long Voyage Home."

In the last decades of his career, Mr.
Wayne became something of an American folk figure, hero to some, villain to

John Wayne was costumed typically for "Rio Lobo" in 1971

others, for his outspoken views. He was
politically a conservative and, although
he scorned politics as a way of life for
himself, he enthusiastically supported
Richard M. Nixon, Barry Goldwater,
Spiro T. Agnew, Ronald Reagan and
others who, he felt, fought for his concept
of Americanism and anti-Communism.

But it was for millions of moviegoers
who saw him only on the big screen that
John Wayne really existed. He had not
created the western with its clear-cut
conflict between good and bad, right and
wrong, but it was impossible to mention

Continued on Page B8, Column 1

...........C6-7
ple C6
...........D19
...........A15
...........C1-3
...........B6
....C10-13
...........C14
...........C7
...........C15
...........A8
...........D18
ews ..A12
e B1

MCLAW MAY
1215 Club at

COMPARING DEATH CERTIFICATE DATA WITH SOCIAL SECURITY APPLICATION DATA

Nels Wullum and Mary Swendsen are siblings, but only by comparing the death certificates and the Social Security applications can you prove their relationship to one another.

Born in Denmark

Names of parents unknown

Nels Christianson Wullum, death certificate number 012943 (1970), Minnesota Department of Health, Minneapolis, Minnesota

Nels Wullum, Social Security application

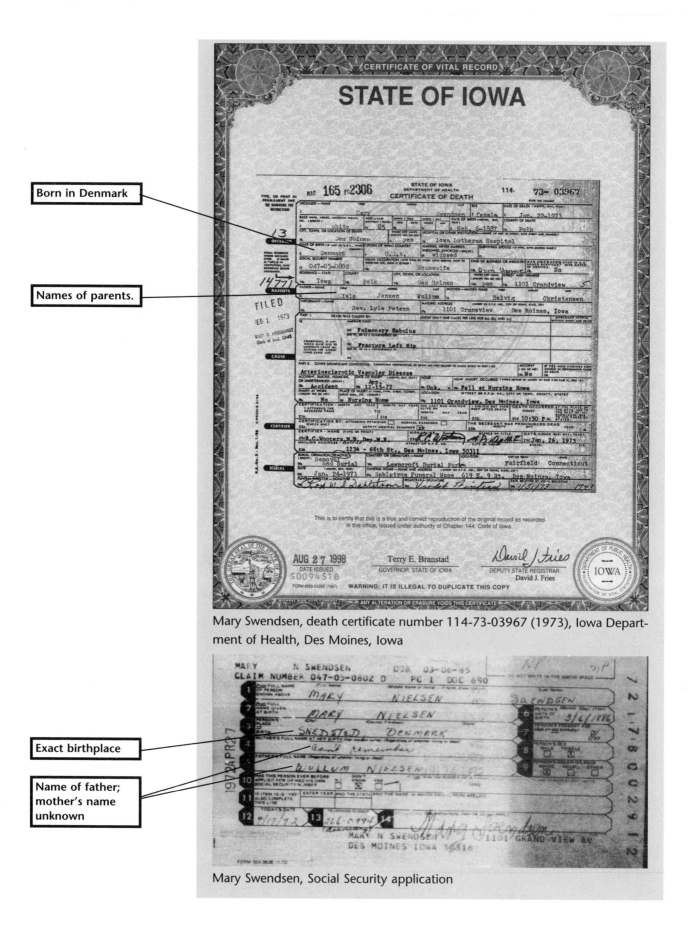

Born in Denmark

Names of parents.

Mary Swendsen, death certificate number 114-73-03967 (1973), Iowa Department of Health, Des Moines, Iowa

Exact birthplace

Name of father; mother's name unknown

Mary Swendsen, Social Security application

Mary completed her Social Security application nine months prior to her death in 1973. She was a resident of the Valborg Lutheran Home. Although neither the death certificate or the Social Security application name the nursing home, you can determine its name by using the address search feature of telephone directories (see chapter two). The home's address, 1101 Grandview Avenue, Des Moines, Iowa, appears on both documents.

COMPARING DEATH CERTIFICATE DATA WITH SOCIAL SECURITY APPLICATION DATA

	Nels Wullum Death Certificate (1970)	Nels Wullum SS-5 (1941)	Mary Swendsen Death Certificate (1973)	Mary Swendsen SS-5 (1972)
Name	Nels Christianson Wullum	Nels Christensen Wellum	Mary Swendsen	Mary Nielsen Swendsen
Date of Birth	14 June 1888	14 June 1888	6 March 1887	6 March 1886
Place of Birth	Denmark	Gjersbol, Snedsted Thy, Denmark	Denmark	Snedsted, Denmark
Father	Unknown	Nels Jensen Wullum	Niels Jensen Wullum	Wullum Nielsen
Mother	Unknown	Hedevig Christensen	Helvig Christensen	Can't Remember

The exact place of birth for both individuals was only available from the Social Security applications.

By comparing the information in the SS-5 for Nels Wullum with the death certificate data of Mary Swendsen, the brother/sister relationship is proven.

BROWSING THE SSDI

The only version of the SSDI that allows a user to browse is the SSDI at the Family History Library (use the Page Up and Page Down keys). The indexes on the Internet do not have this feature.

The ability to browse the SSDI can be extremely helpful when searching for possible spelling errors in surnames and given names. In the example on page 68, if you had typed the surname Wullum into search engines on the Internet, you would have received only Wullum listings. In the index at the Family History Library, you can page up and down and study spellings of surnames and given names. Fishing in this manner can sometimes produce surprising and valuable results.

It is possible to use the data in the SSDI in conjunction with a linkage-based database (World Family Tree in the case on page 69) to show probable family relationships. You must be careful, of course, and not accept the SSDI or the World Family Tree as *proof* of relationships. All data should be documented with sources such as birth, marriage and death records; probate records; obituaries; census records; etc. But these two commonly used indexes are excellent

Brick Wall Buster

```
                         U.S. Social Security Death Index 1.30                02 JUL 1998
                    Esc=Exit  F1=Help  F2=Print/Holding File  F4=Search  F5=Record Offices

              INDEX     Use      PgDn PgUp and press Enter for details.

                (-Name Group-) Name          Birth   Issuance Place   Death   Residence
                  William WULLSCHLEGER ......  1968    South Carolina   1995    Oklahoma
                -WULLSON-
                  Harry WULLSON .............  1881    New Jersey       1967    New Jersey
                -WULLSTEIN-
                  Donald WULLSTEIN .........   1923    South Dakota     1996    Colorado
                  Fred WULLSTEIN ...........   1897    New York         1967    New York
                  Henry WULLSTEIN ..........   1896    Nebraska         1983    Nebraska
                  Irene WULLSTEIN ..........   1903    New York         1984    New York
                  Mary WULLSTEIN ...........   1901    Nebraska         1973    Nebraska
                  William WULLSTEIN ........   1920    South Dakota     1975
                -WULLUM-
                  Arne WULLUM ..............   1903    New Jersey       1980    Norway
                  Avis WULLUM ..............   1899    Washington       1971    Washington
                  Herbert WULLUM ...........   1914    Colorado         1982    California
                  Herbert WULLUM ...........   1914    Colorado         1982    California
                  Inga WULLUM ..............   1881    Montana          1967    Montana
                  Lorraine WULLUM ..........   1920    Minnesota        1969    Minnesota
                  Nels WULLUM ..............   1888    Minnesota        1970    Minnesota
                  Nydia WULLUM .............   1904    California       1975    California
                -WULLUS-
                  Emma WULLUS ..............   1900    Montana          1995    Montana
                  James WULLUS .............   1930    Montana          1996    Montana
                -WULLWEBER-
                  Adele WULLWEBER ..........   1885    Iowa             1974    Iowa
                  Arnold WULLWEBER .........   1918    Illinois         1984    Colorado
                  Bernard WULLWEBER ........   1900    Illinois         1978    Illinois
                  Doris WULLWEBER ..........   1921    Arkansas         1996    Colorado
                  Fred WULLWEBER ...........   1891    Illinois         1965
                  Harriett WULLWEBER .......   1903    Illinois         1993    Illinois
                  Leo WULLWEBER ............   1892    Illinois         1982    Illinois
                  Louis WULLWEBER ..........   1891    Illinois         1963
                  Magdalene WULLWEBER ......   1921    Illinois         1990
```

> **Some death residences are out of the country. The FamilySearch version of the SSDI at the Family History Library is the only index that gives this information.**

> **Is there an error here? Should Inga Wullum be indexed as Inga Wullus? The Montana references suggest this is a possibility (or perhaps Wullus should be Wullum). This is an example of the value of the browse feature with FamilySearch. You can study the index and find items that appear out of place due to a typo or other types of errors.**

The information on this printout is from the United States government records and is in the public domain. No claim to copyright is expressed or implied.

tools to study family groupings and obtain clues to locate proper documentation.

The spousal relationship of Anna and John Zwingelberg, as shown on page 69, is more obvious because of the common death residence; however, the marriage between Anna and Fred is not since their death residences were in different states. The fact that Lloyd Zwingelberg was the son of Anna and Fred could not be speculated with the SSDI only.

SEARCHING THE SSDI BY GIVEN NAME

Brick Wall Buster

As mentioned before, women are difficult to trace because they change their names through marriage—sometimes several times. **The SSDI is a powerful research tool to identify women with the same given name and birth date as the person you seek.** For example, if you are searching for Mildred born 30 July 1920, the SSDI gives the report on page 70.

Searches for women with common names such as Mary or Elizabeth will produce too many hits to be effective. But this technique can be extremely productive for unusual names and is particularly useful when trying to locate birth mothers. The searches can also be filtered by year of birth (rather than exact birth date) and limited to those who died in a specific state.

Given-name searches such as this one cannot be done in FamilySearch at the Family History Library. Their software requires an entry in the surname field. It can, however, be done on the Internet at http://www.ancestry.com and http://familytreemaker.com.

World Family Tree	Social Security Death Index Zwingelberg Surname				
Relationships in Family Group Sheets	Name	Birth Date	Issuance Place	Death Date	Death Residence
WIFE of Fred born 1895	ZWINGELBERG Anna	25 May 1891	Kansas	Feb 1974	Littleton, Colorado
WIFE of John born 1903	ZWINGELBERG Anna	25 Dec 1909	South Dakota	Aug 1987	Flandreau, South Dakota
	ZWINGELBERG August	24 May 1898	Minnesota	Dec 1985	San Stone, Minnesota
	ZWINGELBERG Clara	31 Dec 1906	South Dakota	2 Dec 1996	Stockton, California
	ZWINGELBERG Eleanor	23 Sep 1909	Minnesota	20 May 1991	
	ZWINGELBERG Florence	17 Apr 1906	Minnesota	Nov 1990	
HUSBAND of Anna born 1891	ZWINGELBERG Fred	4 Nov 1895	Minnesota	Mar 1969	Independence, Kansas
	ZWINGELBERG Herman	22 Oct 1903	Minnesota	Aug 1976	Cleveland, Ohio
HUSBAND of Anna born 1909	ZWINGELBERG John	19 May 1903	South Dakota	Jul 1984	Flandreau, South Dakota
SON of Fred and Anna	ZWINGELBERG Lloyd	26 Sep 1928	Kansas	Jul 1977	
	ZWINGELBERG Otto	26 Jul 1902	Minnesota	Dec 1976	Cohasset, Minnesota

Searches by given name and date of birth for living persons can be accomplished with some non-SSDI subscription databases (see chapter seventeen).

THE MISUNDERSTOOD SSDI

Although the SSDI is one of the most widely used tools in twentieth-century research, it is greatly misunderstood. Here is the truth about some of the rumors, myths, and misconceptions:

The SSDI is not a complete death index. Several factors affect inclusion in the SSDI. The most obvious is that the database is created by the SSA; therefore, only individuals who had a Social Security number are eligible. Some government workers and self-employed individuals never obtained a SSN. Also, most people in the SSDI were born after 1870.

The SSDI is not about Social Security benefits. The SSDI is sometimes called the Social Security Death Benefits Index, implying that only persons who either collected benefits or had survivors who applied for benefits are in the index. The majority of persons in the SSDI received benefits from the SSA, but not all of them did.

Name	Birth Date	Death Date	Death Residence
Mildred Alter	30 Jul 1920	05 May 1994	San Antonio, Texas
Mildred Boyens	30 Jul 1920	08 Dec 1992	Charter Oak, Iowa
Mildred Byrd	30 Jul 1920	15 Jan 1997	Dunn, North Carolina
Mildred Cook	30 Jul 1920	Jan 1987	Detroit, Michigan
Mildred Deluca	30 Jul 1920	22 Sep 1996	Bristol, Pennsylvania
Mildred Gutrich	30 Jul 1920	Dec 1988	Chicago Ridge, Illinois
Mildred Kastroll	30 Jul 1920	25 Mar 1995	Clearwater, Florida
Mildred Knox	30 Jul 1920	09 Nov 1994	Trenton, New Jersey
Mildred Manupelli	30 Jul 1920	14 Jun 1993	Stormville, New York
Mildred Maska	30 Jul 1920	Jul 1995	Hays, Kansas
Mildred Mauney	30 Jul 1920	Nov 1994	Gastonia, North Carolina
Mildred Newell	30 Jul 1920	Mar 1984	Springfield, Illinois
Mildred Rebillot	30 Jul 1920	17 Dec 1991	(location not given)
Mildred Roney	30 Jul 1920	Oct 1979	Lima, Ohio
Mildred Shell	30 Jul 1920	Apr 1970	Chicago, Illinois
Mildred Walker	30 Jul 1920	Dec 1981	Atlanta, Georgia

The SSDI does not report birthplace. The state of issuance of the Social Security number is often misinterpreted as the person's place of birth. The state of issuance is not necessarily the person's birthplace.

"Death residence" is not the same as "place of death." The SSDI reports death residence and death benefit localities. The death or benefit residence is often the place of death, but not always.

The death residence may be incorrect. When the DMF comes from the government, it gives only a zip code for the death residence, not the actual city name (e.g., 98466 instead of Tacoma, Washington). The various vendors who post the SSDI treat this field differently. Each may (and probably do) have a completely different table for translating zip codes to locations, which means different versions of the SSDI may list a different death residence for the same person. An example: Anthon Burbidge, who died in zip code 98466. Ancestry interprets the zip code as Tacoma, Washington, but Ultimate Family Tree lists the residence as Fircrest, Washington, an adjoining town that shares the same zip code as Tacoma. Family Search at the Family History Library, Salt Lake City, lists both cities.

The SSDI is an index, not a source. The data collected in the SSDI should be documented with death certificates, obituaries, Social Security applications or other records.

Errors in the SSDI

Databases are created by humans typing data into computers. This always causes a margin of error, and the SSDI is no exception. There are entries in the

```
Social Security Death Index - 1996 Edition - Version 1.30

                    INDIVIDUAL RECORD

29 JUN 1998                                    Page 1

============================================================
NAME: PR&ELL, M&Rg&Ret
------------------------------------------------------------
Birth Date              Social Security Number
12 Dec 1887             062-42-1138

State of Issuance of Social Security Number
New York

Death Date
Jul 1969

Death Residence Localities
10522
Dobbs Ferry, Westchester, New York


============================================================

The information on this printout is from the United States government records
and is in the public domain.  No claim to copyright is expressed or implied.
```

This type of error in an SSDI individual record makes it impossible to retrieve the record in the SSDI searches on the Internet, but it can be found by browsing in FamilySearch.

SSDI that begin with symbols or numbers or have plain, old-fashioned typos. The chart on page 72 includes a sampling of errors. A more complete list can be found at http://www.familydetective.com.

Many errors found in the SSDI suggest that the first character in the surname field is actually the middle initial of the individual. For example, Robert BBENNETT and Felicia BBROWN in the chart may actually be Robert B. Bennett and Felicia B. Brown. When you cannot find an individual in the SSDI, try attaching the middle initial to the surname.

There are also errors in dates of birth. For example, 17 Jan 1000 is given for Walter Fitzpatrick who died in February 1962. The SSDI reports that Oakley Agurs, born 20 January 1822, died October 1900 and lists a Social Security number. This is impossible since Social Security numbers were not issued until 1937. There are several other individuals in the database with similar date conflicts. Some of the errors may be one hundred years off, e.g., someone listed as born in 1815 may well have been born in 1915. Remember the possibility of such errors when conducting your searches.

SOCIAL SECURITY DEATH INDEX RESEARCH TIPS

- **The SSA will answer questions about the SSDI at (800) 772-1213.**
- Social Security numbers are sometimes reversed for husband and wife. Both persons may be in the index under each other's number *or* with the same number.
- If you do not find the person you seek, check names with initials only. For example, if you do not find Charles Smith, search for C. Smith.
- If the surname is more than twelve characters or the given name is more than ten characters, and the index reports there are no entries with that name, reduce the name to twelve or ten characters.

For More Info

Surname	Given Name	Birth	Issuance	Death	Residence
&RANMO	Mary	1908	Minnesota	1985	Minnesota
0NEIL (Begins with zero rather than letter o)	Rose	1909	New York	1978	New Jersey
2ARGOLIS	Abe	1890	New York	1979	New York
56DL MICELI	Catherine	1886	New Jersey	1979	New York
6ATSON	Joseph	1886	California	1963	
7CALEXANDER	Henry	1893	Arizona	1965	
7ENDONCA	Mamie	1918	California	1986	California
8RUE	Ray	1904	California	1970	California
BBENNETT	Robert	1910	Maine	1974	Maine
BBROWN	Felicia	1907	California	1978	California
CCOGGSWELL	Richard	1939	Massachusetts	1994	
CCOK	Kaitlyn	1994	Illinois	1995	
CCOOK	Leslie	1923	Minnesota	1988	North Dakota
DDUKE	Werner	1911	Texas	1982	New Mexico
EEDMUNDS	Marguerite	1898	Dist Columbia	1983	Dist Columbia
ZA8ROBSKY	James	1893	Illinois	1963	
ZZNG	Margaret	1908	Pennsylvania	1980	Pennsylvania

- Do not assume that someone is deceased if he or she is more than one hundred years old. The average age of Americans has climbed from forty-seven in 1900 to seventy-six today. About sixty thousand people reached age one hundred in 1997, and four million were older than age eighty-five. By 2020, the U.S. Census Bureau expects 214,000 centenarians and between seven million and eight million people over age eighty-five. One in nine baby boomers may live a century.

EIGHT

Twentieth-Century Census Records

T
wentieth-century census records provide identifiers needed to locate some living persons. As discussed in chapter six, the methodology to locate a living person can often require researching the parents and siblings of an individual. The census schedules will place the person into a family group and give names and ages of parents, siblings or other relatives.

Gathering data on families through census records, that is, learning the names and ages of someone's parents, siblings or other relatives, can help you locate living persons. For example, if you were trying to locate Josephine Tint (line 29 in the 1920 census on page 74), the information about her father, grandparents, aunts and uncles will help tremendously. Following those people forward into time through marriage and death records, obituaries and probates will identify their children or grandchildren. **As explained earlier, no one is an island. The more you know about the family, the better your odds in locating whomever you seek.**

Reminder

FEDERAL CENSUS

The federal census is a counting of the U.S. population taken every ten years since 1790. The information in each schedule (or questionnaire) varies slightly. Schedules from 1790 to 1840 name only the head of the household (usually the husband) and give statistics on the number and ages of other household members. Beginning in 1850 the name of each individual in the household and that person's age, sex, state or country of birth, and occupation are listed. More questions were added in later years.

On page 75 is a table indicating the type of information available for twentieth-century census records that is pertinent to locating living persons. Census schedules from 1900 to 1920 are open to the public; schedules from 1930 to 1990 have search restrictions explained later in the chapter.

Hermann owns (mortgaged) his home. This is a prompt to research real estate records (see chapter ten). The sale of the home may occur upon the death of a spouse or when they move to another residence.

The year of immigration and naturalization data is needed to search other records (see chapter sixteen).

William Robertson is a brother-in-law to James Tint. He could be the brother of Harriet, James's wife, but he could also be the husband of one of James's sisters. Documentation is always needed to prove a hypothesis. Note that Harriet and William are both sixty-one years old and both born in Canada. Perhaps they are twins.

Marie Home is the mother-in-law of Daniel H. Love, suggesting Elsie's (Daniel's wife) maiden name is Home. But it is also possible that Elsie's mother remarried later in life and Home is not Elsie's maiden name. Documents such as birth, marriage and death records will prove the maiden name.

Portion (columns 21–29 not shown) of 1920 U.S. Census, Assembly district 28, Precincts 38,41, San Francisco County, California, E.D. 291, sheet 6A. National Archives micropublication T625, roll 141.

Availability of Federal Census Schedules, 1790–1920

Surviving census schedules from 1790 through 1920 are available (microfilm copies) to the public at many archives and libraries. However, most public libraries and archives only have selected censuses for their county, state or neighboring states. The National Archives and its branches (listed in the sidebar on page 76), plus the Family History Library, have complete collections of the census, including every available year for every state.

The National Archives also has a choice of two microfilm rental programs. The first is a direct program with the National Archives wherein you purchase a start-up kit. The kit includes census catalogs and discounts on rental fees. The second option allows you to use the interlibrary loan division of your local

Federal Census Data Comparison										
	1900	1910	1920	1930	1940	1950	1960	1970	1980	1990
Address	x	x	x	x	x	x	x	x	x	x
Home Owned/Rented	x		x	x	x					
Name	x	x	x	x	x	x	x	x	x	x
Relationship to Head	x	x	x	x	x	x	x	x	x	x
Age	x	x	x	x	x	x	x	x	x	x
Month/Year of Birth	x									
Marital Status	x	x	x	x	x	x	x	x	x	x
Number of Years Married	x	x								
Age at First Marriage				x						
Number of Children Born to Wife and Number Now Living	x	x								
State/Country of Birth	x	x	x	x	x	x				
State/Country of Birth of Parents	x	x	x	x						
Year of Immigration	x	x	x	x						
Number of Years in the United States	x									
Citizenship Status	x	x	x	x	x	x				
Year of Naturalization			x							
Occupation	x	x	x	x	x	x				
Veteran Status		x		x						
Indian: Full or Mixed Blood and Tribal Affiliation				x						
Location of Residence Five Years Ago					x					

Note: In 1990, a long form with additional questions was sent to 17 percent of all housing units. Additional questions included place of birth, citizenship status, year of immigration, place of residence five years ago, veteran status and occupation.

library, if it is one of the more than six thousand libraries nationwide that participate in the program. For information on rental fees and availability, call your library, call the National Archives at (301) 604-3699, or access http://www.nara.gov/publications/microfilm/micrent.html.

Also, the USGenWeb Census Project began in February 1997 with the mission of **transcribing all of the U.S. federal census records and making them available on-line in the USGenWeb Archives** (http://www.rootsweb.com/~usgenweb). To learn which records are now on-line, visit http://www.usgenweb.org/census/states.html.

Internet Source

Availability of Federal Census Schedules, 1930–1990
Privacy laws require census schedules be kept confidential for seventy-two years, which is why the 1920 census is the most current census available for

Library/Archive Source

NATIONAL ARCHIVES REGIONAL BRANCHES

The National Archives, located in Washington, DC and on the Internet at http://www.nara.gov, has regional branches in these cities:

College Park, Maryland
Waltham, Massachusetts
Pittsfield, Massachusetts
New York, New York
Philadelphia, Pennsylvania
East Point, Georgia
Chicago, Illinois
Kansas City, Missouri
Fort Worth, Texas
Denver, Colorado
Laguna Niguel, California
San Bruno, California
Seattle, Washington
Anchorage, Alaska

For addresses and more information, see appendix B, on page 142.

public inspection. The 1930 enumeration will be released in 2002; the 1940 census will not be public until the year 2012.

There are, however, special procedures that allow you to obtain information from the census records collected from 1930 to 1990. The Census Bureau provides an age search service for the public (http://www.census.gov/genealogy/www/agesearch.html). The service is called "Age Search" because it was developed to assist individuals trying to prove their age for retirement benefits, passport applications or other age-related issues.

The Census Bureau will search the census and issue an official transcript of the results, but the information will be released *only* to the named person, heirs of the named person, or a legal representative. Here is a summary of their requirements and service:

- A completed application for Search of Census Records, Form BC-600. The form can be obtained by writing the U.S. Department of Commerce, P.O. Box 1545, Jefferson, IN 47131, or by requesting it at http://www.census.gov/genealogy/www/agesearch.html.
- If the named person is deceased, a copy of the death certificate. An immediate family member (parent, child, sibling, grandparent), the surviving spouse, the administrator or executor of an estate or the beneficiary by will or insurance can then apply for the information, and their relationship must be stated on the application. Legal representatives must furnish a copy of the court order naming them as a legal representative; beneficiaries must also furnish legal evidence.
- The official transcript will list the person's name, relationship to household head, age and state/country of birth. Date of citizenship will also be provided if the person was foreign born. The search fee is currently forty dollars for one census for one person, plus an additional ten dollars for a full schedule. Information on other family members requires another forty- to fifty-dollar fee each. Full schedules are not available for 1970, 1980 and 1990. Personal checks and money orders are accepted (no credit cards). Processing time is three to four weeks.

USING SOUNDEX TO ACCESS THE 1900 TO 1920 CENSUSES

To locate the exact page number of someone in the 1900 to 1920 censuses, you must use an index called Soundex. **Soundex is a system to code the surname based upon the phonetic sounds of the consonants rather than the spelling.** (The 1910 census uses a "Miracode" which is actually the same principle as Soundex. The difference is only in how the page number, enumeration number, family number, etc., are reported on the index card.)

The Soundex method of indexing was created during the Great Depression by the Works Progress Administration (WPA). In order to collect Social Security when it started in 1935, a person needed to have been born in 1870 or later; therefore, the WPA indexed (Soundexed) the 1880 census for people that had children ages 10 and under. They also Soundexed the 1900 and 1920 censuses

\di'fin\ *vb*

Definitions

(all ages). For the 1910 census they only indexed twenty-one states—those states that did not have state vital records offices in existence at the time.

Soundex is published by state; therefore, you must also know at least the state of residence in order to search for someone.

The first step to find someone in Soundex/Miracode is to work out the person's surname code. Every Soundex code consists of a letter and three numbers. The letter is always the first letter of the surname, and the three numbers are assigned according to the Soundex coding guide:

NUMBER	REPRESENTS LETTERS
1	B, F, P, V
2	C, G, J, K, Q, S, X, Z
3	D, T
4	L
5	M, N
6	R

Disregard letters A, E, I, O, U, H, W and Y

If fewer than three letters of the surname are used in the coding, the remaining numbers become zero. You never code beyond three letters. Letters beyond that point are ignored. Some examples are Smith, S-530; Johnson, J-525; and Anderson, A-536.

Soundex codes can be calculated with the aid of a computer. Some libraries have the program available at a research station, and the National Archives Web site also features the automatic coding at http://www.nara.gov/genealogy/soundex/soundex.html.

Using movie star John Wayne as an example (as we did in chapter seven), several surnames have the same code as *Wayne* because they are phonetically the same:

W A̶ I̶ N	=	W-500
W A Y̶ N E̶	=	W-500
W E̶ A N	=	W-500
W E̶ I̶ N	=	W-500
W E̶ N E̶	=	W-500
W E̶ Y̶ E̶ N	=	W-500
W E̶ Y̶ N	=	W-500
W H̶ A Y̶ N E̶	=	W-500
W I̶ O̶ N	=	W-500
W Y̶ N E̶	=	W-500

The census Soundex cards for each state are grouped by Soundex code (such as W-500), but placed in alphabetical order by given name of the head of the household. This head is usually the husband, but can also be a widow, grandmother, hotel proprietor, etc. If you do not know the name of the head of the household, it will be necessary to carefully examine the family members named on each index card. The W-500 cards would appear similar to the following:

Weyn, Albert

Wayne, Charles

Wain, Chuck

Wayne, David

Wayne, Elizabeth

Weyen, Mary

Weyn, Wesley

Wion, William

There are Soundex indexes for all states for the 1900 and 1920 censuses. The twenty-one states Soundexed for the 1910 census are Alabama, Arkansas, California, Florida, Georgia, Illinois, Kansas, Kentucky, Lousiana, Michigan, Mississippi, Missouri, North Carolina, Ohio, Oklahoma, Pennsylvania, South Carolina, Tennessee, Texas, Virginia and West Virginia.

Only ten southern states are indexed for the 1930 census. The Works Projects Administration was indexing this census, but stopped when World War II began.

1910 Finding Aid

The Census Bureau created an index to city streets and census enumeration districts for thirty-nine cities in the 1910 census. If you have a specific street address, the index translates it into the appropriate enumeration district number of the census. This consequently narrows the search into a few pages in the census, rather than hundreds of pages for large cities. This finding aid is available at the National Archives regional branches (see page 142) and the Family History Library. The thirty-nine cities are:

xARIZONA
Phoenix
CALIFORNIA
Long Beach
Los Angeles and Los
Angeles County
San Diego
San Francisco
xCOLORADO
Denver
xDISTRICT OF COLUMBIA
FLORIDA
Tampa
GEORGIA
Atlanta
ILLINOIS
Chicago
Peoria
INDIANA
Fort Wayne
Gary

Indianapolis
South Bend
KANSAS
Kansas City
Wichita
xMARYLAND
Baltimore
MICHIGAN
Detroit
Grand Rapids
xNEBRASKA
Omaha
xNEW JERSEY
Elizabeth
Newark
Paterson
xNEW YORK
New York City
(excluding Queens)
NORTH CAROLINA
Charlotte

OHIO
Akron
Canton
Cleveland
Dayton
Youngstown
OKLAHOMA
Oklahoma City
Tulsa
PENNSYLVANIA
Erie
Philadelphia
Reading
TEXAS
San Antonio
VIRGINIA
Richmond
xWASHINGTON
Seattle

The states marked with an (x) are not indexed using Soundex/Miracode; therefore, this finding aid is especially important when researching within those cities. The finding aid for the other cities can serve as a second source for locating someone when they are not found in the regular Soundex.

The Family History Library has a guide to five additional cities in the 1910 census: Boston, Des Moines, Minneapolis, New York City's Queens borough, and Salt Lake City. *Street Indexes to Unindexed Cities in the U.S. 1910 Federal Census*, compiled by Emil and Maurine Malmberg, is arranged by city, then by street name and street numbers. It gives the page numbers, enumeration district and library's microfilm number for most addresses.

CENSUS ROLLS FROM BUREAU OF INDIAN AFFAIRS

Special census enumerations of the Indian population have been taken by the Bureau of Indian Affairs. Below is an inventory of census rolls that are available at the Family History Library. Originals are in the National Archives in Washington, DC, and/or the regional branch that serves the particular state.

KANSAS
1927–1930: Potawatomi, Kickapoo, Iowa, Sac and Fox
1931: Potawatomi, Kickapoo, Iowa, Sac and Fox and supplemental rolls for additions, deductions, deaths, births (1924–1931)
1932–1934: Potawatomi, Kickapoo, Iowa, Sac and Fox with supplemental rolls for additions, deductions, births, deaths

MINNESOTA
1892–1939: Flandreau
1876–1953: Consolidated Chippewa Agency
1925–1938: Red Lake Agency, Chippewa Indians

NEW MEXICO
1929–1935: Eastern Navajo
1904–1935: Zuni

NEW YORK
1969: Cayuga Indian Tribe

NORTH DAKOTA
1889–1939: Fort Berthold
1906–1939: Fort Totten
1910–1939: Turtle Mountain
1876–1939: Standing Rock Agency
All census rolls include births, marriages and deaths.

SOUTH DAKOTA
1926: Sisseton Agency
1976: Census of Rosebud Tribal membership for burial insurance

STATE CENSUS SCHEDULES

State censuses have been taken in years between the federal enumerations, but not by all states and not at regular intervals. Beginning on page 80 is a list of state census schedules after 1920, plus the contents of each:

ALABAMA: 1921

This census of Confederate pensioners in Alabama was taken by mail. Each pensioner was asked to complete the form and return it to the state. The original forms may be examined at the Alabama Department of Archives and History, 624 Washington Ave., Montgomery, AL 36130.

FLORIDA: 1935 AND 1945

Lists name, address, age, sex, race, relationship to family head, state or country of birth, degree of education, home ownership or rental, and occupation.

Case Study

CENSUS RECORDS LOCATE HEIRS

In 1920, an individual executed a title transfer for some real estate in Colorado. He died in 1969, and in 1998 the real estate went into litigation. We were asked to locate his heirs so they could execute a quitclaim deed to settle the dispute.

The deceased had no children nor a surviving spouse. His death certificate gave his birth date and place as 1881 in Minnesota. It was unknown whether the person who provided the information for the death certificate was a relative, friend or hospital administrator. (The relationship of the informant to the deceased is usually stated on death certificates, but in this case, it was not.) The name of the informant and address, however, were noted as clues that might be useful in analyzing future research results. Attempts were made to locate the informant, but without success.

To locate the heirs of the deceased, the identity of his parents and siblings needed to be determined. Any surviving siblings would be heirs, as would any children of his siblings (his nieces and nephews). The census is the best source for piecing together family relationships and gathering information on birth dates, places, etc.

According to the 1900 census, the individual, then nineteen years old, was living with his parents and siblings in Minnesota. This was an important base of information to prove identities in other documents.

The deceased was next located in the 1920 Colorado census. (The 1910 census was not researched because the states of Minnesota and Colorado are not Soundexed [see page 77]). He was thirty-eight years old, married and had no children. The family next door had the same surname as the informant on the death certificate. Closer examination of the entry indicated that the wife of the next-door neighbor had the same given name as a sister of the individual who was also named in the 1900 records. The woman next door was also born in Minnesota, and one of her children's given names matched that of the informant. That child, one year old in the 1920 census, turned out to be the informant for the 1969 death certificate and a nephew of the deceased. Using the information on the names of the informant's siblings and parents, the heirs were located.

The original schedules are arranged alphabetically by county and then by election precinct. (There is no index.) They are available at Florida State Archives and Library, 500 S. Bronough St., Tallahassee, FL 32399.

INDIANA: 1925, 1931 AND 1937 (HENRY COUNTY ONLY)

Enumeration of white and colored males. Censuses are located at the Indiana State Library, 140 N. Senate Ave., Indianapolis, IN 46204. They are also available at the Family History Library, Salt Lake City, but circulation to Family History Centers is not allowed.

IOWA: 1925

Lists name, relationship, sex, race, age, marital status, property ownership, citizenship, education, names of parents (including mother's maiden name), nativity of parents, place of marriage of parents, military service, occupation and religion. Arranged by locality, then alphabetical. The census has been microfilmed and can be purchased. It is available for research at the State Historical Society of Iowa, 600 E. Locust, Des Moines, IA 50319, and at the Family History Library in Salt Lake City.

KANSAS: 1925

Lists name, address, age, sex, race, marital status, occupation, state or country of birth, and citizenship (year of immigration and year of naturalization). The census also asks where the family moved from (state or country) to Kansas. Available at Kansas State Historical Society, 120 W. Tenth, Topeka, KS 66612.

NEW YORK: 1925

Lists name, race, sex, age, country of birth, number of years in the U.S., citizenship, when and where naturalized, occupation and previous residence. Available at New York State Library, Cultural Education Center, Seventh Floor, Empire State Plaza, Albany, NY 12230. Bronx and Broome County are available on microfilm at the Family History Library, Salt Lake City.

NORTH DAKOTA: 1925

Names all members of the household and is not indexed. Available on microfilm at the North Dakota State Archives and Historical Research Library, Heritage Center, 612 E. Boulevard Ave., Bismarck, ND 58505.

RHODE ISLAND: 1925 AND 1935

The 1925 census names all members of the household, relationship to head, sex, race, place of birth, and citizenship. The 1935 census gives the same information as the 1925 census, plus marital status and occupation. The censuses are available at the Rhode Island State Archives, 337 Westminster St., Providence, RI 02903, and at the Family History Library in Salt Lake City.

SOUTH DAKOTA: 1925, 1935, AND 1945

Card file index, arranged alphabetically, at the South Dakota Historical Society, Cultural Heritage Center, 900 Governors Dr., Pierre, SD 57501.

CENSUS RESEARCH TIPS

- Take your time. It is easy to miss a name in the handwritten records.
- If you do not find the name you seek, try an alternate spelling for the surname (it may create a different Soundex code).

Notes

CHALLENGING NAMES

Common surnames are difficult to research. Below are the twenty most common surnames in the 1990 census enumeration:

1. Smith
2. Johnson
3. Williams
4. Jones
5. Brown
6. Davis
7. Miller
8. Wilson
9. Moore
10. Taylor
11. Anderson
12. Thomas
13. Jackson
14. White
15. Harris
16. Martin
17. Thompson
18. Garcia
19. Martinez
20. Robinson

Tip

- Be sure to check for nicknames and abbreviations, such as "Chas." for Charles.
- **Make a photocopy of the census page. Quite often the next-door neighbor is related, but you may not know that until further research has been done.**
- Remember that no census enumeration is 100 percent complete or 100 percent accurate. Families were missed, and people (particularly women) seemed to have not aged ten years between census years.

NINE

Military Records

N early one-third of the nation's population—approximately seventy million people—are potentially eligible for veteran's benefits and services. Of those seventy million, about twenty-eight million are living veterans; the rest are dependents and survivors. Vietnam vets number 8.2 million, followed by World War II vets at 8.1 million, 6.1 million peacetime-only vets and 4.7 million Korean War vets. There are more than one million Gulf War veterans, and there are a few surviving veterans from World War I. More than 1.5 million persons are serving on active duty, including the reserves and the National Guard.

What does this mean to you? It means the odds are good that the individuals you seek have a military connection. Perhaps they receive pension payments or belong to a veteran's organization. Maybe the father of the person you are seeking is buried in a national cemetery. Obtaining the death date and obituary of the father will help you find the son or daughter. Sometimes an exact birth date is the identifier you need to pinpoint someone, and a military record may supply that data.

DRAFT CLASSIFICATION AND REGISTRATION

When the U.S. entered World War I, Congress enacted legislation to create a Selective Service System under the umbrella of the Office of the Provost Marshal. Following the war (by 31 May 1919), all draft boards were closed and further registration ceased.

In 1940, President Franklin Roosevelt signed the Selective Training and Service Act and established the Selective Service System as an independent federal agency. From 1948 until 1973, men were drafted to fill vacancies in the armed forces. In 1973, the draft ended and the U.S. converted to an all-volunteer force.

The registration requirement was suspended in April 1975, then reinstated in 1980 by President Carter in response to the Soviet invasion of Afghanistan.

"On these stones are engraved the names of the most famous Americans and those who are familiar only to their families and loved ones. On each tablet is a name, a date of birth, a date of death, the name of a state, a religious symbol, perhaps a few details about rank and service—simple facts on simple stones, each standing for a person who believed the idea of America was worth fighting for. And all the stones standing together are the enduring monument to our greatness and eternal promise, including the stones which have no names."

—President Bill Clinton at Arlington National Cemetery on Memorial Day, 1998

PRIVACY LAWS

You cannot obtain a current address, telephone number, Social Security number or medical information from a military file without the written consent of the individual. If the veteran is deceased, a copy of the death certificate must accompany any requests for information, plus written consent of the next of kin. Privacy laws make military searches more difficult—but not impossible. More information on how to obtain information on living or deceased veterans is given with each record type within this chapter.

Not all men who registered for the draft actually served in the military, and not all men who served in the military registered for the draft. In other words, some men were not inducted into service, and those who were already in the military did not register. Aliens were required to register but were not subject to induction.

Registration continues today for all males, ages eighteen through twenty-five who are U.S. citizens or aliens living in the U.S. Women are not, nor have ever been, required to register for the draft. Selective Service law refers specifically to "male persons."

DRAFT REGISTRATION: WORLD WAR I

More than twenty-four million men born between 1873 and 1900 (approximately 23 percent of the population) registered in one of the three World War I (WWI) drafts. The form was revised during each registration; therefore, the data varies. Registrations contain the name and residence of the person, date of birth, race, citizenship, occupation, employer, marital status, draft exemption claims and reasons, physical description and the signature of the registrant.

The first draft, dated 5 June 1917, required the registration of all male citizens and all aliens who had declared their intent to become a citizen born between 6 June 1886 and 5 June 1896 (twenty-one to thirty-one years old). This form included birth date, exact birthplace, occupation, dependents (names were not usually given but relationships stated such as wife, mother, child, etc.), nearest relative and details of previous military experience.

The second draft, dated 5 June 1918, covered all men who had become twenty-one years of age since the previous registration. A supplemental registration, dated 24 August 1918, covered all men who had become twenty-one years of age after 5 June 1918. This is the only registration (including supplemental) that asked for the registrant's father's birthplace.

The third draft, dated 12 September 1918, covered all men aged eighteen to twenty-one (born 1897 to 1900) and thirty-one to forty-five (born 1873 to 1887). This registration asked for occupation, country to which alien is subject, and nearest relative. An important question for anyone wanting to prove Native American ancestry appears only on the third registration, asking whether the registrant is an Indian citizen or noncitizen.

Location of Original and Microfilmed WWI Draft Cards

The original WWI draft registration cards are at the National Archives, Southeast Region, in East Point, Georgia. Staff will research and photocopy requested records; however, you must have the full name of the person and his city, county and state of residence at the time of registration.

Microfilm copies for all states are available at the National Archives in Washington, DC. The Regional Archives (see page 142) have films for the states corresponding to their regions. For example, the Central Plains Region in Kansas City, Missouri, has microfilm copies of the draft registrations for the states of Iowa, Kansas, Missouri and Nebraska.

A complete collection is available at the Family History Library or through their Family History Centers (see page 26). They are cataloged under "United States—World War I Selective Service System Draft Registration Cards, 1917–1918."

REGISTRATION CARD

1 Name in full ... Mike Steiner

2 Home address ... 601 3rd Ave South South St. Paul Minn

3 Date of birth ... June 13, 1885

4 Are you (1) a natural-born citizen, (2) a naturalized citizen, (3) an alien, (4) or have you declared your intention (specify which)? ... Has 1st Papers

5 Where were you born? ... Rodki Czacikowice Poland

6 If not a citizen, of what country are you a citizen or subject? ...

7 What is your present trade, occupation, or office? ... Butcher 12

8 By whom employed? ... Swift & Co. Where employed? ... South St. Paul

9 Have you a father, mother, wife, child under 12, or a sister or brother under 12, solely dependent on you for support (specify which)? ... Wife & Child

10 Married or single (which)? ... Married Race (specify which)? ... Caucasian

11 What military service have you had? Rank ... Private branch ... Infantry years ... 2 Nation or State ... Austria

12 Do you claim exemption from draft (specify grounds)? ... Rupture

I affirm that I have verified above answers and that they are true.

Mikal Steiner
(Signature or mark)

The exact date of birth may be helpful in separating identities of persons with the same name in the Social Security Death Index or other databases.

Mike Steiner has filed "First Papers," which means he has begun the naturalization process. (See chapter sixteen.)

The exact place of birth can be difficult to determine when researching immigrants. The draft registration cards are an excellent source for obtaining this data.

St. Paul, Minnesota, WWI Draft Registration Card

Researching WWI Draft Registration Cards

The draft registration cards are arranged alphabetically by state, including Alaska, Hawaii, Puerto Rico and the District of Columbia. Within the states, the cards are filed alphabetically by county or city, numerically by local draft board, then alphabetically by name of registrant.

Local draft boards were established for districts of approximately thirty thousand persons in each city or county with a population of more than thirty thousand. Registrants residing in rural areas are comparatively easy to locate because each county had only one draft board. New York City, on the other hand, had 189 boards; Chicago, 86; and Boston, 25. **To search large cities, you must determine the correct draft board, which requires a registrant's exact street address in 1917 or 1918.** If you cannot determine the correct draft

Important

The nearest relative to Stephen Peter Walner is his brother, Peter J. Walner, residing in Anaconda, Butte County, Montana. Relationship proof such as this may be important if you are searching for either one's children, grandchildren or nieces and nephews. This also demonstrates the value of researching collateral relatives. For example, if your focus was Peter J. Walner and you were unable to locate records about him, redirecting the research to his brother (a collateral relative) may help locate and identify Peter.

This WWI draft registration (front and reverse) from Butte County, Montana, dated 12 September 1918, is from the third registration. It does not give place of birth, as do forms from the first and second registration.

DRAFT BOARD MAPS AT NATIONAL ARCHIVES

City	Number of Draft Boards	City	Number of Draft Boards
Albany, New York	4	Milwaukee, Wisconsin	15
Allegheny County, Pennsylvania	18	Minneapolis, Minnesota	13
Atlanta, Georgia	7	New Haven, Connecticut	6
Baltimore, Maryland	24	New Orleans, Louisiana	13
Birmingham, Alabama	6	New York, New York The Web page by the Italian Genealogical Group (http://www.italiangen.org/igg011.htm) lists the address for each New York City draft board	189
Boston, Massachusetts	25		
Bridgeport, Connecticut	6		
Buffalo, New York	16		
Chicago, Illinois	86	Newark, New Jersey	14
Cincinnati, Ohio	10	Philadelphia, Pennsylvania	51
Cleveland, Ohio	18	Pittsburgh, Pennsylvania	8
Dallas, Texas	4	Rochester, New York	8
Denver, Colorado	9	San Diego, California	2
Hartford, Connecticut	3	St. Paul, Minnesota	11
Indianapolis, Indiana	10	Schenectady, New York	4
Jersey City, New Jersey	10	Scranton, Pennsylvania	5
Kansas City, Kansas	4	Seattle, Washington	12
Louisville, Kentucky	7	Syracuse, New York	5
Los Angeles, California	18	Toledo, Ohio	6
Luzerne County, Pennsylvania	11	Washington, DC	11
Wilkes-Barre, Luzerne County, Pennsylvania	3		

board, it is still possible to search the microfilm; it will just take considerably longer to search alphabetically within each draft board.

City directories (see chapter three) are the most logical source to obtain an address. If that is unsuccessful, try alternate sources such as vital records (birth, marriage, divorce, death), voter registrations and naturalization records. The address of the registrant in the 1920 census (see chapter eight) may be helpful if the family did not move between 1917 and 1920.

The original draft board maps are located at the National Archives in Washington, DC. Microfilms are also available at the Family History Library (film number 1,498,803) and its Family History Centers. Some of the maps show the boundaries of the draft boards while others are just street and road maps. A table of the cities and number of local draft boards appears above.

Raymond H. Banks is extracting the registrant's name and birth date from the WWI draft registration cards. The database created from his extractions is available on the Internet at http://www.ancestry.com and represents approximately 8.5 percent of all counties nationwide. The states of Alaska, Delaware,

Research Tip

Italian emigrants often wrote their last names first, therefore search alphabetically by the surname *and* the given name. Cards of Hispanics may be filed under the mother's maiden name if they gave both parents' surnames.

Idaho and Nevada are completely indexed, and California, Colorado, Florida, Kansas, Mississippi, Nebraska, South Dakota, Texas and Utah are partially indexed.

DRAFT CLASSIFICATION AND REGISTRATION: WORLD WAR II

The Selective Service System for World War II (WWII) was established by executive order on 23 September 1940. Local draft boards were formed to register, classify and select for induction male citizens and aliens subject to service. From 1940 to 1947, more than ten million men were inducted into the armed forces from a pool of almost fifty-one million men who registered in one of seven registrations.

The first draft, dated 16 October 1940, required the reigstration of all males ages twenty-one to thirty-five. More than sixteen million men registered within the forty-eight states and the District of Columbia. Registrations for the Territories were held later: Hawaii on 26 October 1940, Puerto Rico on 20 November 1940, and Alaska on 22 January 1941.

The second draft, 1 July 1941, covered all males who had reached twenty-one years of age since the first registration. Nearly 790,000 names were added.

The third draft, 16 February 1942, covered males ages twenty to forty-five who had not previously registered. Nearly nine million men registered.

The fourth draft, 27 April 1942, covered males ages forty-five to sixty-five (born between 28 April 1877 and 16 February 1897). Over fourteen million men previously not eligible for military service registered. (These draft records are now open to the public because of the men's ages. See details later in this chapter.)

The fifth draft, 30 June 1942, covered males ages eighteen to twenty. Nearly three million men (who were not liable for military service until age twenty) registered.

The sixth draft, 10–31 December 1942, covered all males who had reached age eighteen after 12 November 1942.

The seventh draft, 16 November 1943 through 31 December 1943, required the registration of citizens living abroad, ages eighteen to forty-five.

World War II registration cards (except the fourth registration as explained below) are protected under the Privacy Act. To obtain a copy, you must have written permission from the registrant. If the person is deceased, a copy of the death certificate (or other proof of death, such as an obituary or probate record) must accompany the request, plus the registrant's full name, date of birth and address at the time of registration. An exact address is required for New York City; Washington, DC; Chicago; Detroit; and Los Angeles. Send requests to The Records Division, Selective Service National Headquarters, Arlington, VA 22209-2425 (phone number [703] 605-4047).

Fourth WWII Registration Records Open to the Public

The fourth draft registration (April 1942) was for men born between 28 April 1877 and 16 February 1897 (ages forty-five to sixty-five). Because of the ages

SERIAL NUMBER	1. NAME (Print)			ORDER NUMBER
884	Glen (First)	LeRoy (Middle)	Westberg. (Last)	2975

2. ADDRESS (Print)
1204 Ludington   Escanaba   Delta   Mich
(Number and street or R. F. D. number)   (Town)   (County)   (State)

3. TELEPHONE	4. AGE IN YEARS	5. PLACE OF BIRTH	6. COUNTRY OF CITIZENSHIP
654. (Exchange) (Number)	22	Grandy (Town or county)	U. S.
	DATE OF BIRTH 11 22 1918 (Mo.) (Day) (Yr.)	Minn. (State or country)	

7. NAME OF PERSON WHO WILL ALWAYS KNOW YOUR ADDRESS   **8. RELATIONSHIP OF THAT PERSON**
Mrs. (Mr., Mrs., Miss)   Mildred (First)   K. (Middle)   Westberg (Last)   Wife.

9. ADDRESS OF THAT PERSON
1204 Ludington   Escanaba   Delta   Mich.
(Number and street or R. F. D. number)   (Town)   (County)   (State)

10. EMPLOYER'S NAME
Glen. LeRoy Westberg.

11. PLACE OF EMPLOYMENT OR BUSINESS
1204 Ludington. Main Hotel. Escanaba. Mich
(Number and street or R. F. D. number)   (Town)   (County)   (State)

I AFFIRM THAT I HAVE VERIFIED ABOVE ANSWERS AND THAT THEY ARE TRUE.

REGISTRATION CARD
D. S. S. Form 1   (over)   10—17105   Glen LeRoy Westberg
(Registrant's signature)

> The year of birth is incorrect; it should 1917. Always question dates, as errors are made in official and unoffical documents.

This WWII registration card is from the first draft.

of these men (see page 88), the registration cards are now open to the public and available at the respective regions of the National Archives, Record Group 147. (Refer to the table on page 90.) The cards are arranged primarily by Selective Service Board number, then alphabetically by name of applicant. Counties with only one draft board are therefore in one alphabetical group, whereas larger cities will have multiple groups.

Draft Classification: World War II

After a man registered for Selective Service in World War II, he was classified by his local board as follows:

Class I	Available for training and service.
Class I-A	Eligible to be inducted for unlimited service.
Class I-B	Available for limited service.
Class I-B-O	Available for limited service.
Class II	Available for training but deferred for periods up to six months. This class included farmers and men deferred because of industrial skills.
Class III	Men who had dependents.
Class IV	Registrants who had completed certain types of military service, officials deferred by law, aliens who had not filed first papers (intent to become a citizen), ordained ministers and theological students, conscientious objectors, men having dishonorable discharges from the armed services, men convicted of certain crimes, men morally unfit for military

service, men discharged from the armed services because of undesirable habits or traits of character, and men found physically or mentally unfit for military service after physical examination.

The classification record is public information and available to anyone who requests it. The record shows the registrant's name, local board number, his classification and the dates he received the classifications.

To request the record, you must provide the registrant's full name, date of birth and address at the time of registration. Send requests to: The Records Division, Selective Service National Headquarters, Arlington, VA 22209-2425 (phone number [703] 605-4047).

LOCATION OF WWII FOURTH DRAFT REGISTRATION CARDS

National Archives and Records Administration Regional Facility	States
Central Plains Region Kansas City, Missouri	Iowa, Kansas, Minnesota, Missouri, Nebraska, North Dakota, South Dakota
Great Lakes Region Chicago, Illinois	Illinois, Indiana, Michigan, Ohio, Wisconsin
Mid-Atlantic Region Center City/Philadelphia, Pennsylvania	Delaware, Maryland, Pennsylvania, Virginia, West Virginia
Northeast Region Waltham, Massachusetts	Connecticut, New Hampshire, Rhode Island, Vermont (Cards for Maine and Massachusetts have not yet been accessioned because these two states filed the cards for all the registrations into one single series.)
Northeast Region New York, New York	The cards for New Jersey and New York have not been accessioned.
Pacific Alaska Region Anchorage, Alaska	Alaska
Pacific Alaska Region Seattle, Washington	Idaho, Oregon, Washington
Pacific Region San Bruno, California	California, Hawaii, Nevada (The California cards for surnames beginning with the letter A are arranged alphabetically regardless of board number. The remaining cards for California are arranged primarily by Selective Service Board number as in other states. Hawaii cards are arranged alphabetically by name of registrant.)
Rocky Mountain Region Denver, Colorado	Arizona, Colorado, Montana, Utah, Wyoming
Southeast Region East Point, Georgia	The Atlanta (East Point) Federal Records Center destroyed the records in 1983 for the states of Alabama, Florida, Georgia, Kentucky, Mississippi, North Carolina, South Carolina and Tennessee.
Southwest Region Fort Worth, Texas	Arkansas, Louisiana, New Mexico, Oklahoma, Texas

Cards from the fourth draft registration for Maine, Massachusetts, New Jersey and New York can only be accessed through the Selective Service System by sending proof of registrant's death, plus registrant's full name, date of birth and address at the time of registration. An exact address is required for New York City. Send requests to The Records Division, Selective Service National Headquarters, Arlington, VA 22209-2425 (phone number [703] 605-4047).

REGISTRATION CARD—(Men born on or after April 28, 1877 and on or before February 16, 1897)   6

SERIAL NUMBER 3302	1. NAME (Print)	(initial only)	ORDER NUMBER
U.	William (First)	A. (Middle) Hopkins (Last)	

2. PLACE OF RESIDENCE (Print)
1108 22nd Street   Denver   Denver   Colorado
(Number and street)   (Town, township, village, or city)   (County)   (State)
[THE PLACE OF RESIDENCE GIVEN ON THE LINE ABOVE WILL DETERMINE LOCAL BOARD JURISDICTION; LINE 2 OF REGISTRATION CERTIFICATE WILL BE IDENTICAL]

3. MAILING ADDRESS   Same
[Mailing address if other than place indicated on line 2. If same insert word same]

4. TELEPHONE	5. AGE IN YEARS 55	6. PLACE OF BIRTH Uninon County (Town or county)
Main 9746 (Exchange) (Number)	DATE OF BIRTH June 6, 1886 (Mo.) (Day) (Yr.)	Mississippi (State or country)

7. NAME AND ADDRESS OF PERSON WHO WILL ALWAYS KNOW YOUR ADDRESS
Mrs. Otis Morgan   1664 Pearl St   Wichita Falls, Texas

8. EMPLOYER'S NAME AND ADDRESS
Unemployed

9. PLACE OF EMPLOYMENT OR BUSINESS
Unemployed   Amarillo
(Number and street or R.F.D. number)   (Town)   (County)   (State)

I AFFIRM THAT I HAVE VERIFIED ABOVE ANSWERS AND THAT THEY ARE TRUE.

D. S. S. Form 1   16—21630-2   W. A. Hopkins
(Revised 4-1-42)   (over)   (Registrant's signature)

> Mrs. Otis Morgan may be a relative of William A. Hopkins. This is a valuable clue to conduct further research.

REGISTRAR'S REPORT

DESCRIPTION OF REGISTRANT

RACE		HEIGHT (Approx.)	WEIGHT (Approx.)	COMPLEXION	
White	X	5'8½"	156	Sallow	
		EYES	HAIR	Light	
Negro		Blue	Blonde	Ruddy	X
		Gray	Red	Dark	
Oriental		Hazel	Brown	Freckled	
		Brown X	Black X	Light brown	
Indian		Black	Gray X	Dark brown	
			Bald	Black	
Filipino					

Other obvious physical characteristics that will aid in identification
right arm off at wrist joint

I certify that my answers are true; that the person registered has read or has had read to him his own answers; that I have witnessed his signature or mark and that all of his answers of which I have knowledge are true, except as follows:

none to my knowledge

M. Darrell Grundy
(Signature of registrar)

Registrar for Local Board Potter County Texas
(Number)   (City or county)   (State)

Date of registration April 27, 1942

Local Board No. 6	82
Denver County	031
	006

(STAMP OF LOCAL BOARD)
619 14th Street
Denver Colorado
(The stamp of the Local Board having jurisdiction of the registrant shall be placed in the above space)
16—21630-1

> Disabled men also registered for the draft.

Colorado WWII (fourth registration) Draft Registration Cards. National Archives Rocky Mountain Region, Denver, Colorado.

Case Study

THE JOY OF COMPARING

Comparing the information found in different sources can often lead you to a more complete picture of the person you are tracking. For instance, the draft registration card provides the complete name of John Emil Conrad Hoppe; the 1945 Denver City Directory lists his initials only—J.E.C. Hoppe. The 1939 city directory listed him as E.C. Hoppe, suggesting that he may have been known as Emil Hoppe. If so, some records, such as a marriage index, may be indexed as Emil Hoppe, rather than John E. C. Hoppe.

Also, Mr. Curtis Eagan was identified as a person who would always know the address of John Emil Conrad Hoppe. The address indicates he was a next-door neighbor. But was he just a neighbor or also a relative? Perhaps a brother-in-law or son-in-law? Information such as this should be used as a clue to future research.

German-born persons registered for the draft. Do not assume otherwise.

REGISTRATION CARD—(Men born on or after April 28, 1877 and on or before February 16, 1897)   6

SERIAL NUMBER | 1. NAME (Print) | ORDER NUMBER

U   3883   *John Emil Conrad Hoppe*

(First)   (Middle)   (Last)

2 PLACE OF RESIDENCE (Print)

1129 17th St.   Denver   Colo.

(Number and street)   (Town, township, village, or city)   (County)   (State)

[THE PLACE OF RESIDENCE GIVEN ON THE LINE ABOVE WILL DETERMINE LOCAL BOARD JURISDICTION; LINE 2 OF REGISTRATION CERTIFICATE WILL BE IDENTICAL]

3. MAILING ADDRESS   *Same.*

[Mailing address if other than place indicated on line 2. If same insert word same]

4. TELEPHONE   *Ma. 5085*   5. AGE IN YEARS   *45*   6. PLACE OF BIRTH   *Altona E. Hamburg*

(Town or county)

DATE OF BIRTH   *Aug. 14 1896   Germany*

(Exchange)   (Number)   (Mo.)   (Day)   (Yr.)   (State or country)

7. NAME AND ADDRESS OF PERSON WHO WILL ALWAYS KNOW YOUR ADDRESS

1131 17th St.   Mr. Curtis Eagan.

8. EMPLOYER'S NAME AND ADDRESS   *Watch repairing 1129 17th St.*

9. PLACE OF EMPLOYMENT OR BUSINESS   *1129 17th   Denver   Colo.*

(Number and street or R.F.D. number)   (Town)   (County)   (State)

I AFFIRM THAT I HAVE VERIFIED ABOVE ANSWERS AND THAT THEY ARE TRUE.

D. S. S. Form 1   (Revised 4-1-42)   (over)   16—21630-2   *J.E.C. Hoppe*

(Registrant's signature)

This excerpt from the 1945 Denver City Directory lists initials only for J.E.C. Hoppe.

Hoppe Chas (Marie) USA n1310 Stout apt 311
" J E C instrument mkr 1129 17th R7 h do
" L Pearl Mrs (American Beauty Salon) h1519 E Colfax
" Lena J (wid Geo) r2391 Hudson
" M R Capt (Lois M) USA h1415 Cherry
" Marg maid 788 Milwaukee
" Mary E r900 Sherman apt C22
" Oscar P (Emily) asst supvr Prudential Ins Co h975 Monroe
" Ralph N mech Denver Buick r94 Sherman

SELECTIVE SERVICE SYSTEM: KOREAN WAR AND LATER

The Selective Service System's Web page (http://www.sss.gov/records.htm) gives instructions on obtaining draft classification and registration information on veterans since World War II. The instructions vary slightly according to the birth date of the veteran:

Men born on or before 29 March 1957: The classification record is public information and available to anyone who requests it. The record shows the registrant's name, Local Board number, his classification and the dates he received the classifications. To request the record, you must provide the registrant's full name, date of birth–and address at the time of registration.

The registration cards are protected under the Privacy Act. To obtain a copy, you must have written permission from the registrant. If the person is deceased, a copy of the death certificate (or other proof of death) must accompany the request, and include the registrant's full name, date of birth and address at the time of registration.

You need an exact address if you are requesting a classification record or registration card for anyone residing in New York City; Washington, DC; Chicago; Detroit; or Los Angeles. Send requests to The Records Division, Selective Service National Headquarters, Arlington, VA 22209-2425 (phone number [703] 605-4047).

Men born from 29 March 1957 to 31 December 1959: Registration was suspended in the late 1970s, and men born between these dates were not required to register.

Men born on or after 1 January 1960: The registration card shows the registrant's name, date of birth, home address, telephone number, Social Security number and Selective Service registration number. The registration cards are protected under the Privacy Act. To obtain a copy, you must have written permission from the registrant. If the person is deceased, a copy of the death certificate (or other proof of death) must accompany the request.

The Selective Service will verify that a man is registered and provide the registrant's Selective Service number if you provide the Social Security number and date of birth of the registrant. The information can be obtained by calling the Agency at (847) 688-6888 or writing to Selective Service Data Management Center, P.O. Box 94638, Palatine, IL 60094-4638.

SERVICE RECORDS

Nearly all records pertaining to persons discharged from the army before 1960 and about three-quarters of the records pertaining to persons discharged from the air force before 1964 were destroyed in a 1973 fire at the National Personnel Records Center (NPRC) in St. Louis, Missouri. The fire destroyed approximately sixteen million to eighteen million official military personnel files. There were no duplicate copies of the records, nor were they ever microfilmed or indexed. A complete listing of the records that were destroyed is not available, except for these general statistics:

Army (80 percent loss): Personnel discharged 1 November 1912 to 1 January 1960.

Air Force (75 percent loss): Personnel (names following Hubbard, James E. alphabetically) discharged 25 September 1947 to 1 January 1964.

When proof of military service is needed, the NPRC attempts to reconstruct basic data from alternative sources, such as their collection of nineteen million final pay vouchers. These records provide name, service number, dates of service and character of service. By combining this data with other organizational records (enlistment ledgers, service number indexes, etc.), they can usually verify military service and provide a Certification of Military Service.

A collection of computer tapes containing ten million hospital/treatment facility admission records was discovered by the National Academy of Sciences in 1988 and offered to the National Archives for use by the Medical Personnel Records of the NPRC. Over 7.8 million records were salvaged for active duty army and army air corps personnel in service between 1942 and 1945, and active duty army personnel who served between 1950 and 1954. About 5 percent of the files are for marine corps, navy, air force and military cadet personnel, 1950 to 1954.

The records do not show the patient's name, but are identified by military service number. Personal data includes age, race, sex and place of birth. The listings are not complete because the records were collected as a sampling for statistical purposes. Written permission from the patient (or proof of death) must be given to access these records. And, of course, the military service number is required. This can be found on discharge papers, which I discuss next.

All requests for information from the NPRC must be submitted on Standard Form 180 (Rev. 4/96), Request Pertaining to Military Records. The form can be downloaded from NARA at http://www.nara.gov/regional/mprsf180.html or requested from their fax-on-demand system at (301) 713-6905, document number 2255.

DISCHARGE PAPERS

Tip

Soldiers and sailors who were honorably discharged from WWI often recorded their discharge at the local county courthouse as proof of their veteran status. The discharges were usually recorded with the land deeds, although some courts kept a separate volume of military discharges. This practice continued through WWII and Vietnam and remains a common practice today. Below is a description of how these records are indexed and stored in Denver, Colorado; other states and counties may have similar methods.

- World War I: Recorded in grantor indexes at the county recorder of deeds office. In other words, the military discharges were intermingled with the deeds. Alphabetical by first letter of surname only, thereafter chronologically.
- October 1945 to July 1986: Three volumes at the county recorder of

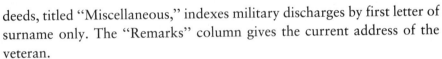

WWII OFFICIAL ARMY REGISTER PROVIDES KEY TO SEARCH

A researcher wanted to learn more about an aide to Gen. George Patton and hoped to interview any surviving relatives. The aide—Richard N. Jenson—was killed in action during WWII, but the exact date of his death was unknown. Jenson had a very common surname, his marital status was unknown, and the names of his parents and siblings were unknown.

Since Jenson worked for General Patton, we thought his death might have made headlines. *The New York Times* indexes were examined, but he was not included. Since Jenson was from the Los Angeles area, the *Los Angeles Times* index was checked, but also without success. The Los Angeles County veteran's burial cards were checked, but the index ended in 1940, prior to the aide's death. We still needed an exact death date to locate an obituary or death notice.

The 1943 edition of the Official Army Register listed General Patton's aide, and Jenson was on the casualty list in the 1944 edition. Once the exact death date was known, an extensive newspaper report was located detailing his death. His mother, grandmother and aunt were named in the report, providing information that allowed us to locate the family.

deeds, titled "Miscellaneous," indexes military discharges by first letter of surname only. The "Remarks" column gives the current address of the veteran.

- July 1986 to Current: All military discharges are indexed via computer, along with deeds, powers of attorney, etc.

The records may contain the individual's name, race, rank, serial number, reason for discharge, birthplace, age at time of enlistment, occupation and a personal description. The service record, sometimes included with the discharge record, gives the length of service, prior service, marital status, battles, decorations, honors, leaves of absence, physical condition and character evaluation.

The discharge record for a WWII veteran appears on page 96; the discharge for a Vietnam veteran appears on page 97.

OFFICIAL ARMY AND AIR FORCE REGISTERS FOR THE WORLD WAR II ERA

Official Army and Air Force Registers (there are also Navy and National Guard Registers) were published by the Superintendent of Documents, U.S. Government Printing Office. These registers list active-duty officers, retired officers and casualties. Information includes date and state of birth, details of place, and degree of education, and appointment data. These registers are difficult to locate because they were not distributed to the public, but instead placed in public libraries that are official government document repositories.

The serial or service number may be required to access other military records.

Exact date of birth and place of birth are always important identifiers.

Although this veteran is a Colorado resident, he gives a permanent address of Brooklyn, New York. This is a clue for identifying and locating relatives.

Clues are sometimes hidden. Note the dates he was AWOL. This is when Vincent J. Ranieri married. Comparing the dates with the marriage record verify this.

This World War II military discharge was recorded in Denver County, Colorado, on 29 May 1946. (Permission to reprint given by Vincent J. Ranieri.)

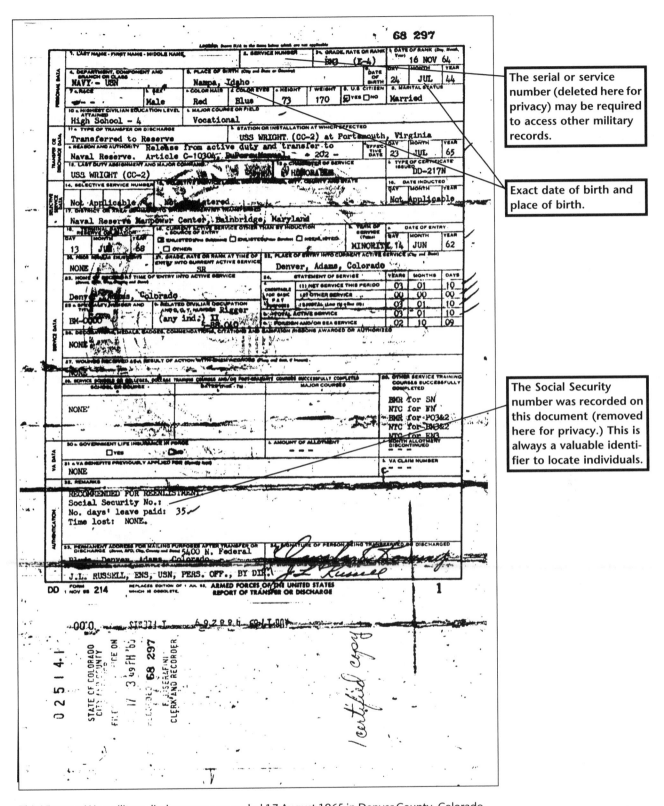

The serial or service number (deleted here for privacy) may be required to access other military records.

Exact date of birth and place of birth.

The Social Security number was recorded on this document (removed here for privacy.) This is always a valuable identifier to locate individuals.

This Vietnam War military discharge was recorded 17 August 1965 in Denver County, Colorado. The name has been removed for privacy.

CASUALTY LISTS

Casualty lists for the Korean and Vietnam wars can be accessed on-line at http://www.nara.gov/nara/electronic/korvnsta.html. The same data is available in FamilySearch at the Family History Library and its Family History Centers. **The FamilySearch CD-ROM version, however, gives extra information.** For example, a list of Korean War casualties from Wyoming, taken from the Internet page, appears on page 99.

The U.S. Military Index that is part of FamilySearch allows filtering by state. When filling out the opening search form, enter a given name (any name will work) and leave the surname field blank. Sort by name of state, and a statewide list such as this results. Comparing this list with the Wyoming list from the Internet shows the same names.

CD Source

```
                     Military Index 2.02 - Korea
        Esc=Exit  F1=Help  F2=Print/Holding File  F4=Search        21 JUL 1998

        INDEX     Use      PgDn PgUp and press Enter for details.

          (-Name Group-) Name       Birth Year & Home of Record  Death Year & Place

          -ANDERSON-
            Allen G ANDERSON .........  1930   Wyoming       1951   Korea
          -BAKER-
            Clifford E BAKER .........  1926   Wyoming       1953   Korea
          -BARNES-
            Ted U BARNES .............  1921   Wyoming       1950   Korea
          -BARNHILL-
            Kenneth R BARNHILL .......  1928   Wyoming       1951   Korea
          -BAXTER-
            Neil B BAXTER ............  1923   Wyoming       1950   Korea
          -BOD-
            Malcolm Lloyd BUDD .......  1930   Wyoming       1950   Korea
          -CLARK-
            Leonard W CLARK ..........  1928   Wyoming       1951   Korea
          -CLAY-
            James E CLAY .............  1925   Wyoming       1952   Korea
          -COWDEN-
```

The information on this printout is from the United States government records and is in the public domain. No claim to copyright is expressed or implied.

The big difference between the Internet list and FamilySearch is that you can get a detailed record for each person, such as the following for Kenneth R. Barnhill:

Sources

```
        Military Index, Version 2.02 - Korea

                            INDIVIDUAL RECORD

        21 JUL 1998
        ==============================================================================
        NAME: BARNHILL, Kenneth R
        ------------------------------------------------------------------------------
                      Sex:  M

               Birth Date:  1928
        Home of Residence:  Platte, Wyoming

                   Branch:  U S Army
                     Rank:  PVT
              Service No.:  55079126

               Death Date:  3 Sep 1951
                    Place:  Korea

           Marital Status:  Unknown
                     Race:  Caucasian

        ==============================================================================
```

The information on this printout is from the United States government records and is in the public domain. No claim to copyright is expressed or implied.

VETERANS ORGANIZATIONS AND ASSOCIATIONS

Disabled American Veterans
National Headquarters
P.O. Box 14301
Cincinnati, OH 45250-0301
(606) 441-7300
fax: (606) 441-9521
E-mail: ahdav@one.net
http://www.dav.org

The American Legion
P.O. Box 1055
Indianapolis, IN 46206
(317) 630-1366
fax: (317) 630-1241
http://www.legion.org/index.htm

National Archives and Records Administration
Center for Electronic Records

WY

ANDERSON ALLEN G	PVT	ARMY	SHERIDAN	WYOMING
BAKER CLIFFORD E	1LT	ARMY	BIG HORN	WYOMING
BARNES TED U	CAPT	ARMY	COSHEN	WYOMING
BARNHILL KENNETH R	PVT	ARMY	PLATTE	WYOMING
BAXTER NEIL B	1LT	ARMY	SHERIDAN	WYOMING
BUDD MALCOLM LLOYD	SGT	MARINES	BIG PINEY	WYOMING
CLARK LEONARD W	PVT	ARMY	SWEETWATER	WYOMING
CLAY JAMES E	1LT	AIR FORCE	LARAMIE	WYOMING
COWDIN RAY P	PFC	ARMY	CARBON	WYOMING
DAVIS COURTENAY C	2LT	ARMY	LARAMIE	WYOMING
DEWEES DONALD L	PFC	ARMY	ALBANY	WYOMING
DIANA PAUL R	CAPT	MARINES	NEW CASTLE	WYOMING
DURAM ANTHONY DOMINGO	CPL	MARINES	POWELL	WYOMING
ELSOM BILL	CAPT	AIR FORCE	CHEYENNE	WYOMING
FINCH ROBERT A	1LT	ARMY	FREMONT	WYOMING
FINLAYSON KENNETH	CPL	ARMY	FREMONT	WYOMING
FRIEDLUND RICHARD	1LT	ARMY	WASHAKIE	WYOMING
GARCIA FRED N	PFC	ARMY	WASHAKIE	WYOMING
GARCIA JOSEPH G	CPL	ARMY	CARBON	WYOMING
GREEN JOHN H	1LT	ARMY	SWEETWATER	WYOMING
HARPER EDWARD W	SGT	ARMY	SHERIDAN	WYOMING
HARRIS THOMAS R	SGT	ARMY	SWEETWATER	WYOMING
HESSENFLOW ROBERT	PFC	ARMY	NATRONA	WYOMING
HILL DONALD G	PVT	ARMY	FREMONT	WYOMING
HITTNER GEORGE B	SGT	ARMY	CARBON	WYOMING
HOKE JOHN DAVID	1LT	AIR FORCE	CHEYENNE	WYOMING
HORN JOHN LUCIUS	CAPT	AIR FORCE	CHEYENNE	WYOMING
JARAMILLO ROSELIO	PFC	ARMY	CAMPBELL	WYOMING
JOHNSON KENNETH C	CPL	ARMY	FREMONT	WYOMING
JONES JAMES L	PVT	ARMY	PARK	WYOMING
KIRTLEY DEMARET	PFC	ARMY	JOHNSON	WYOMING
KUIPER DAVID H	PFC	ARMY	SHERIDAN	WYOMING
LARSON EDGAR J	PVT	ARMY	FREMONT	WYOMING
LEWIS ROBERT I SR	CPL	ARMY	PARK	WYOMING
LIEB RAYMOND J	1LT	ARMY	PLATTE	WYOMING
LUNBECK CHARLES E	PFC	ARMY	SUBLETTE	WYOMING
MC LAUGHLIN CLINTO	PFC	ARMY	UINTA	WYOMING
MITCHELSON THOMAS	PFC	ARMY	SWEETWATER	WYOMING
NEARY PHILIP PATRICK	PFC	MARINES	LANCE CREEK	WYOMING
PEREA CAMERINO	PFC	ARMY	ALBANY	WYOMING
PRATT CLIFFORD F	1LT	AIR FORCE	CHEYENNE	WYOMING
ROBB CHARLES E	PVT	ARMY	CAMPBELL	WYOMING
ROGERS LLOYD G	PVT	ARMY	LARAMIE	WYOMING
ROSZEK ROBERT L	SGT	ARMY	CARBON	WYOMING
RUSTH HELMAR O	SFC	ARMY	PARK	WYOMING
SMITH RUSSELL EVERETT	PFC	MARINES	BOSLER	WYOMING
SONNAMAKER WILLIAM	SGT	ARMY	SHERIDAN	WYOMING
SWANSON JOHN A	1LT	AIR FORCE	TORRINGTON	WYOMING
TAYLOR ERVIN JOHN	PFC	MARINES	LARAMIE	WYOMING
THOMPSON MAYNARD H	PFC	ARMY	WASHAKIE	WYOMING
TILTON CLARK M	SGT	ARMY	SHERIDAN	WYOMING
TONER EDWARD E	PFC	ARMY	SWEETWATER	WYOMING
URBANSKI DAROLD D	PFC	ARMY	PARK	WYOMING
VIGIL PABLO J	PFC	ARMY	SWEETWATER	WYOMING
WADSWORTH FREEMAN	PVT	ARMY	LARAMIE	WYOMING
WELLS ELMER L	PFC	ARMY	CROOK	WYOMING
WOLF LELAND HENRY	1LT	AIR FORCE	CHEYENNE	WYOMING

Year of birth (exact date of birth is given in the Vietnam database), service number, death date, marital status and race are reported in the FamilySearch version. This information is *not* reported in the on-line version by the National Archives and Records Administration.

Casualty reports, which contain names and addresses of next of kin, will be provided by the following casualty offices:

Air Force	(800) 531-5501
Army	(800) 892-2490
Marine Corps	(800) 847-1597
Navy	(800) 443-9298

NATIONAL CEMETERY SYSTEM

A national system to provide for the proper burial and registration of graves of the Civil War dead was established by Congress and approved by President Abraham Lincoln in 1862. The cemeteries were under the Department of the Army until 1973 when they were transferred (except Arlington) to the Department of Veterans Affairs (VA). In 1978, the VA established the National Cemetery System to administer the cemeteries and related programs.

There are 114 VA national cemeteries in thirty-eight states (and Puerto Rico) [listed in appendix C], with more than seventy thousand interments per year. The annual interments are expected to increase as the veteran population ages. Arlington National Cemetery averages three thousand burials annually and is expected to reach capacity in the year 2020, when more than 250,000 people will have been buried there.

Library/Archive Source

Records pertaining to almost all soldiers and veterans buried in national cemeteries are maintained by the Cemetery Service, National Cemetery System, Department of Veterans Affairs, 810 Vermont Ave., Washington, DC 20420. The names of the deceased are indexed, and information will be furnished upon request. You can also write or telephone individual cemeteries and inquire about burials.

Persons eligible for burial in a VA national cemetery include:

- veterans and members of the armed forces (army, navy, air force, marine corps and coast guard), as well as their spouses, unremarried widow or widower, minor children, and under certain conditions, unmarried adult children
- members of the reserve components of the armed forces—the army and air national guard and the reserve officers' training corps—who die on active duty or have twenty years of service in the reserve components
- commissioned officers of the National Oceanic and Atmospheric Administration
- any commissioned officer of the regular or reserve corps of the Public Health Service who served on full-time duty on or after 29 July 1945
- World War II Merchant Marines

Burials in Foreign Countries

Grave registrations of WWI and WWII soldiers who died overseas are in Record Group 92, Records of the Quartermaster General, in the National Archives. The registrations include the name of the soldier, military organization, date of death, a statement that he was killed in action, name and address of the nearest relative or guardian and name of the chapel.

For a copy of the grave registration write to American Battle Monuments Commission, Pulaski Building, Room 5127, 20 Massachusetts Ave. NW, Washington, DC 20314-0001 (phone numbers [202] 761-0532 and [202] 761-0537).

A list of soldiers classified as missing in action is also in the custody of the National Archives under the Records of American Battle Commission, Record Group 117. The information includes the name of the missing soldier, the unit in which he served and the date of disappearance.

LETTER-FORWARDING SERVICES

Several military organizations will forward letters. The instructions are similar to the Social Security Administration's program (see page 55): Write two letters—one to the person you seek and the second to the administrator explaining why you are requesting their service. (Some groups charge fees; telephone or check the Internet first for details.) The addresses in their files may not be current; it depends on whether the veteran had recent correspondence or business with the organization. Send letter-forwarding requests to either of these two offices:

Tip

VA Records Processing Center
P.O. Box 5020
St. Louis, MO 63115
(800) 827-1000 (will connect you to the nearest regional office)

National Personnel Records Center
9700 Page Blvd.
St. Louis, MO 63132

A 1990 federal court decision directed the NPRC to forward letters to the last known address of veterans who may have fathered illegitimate children who are members of an organization called War Babes. These children were fathered by U.S. servicemen while in Great Britain during WWII.

MILITARY REUNION ORGANIZATIONS

Many groups of veterans have formed reunion organizations to help former comrades stay in touch. **These reunion organizations are an excellent resource when trying to locate a veteran.** For example, the WWII-era 456th Bomb Group Association was formed in the late 1940s with a reunion of the 747th Bomb Squadron in Chicago. Membership is open to all former members who

Tip

served as part of the unit, either in the States or in the combat zone, and to members of their families, either direct or indirect. Yearly reunions have been held ever since, including two in Italy. They publish a newsletter, and in 1994 published a hardcover history of the 456th Bomb Group that included nearly seven hundred biographies with photographs.

To determine if a reunion organization exists for a particular unit or group, contact the National VETS Archives, P.O. Box 901, Columbia, MO 65205-0901, (573) 474-4444. They maintain a database (http://www.vets.org) of more than twelve thousand veterans reunions, as well as a search service to help locate military buddies.

Reunions are also advertised in magazines such as the *Reunions Magazine*, P.O. Box 11727, Milwaukee, WI 53211-0727, (414) 263-4567 (http://www.reunionsmag.com).

MILITARY RECORDS RESEARCH TIPS

Library/Archive Source

- **A veteran is a person who has served on active duty in one or more of the armed forces.** Individuals who served only in the reserves or national guard are not considered veterans.
- For a discussion of U.S. military records from Colonial America to the present, consult James C. Neagles's *U.S. Military Records: A Guide to Federal and State Sources, Colonial America to the Present* (see appendix E).
- Consult Richard S. Johnson's *How to Locate Anyone Who Is or Has Been in the Military: Armed Forces Locator Guide*, 7th edition (Spartanburg, SC: MIE Publishing, ©1996).
- A complete list of U.S. military associations, compiled by Ben N. Myer, U.S. Army Ret., is on the Internet at http://vets.com/inside/assoc.htm. It includes army, air force, navy, coast guard and marine corps and is divided into twenty areas of interest. Select "Table of Contents" at the bottom of the opening page.
- Military City Online (http://www.militarycity.com/) has a fee-based search service for active-duty military personnel. Their database exceeds ten million records.
- An excellent Web site for women in the military is at http://militarywoman.org/homepage.htm.

TEN

Real Estate Records

O wnership of real property creates a paper trail. The deeds, mortgages, powers of attorney, liens and tax assessments provide clues or information on current and former residences. **Real estate records are not limited to those pertaining to ownership of a home.** They can include records of empty lots, cemetery plots, farmland, mineral rights and apartment or business buildings. (See chapter fifteen for information on owners of mobile homes.) Real estate records can also include such supplemental documents as:

Research Tip

- **Death Certificates:** When a home is in joint tenancy (owned by two people, usually husband and wife) and one of them dies, the surviving owner often files a copy of the death certificate with the Recorder of Deeds. This establishes sole ownership and sometimes avoids probate. The death certificate, of course, is a valuable document in researching an individual or family (see chapter six).

- **Powers of Attorney:** When the owners of property are unable to personally attend the closing of a sale of a home, they issue a power of attorney to someone to act on their behalf. The power of attorney may provide a current address of the individual. This is common when the owner moves to another state prior to the final sale of the home.

- **Liens:** A lien on someone's property will supply data on business associates or creditors that may be useful in locating the person you seek. There are several types of liens.

    Architect's Lien: A lien on real estate by the architect who drew the plans and supervised the construction of the real estate; such liens are used to ensure the payment of his fee.

    Attorney's Lien: The right of an attorney at law to hold a client's money or property until the attorney's fee has been paid. It requires no equitable proceeding for its establishment.

Charging Lien: An attorney's lien on the monies a client recovers using the attorney's services.

Retaining Lien: The lien which allows an attorney to keep all his client's papers, deeds, vouchers, etc., until he is paid for professional services.

General Lien: The right to hold on to an asset, etc., until payment is made, not only of any debt due related to that asset, but of any balance that may be due on general account in the same line of business.

Judgment Lien: A lien binding the real estate of a debtor, in favor of the holder of the lien. This lien mandates that the holder of the lien be paid before any others.

Judicial Lien: One obtained by judgment, levy or other legal or equitable process or proceeding.

Mechanic's Lien: A claim used to secure priority of payment for work and materials used in erecting or repairing a building or other structure. Such a lien covers materialmen, tradesmen, suppliers, and the like, who furnish services, labor or materials on construction or improvement of property.

Tax Lien: A lien on real estate, placed by a state or local government for nonpayment of taxes. The majority of the states have adopted the Uniform Federal Tax Lien Registration Act. A federal tax lien is a lien placed on property by the federal government for unpaid federal taxes.

Printed Source

The names, addresses and telephone numbers of all county courthouses in the United States can be found in: *The Handybook for Genealogists*, 9th edition (http://www.everton.com) and Public Record Research Library, *The Librarian's Guide to Public Records: The Complete State, County, and Courthouse Locator* (http://www.brbpub.com). (See appendix E).

LOCATION OF REAL ESTATE AND TAX RECORDS

Transactions related to real estate can be a city, county or state function, but most often they are handled by the county. Therefore, the city offices or county courthouse is where you will find the documents and related indexes. The structure of record keeping varies between states, but the appropriate office is generally referred to as Register of Deeds, Recorder of Deeds, or Clerk and Recorder's Office. The tax assessor's office is separate from the recorder of deeds, but is also usually located in the city or county buildings.

Within those offices, real estate transactions are indexed by both seller (known as the grantor) and buyer (grantee), the two parties in a real estate transaction. The indexes are called grantor and grantee indexes, although they are called direct (seller) and indirect (buyer) indexes by some offices.

Depending on the time period and location of the records, the deeds will be indexed in handwritten paper volumes or on computer. The index will name the parties, the type of instrument (such as Deed of Trust or Warranty Deed) and book and page number where the deed or document is recorded.

The recorder of deeds's office staff will rarely search grantor and grantee indexes for the public. Aside from the time and budget constraints, the primary reason they refuse to conduct such searches is that land records are usually used for legal matters. The staff does not want to take the responsibility of identifying or misidentifying a record or declaring that a record does not exist when it may be misfiled or misindexed.

For this reason, you must visit the office personally or hire a professional researcher (see chapter seventeen) to conduct the research. Of course, if you already know the book and page number, you can write to the courthouse and request a photocopy.

TAX ASSESSOR RECORDS

Real estate is appraised and taxed. The tax assessor maintains the record of tax assessments and a database of property owners. The county treasurer's office maintains the record of payments.

The tax assessor's records are useful in determining the current whereabouts of an individual. For example,

- **City or County Known, Exact Address Unknown, Telephone Nonpublished**

  Telephone the county tax assessor's office and ask whether the person owns any real estate. The address of the real estate and the mailing address of the owner (usually the same) is public record. You will need to research policies from state to state, e.g., some offices require a written request or a personal visit to the office or the payment of a fee.

- **Previous Address Known, Current Address Unknown**

  Write or telephone the county tax assessor's office and ask for the name and address of the current owner of the previous address and the date of purchase. You can then interview the current owner, who may be able to provide information on the whereabouts of the person you seek. The date of purchase is helpful to search the records from the sale of the property and gives you an approximate date of the change of address. This technique works best if the person you seek lived at the previous address within the past five years.

REAL ESTATE RECORDS RESEARCH TIPS

- Many families own a vacation home in the mountains, near the beach, or in another state. Remember this possibility during real estate research. Florida, Arizona and Colorado are popular states for second homes.
- Check for spelling variations in surnames and the use of nicknames instead of given names.
- Combine city directory research (chapter three) with real estate research.
- The Internet is beginning to include databases from county offices. For example, the Hamilton County, Ohio, Web site (http://www.hamiltoncountyauditor.org/) lists real estate records that include owner's name and address, appraised value, photos of improvements and sketches of building outlines.

Case Study

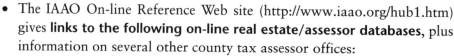

REAL ESTATE RECORDS HELP LOCATE DESCENDANTS OF PREVIOUS OWNERS OF HISTORIC HOME

The current owner of a historic home wanted to restore the interior and exterior to its original design and color. A chronological history of the names of prior owners was compiled using city directories (see chapter three), census enumerations (see chapter eight) and real estate records. The real estate records provided an exact timetable of former residents, as well as clues that helped locate the descendants.

We then identified and lcoated living descendants of the prior residents using death records (see chapter six) and telephone directories (see chapter two). During interviews, the descendants were asked if they had any family photographs that would show architectural features of the home.

The resulting collection of photographs helped the owners accomplish their restoration goal.

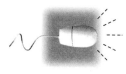

Internet Source

- The IAAO On-line Reference Web site (http://www.iaao.org/hub1.htm) gives **links to the following on-line real estate/assessor databases,** plus information on several other county tax assessor offices:

    Arizona: Pima County and the Arizona State Board of Equalization
    Colorado: Park County
    Florida: Broward, Charlotte, Duval, Hillsborough, Indian River, Lee, Leon, Manatee, Marion, Martin, Orange, Palm Beach, Pinellas, Seminole, St. Johns and Volusia counties
    Iowa: Pottawattamie County
    Indiana: Vanderburgh County
    Kansas: Johnson County
    Massachusetts: Cities of Boston and Cambridge, town of Mashpee
    Maine: Town of Kennebunk
    Nevada: Clark and Douglas counties
    Ohio: Franklin County
    Texas: Bexar, Brazoria, Caldwell, Dallas, Galveston, Guadalupe, Harris, Kendall, Tarrant, Taylor, Travis and Webb counties
    Virginia: Fairfax County
    Wisconsin: City of Milwaukee

ELEVEN

High School and College

 earbooks, reunion memorabilia and alumni publications can help you locate an individual, or at least provide clues that lead to other sources.

YEARBOOKS

Yearbooks are used extensively in adoption searches. When a surname is known for a birth mother, plus an estimated age and place of residence, a list of *possible* individuals can be compiled from the yearbook. This is especially successful when the surname is unusual. If a physical description of the birth mother is also known (such nonidentifying information is often provided by the adoption agency), the yearbook photo can narrow the field of possibilities. A secondary list can be compiled from the same yearbook, noting males with the same surname (who may be brothers or cousins). Follow-up research on the families using city directories, obituaries, etc., may eventually locate the birth family.

Look for yearbooks in each school's library or in the local public library. The public libraries rarely have a complete collection, because they do not purchase the yearbooks—they collect donated copies.

You can determine the location of some yearbook collections by searching the **National Union Catalog of Manuscript Collections**, also known as NUC-MUC. This catalog is located at most large libraries, as well as through the Library of Congress Web site at http://www.lcweb.loc.gov/coll/nucmc/nucmctxt .html. Two examples of search results:

- The Stirling Historical Society of Greenport, New York, houses thirty-seven yearbooks from Greenport High School, 1945–1982.
- The Special Collections Department of the Transylvania University Library, Lexington, Kentucky, has their university yearbook, *Crimson*, for 1897 to 1992.

Research Tip

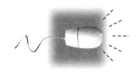

Internet Source

The Yearbook Archives Celebrity Collection contains more than three thousand volumes of high school yearbooks. The yearbooks are from schools attended by students who became prominent politicians, movie stars or other celebrities, although they have also preserved more than five hundred high school yearbooks that don't include a celebrity alumnus (or at least not yet). Additional information can be obtained from Seth Poppel Yearbook Archives, 38 Range Dr., Merrick, NY 11566 or http://www.highschool.com.

REUNION MEMORABILIA

High school and college reunion planners compile and distribute lists of reunion attendees with current addresses, names of children and employment data. Some reunions even publish biographies of alumni, whether or not they attend the reunion. This type of information is valuable in any search to locate a living person.

Local public libraries may have copies of reunion memorabilia. If not, search the newspaper index for announcements of reunions. Such notices usually include the name of an organizer. Hopefully this person will be easy to contact (perhaps as simple as looking in the telephone book) and will release the information you need. If that does not work, determine the names of the individuals who were class officers (from the yearbooks) and locate them. The odds are excellent that the class president or other officers are involved in class reunions and will be able to help you.

ALUMNI PUBLICATIONS

Colleges and universities, and even some high schools, publish alumni directories. The frequency of publication, however, will vary tremendously among institutions. Some major universities publish alumni directories annually. On the other hand, Brown High School, Sturgis, South Dakota, celebrated its hundredth anniversary in 1997 and published its one and only alumni directory. It was indexed alphabetically (including maiden names) and geographically, and listed students by year of graduation. Deceased students were included in the class lists, but the date or place of death was not reported.

Tip

Magazines and newsletters published by universities also include obituaries and news items about alumni. The May/June 1997 *Harvard Magazine*, for example, included 151 obituaries and nine pages of alumni news items, such as awards received, employment, address changes and retirement announcements. This issue also announced that class notes and obituaries would be published on the magazine's Web site (http://www.harvard-magazine.com), unless it was specified that the obituary be published only in the printed edition.

ASSISTANCE FROM ALUMNI OFFICES

The Federal Family Educational Rights and Privacy Act of 1974 (the Buckley Amendment) permits colleges and universities to release or publish, without the

---

UNIVERSITY ARCHIVES PROVIDES BIOGRAPHY AND PHOTOGRAPH

William Lang, one of Denver's best residential architects of all time, built hundreds of buildings from 1885 to 1893. In 1889, Marshall Pugh became his partner. Pugh was not from the Denver area and only remained in Denver about four years.

The historical community wanted to know more about Marshall Pugh, as well as descendants who might have a photograph of him or William Lang.

It was unknown where Marshall Pugh was born, where he was educated, where he came from when he arrived in Denver or where he went after he left Denver. Marshall Pugh was listed in city directories, but it was not known whether he was married or had children.

The 1890 federal census could not be searched, since most of it was destroyed by fire in 1921.

The grantor and grantee indexes (see chapter ten) listed a warranty deed from 1894. The deed was notarized in Bucks County, Pennsylvania, indicating the new residence for Marshall Pugh.

The Pugh family was listed on the 1900, 1910 and 1920 federal census enumerations (see chapter eight) in Pennsylvania. A professional genealogist was hired (see chapter seventeen) to research local records.

Marshall Pugh's Quaker marriage record was located, as well as a published family history that identified children and grandchildren. The family history reported that he attended the University of Pennsylvania. Their alumni collection included a World War I photograph of Marshall Pugh, plus several biographical clippings. There was also a handwritten biographical history written by Marshall Pugh himself—an original record located only at the university.

---

student's consent, items considered to be directory information:
- name
- address (campus and/or permanent) and telephone number
- date and place of birth
- major fields of study
- dates of attendance
- degrees, honors and awards received
- most recent previous educational institution attended
- participation in officially recognized activities, including intercollegiate athletics
- name, weight and height of participants on intercollegiate athletic teams

The Buckley Amendment only applies to universities that accept federal funds; therefore, private institutions are not bound to this law. Schools cannot release a student's Social Security number without their permission. Students may request that any or all personally identifiable information from their records be considered confidential and not open to the public. However, students are cautioned that closing their files may prevent the release of information to potential employers for confirming attendance or degrees earned.

Schools usually insist upon written requests for information and will forward a letter to a former student rather than release the address to you. Information on deceased students can be released since their rights of privacy end upon death.

It's important to note that alumni offices do *not* have current data on all former students. The primary reason they maintain addresses on students is for fund-raising. Therefore, if students do not respond with updated information, the alumni office will not have the data. But even an outdated address for a student can be helpful. Using city and crisscross directories (see chapter three) and real estate records (see chapter ten), you may be able to track an individual forward to a more current address.

The Internet

Universities and high schools are establishing Web sites that include information on alumni. Some schools report births (children of alumni), marriages and deaths in their alumni newsletters, as well as on their Web pages. To find the school of your interest, enter the name of the school in a search engine. If you do not find anything, try again in a month or two. The Internet is constantly growing.

Links to over three thousand college and university home pages can be found at http://www.mit.edu:8001/people/cdemello/univ.html. Current telephone directories of university/college students and faculty can also be found on the Internet. A gateway to nearly four hundred directories is maintained by Northwestern University at http://www.uiuc.edu/cgi-bin/ph/lookup.

HIGH SCHOOL AND COLLEGE RESEARCH TIPS

- When requesting information from an alumni office, be sure to inquire about fees or give a donation to the school for assisting in your research.
- Remember that alumni information on a Web site may not be as complete as that published in their newsletters, magazines or directories.
- Public libraries may have manuscript collections from a school with student lists, directories, yearbooks, etc.
- **Sororities and fraternities, both social and honorary, keep track of alumni** at both the national level and chapter level. The yearbook may indicate if the person you are researching was a member.

Internet Source

MILITARY BRATS ONLINE

Look here for the Military Brats Registry, listing children of military personnel from any branch of service who attended stateside or overseas public or dependent schools. This Web site (http://www.lyn xu.com/brats/index.html) also includes links to alumni organizations.

Internet Source

Idea Generator

TWELVE

Church Records

C hurches maintain better records on individuals than some government agencies. Depending upon the denomination of the church, a record is created when someone is baptized, confirmed, married or buried. The church knows when members joined and when they left or transferred to another church. The church maintains current addresses on all its members.

Church records are therefore an obvious resource for dates of birth, marriage and death; names of parents or other family members; and addresses or telephone numbers. But a church is a private institution and not bound by either privacy or freedom of information laws. Officials can release information or they can refuse such requests.

DETERMINING A PERSON'S RELIGION

You must know the religion or faith of an individual before you can even attempt to locate church records. If you do not have personal knowledge of his or her religion, there are a few ways to make an educated guess or even an exact determination.

- **Marriage Certificate**
  Assuming you have a copy of a marriage certificate (from the county or state government), the name and title of the official who performed the ceremony will be listed. If it was a justice of the peace, this will not be a clue to religion. But if it was Rev. John Smith, you have a clue. Sometimes the name of the church is given on the marriage record, but if it is not, search city directories (see chapter three) to determine the religious affiliation of the minister. If it was *Father* John Smith or *Rabbi* John Smith, you have a more specific clue to the religion and can narrow your search in the city directories. **A church's record of a marriage may or may not have the same information as the civil record.**

- **Ethnicity**
  A person's surname can be a clue to a person's ethnicity. This is not an

Tip

Case Study

CHURCH SECRETARY HELPS ADOPTEE LOCATE BIRTH MOTHER

An adoptee's search for his birth mother was difficult and discouraging. The birth mother had an exceptionally common Hispanic surname and resided in a large metropolitan area when she gave birth.

The adoptee, however, knew the approximate age of his birth mother, as well as the mother's place of birth—which was in another state and in a town with fewer than five hundred residents.

We contacted the Catholic church in this small community and asked if they would search their baptismal records for the birth of the birth mother. We hoped to obtain an exact birth date and names of the parents of the birth mother, which would help in other research tasks. It was *not* concealed that this was an adoption search, as is often recommended.

The secretary at the church was eager to help and located the baptismal record. She recognized the family and offered to contact distant relatives who still resided in the small community. The relatives provided the married name and last known residence (which was in yet another state) of the birth mother. Within twenty-four hours she was located.

Ironically, the birth mother reported that about a year earlier, the adoptee's birth father had contacted her and asked about the child they'd given up for adoption. As the birth mother had never revealed her past to her husband or children, she told the birth father that their child had died at birth. When the adoptee contacted the birth mother, she at first did not want to meet him. Eventually, she changed her mind, and also gave the adoptee the name and address of his birth father. The adoptee was reunited with his birth parents, who were nearly seventy years old.

This reunion might never have occurred without the information and cooperation from the local Catholic church.

absolute method, of course, but the odds are good. The adoption example above used the assumption that the Hispanic family was Catholic and proved to be correct. Other examples: A German-sounding surname may indicate the person is Catholic or Lutheran. An Italian is probably Catholic; an Englishman may be Presbyterian or Methodist. A Scandinavian may be Lutheran, and an Eastern European surname may mean the person is Jewish.

- **Neighborhood**
  What churches are within a five- or ten-mile radius of the individual's home? If there are five Catholic churches and you are researching an individual with an Irish surname, find the Catholic church within an Irish neighborhood.

CHURCH DIRECTORIES

Churches publish directories similar to school yearbooks. Such directories may be published annually, every few years, or to commemorate an anniversary. The directories may include photographs of families and individuals and group photos of the choir, youth group or other organizations within the church. And, of course, the directory lists everyone's current address and telephone number. Ask about these directories when contacting a church. They may even have old issues for sale.

Published Church Records

Genealogical and historical societies often publish abstracts or indexes to church records, including those from the twentieth century. Search the card catalog from the local public library, or ask the church if this has ever been done.

Church Records at the Family History Library

Some church records have been microfilmed and are available through the Family History Library and its Family History Centers. Below is a mere sampling of twentieth-century church records at the library.

GEORGIA (ATLANTA)
Hebrew Benevolent Congregation, 1867–1956

ILLINOIS (CHICAGO)
First St. Paul's German Evangelical Lutheran Congregation, 1833–1971
Sacred Heart Catholic Church (Croatian), 1913–1980
St. Jerome Catholic Church, 1895–1972

INDIANA (ARCOLA)
St. Patrick's Catholic Church, 1873–1957

INDIANA (AUBURN)
Immaculate Conception Catholic Church, 1891–1958

MINNESOTA (HANSKA)
Nora Unitarian Universalist, 1882–1989

MINNESOTA (MANKATO)
First Congregational Church, 1870–1990
Grace Lutheran Church, 1871–1956

NEW YORK (WILLIAMSVILLE)
Methodist Episcopal Church, 1867–1948

NORTH CAROLINA (BREVARD)
East Fork Baptist Church Register, 1842–1969

OREGON (PORTLAND)
Lents Monthly Meeting, Society of Friends, 1909–1975
Reedwood Monthly Meeting, Society of Friends, 1958–1996

SACRAMENTS PERFORMED ON U.S. MILITARY BASES

Sacraments (baptism, marriage) performed on U.S. military bases are recorded by the church that performs the ceremony. The Archdiocese for Military

Services (3311 Toledo Terrace #A201, Hyattsville, MD 20782, [301] 853-0400) maintains the records of Roman Catholic sacraments performed on U.S. military bases worldwide and the four military academies.

There are more than two hundred protestant religions recognized by the military. The regional or national headquarters for each of those denominations can direct you to the location of their records.

CHURCH RECORDS RESEARCH TIPS

For More Info

- For a thorough discussion on the types of American church records and how to locate and use original records of various denominations, **see Richard W. Dougherty's chapter six, "Research in Church Records,"** in *The Source: A Guidebook of American Genealogy*, rev. ed., edited by Loretto Dennis Szucs and Sandra Hargreaves Luebking (see appendix E).
- For an extensive bibliography of published church records, see Richard W. Dougherty's chapter eight, "Published Church Records," in *Printed Sources: A Guide to Published Genealogical Records*, edited by Kory L. Meyerink (see appendix E).
- Virginia Humling's *U.S. Catholic Sources: A Diocesan Research Guide* (see appendix E) lists every archdiocese and diocese in the U.S. and identifies the records available and the archivist at each location.
- If you are trying to determine what churches existed for a particular time period in a particular place, use the city directory (see chapter three). The directories have a section similar to the yellow pages section listing churches alphabetically by denomination.
- Give a donation to the church when requesting information.

THIRTEEN

Court Records

Business is booming in America's courtrooms. And for every courtroom action—from a minor traffic violation to a first-degree murder trial— records are created. For the researcher these records may offer an updated or current address, a birth date, a Social Security number, names of employers or relatives and other information.

U.S. FEDERAL COURT

Federal court includes the U.S. Supreme Court, the U.S. Court of Appeals and U.S. District Courts, including bankruptcy court. There is at least one district court and one bankruptcy court in each state. U.S. District Courts hear civil and criminal cases involving federal law.

The closed case files created by federal courts are archived at the Federal Records Centers. After twenty to thirty years, the records are transferred to the Regional Archives of the National Archives and Records Administration (see appendix B). The case number and accession code must be obtained from the originating court in order to access the files.

U.S. Federal Bankruptcy Court

A record 1.4 million bankruptcies were filed in 1997, with more than 90 percent of those filings made by individuals. Bankruptcies are filed by young and old, and the files are open to the public and searchable by name.

Bankruptcy files may include exact birth dates; current and former addresses; Social Security numbers; names of relatives (from whom the filer may have borrowed money); real estate holdings; stock ownership; employment history; and information about child support, alimony and school loans.

There is at least one U.S. Bankruptcy Court in each state. Check the government blue pages in the local telephone directory for information, or telephone the Federal Information Center at (800) 688-9889. *The Sourcebook of Federal*

NATIONAL CRIME INFORMATION CENTER (NCIC)

Parents attempting to locate a missing child can turn to the National Crime Information Center, available only to law enforcement agencies. The NCIC has seventeen databases containing more than ten million records, plus twenty-four million criminal history records.

The National Child Search Act of 1990 requires law enforcement agencies to record missing children's descriptions into the NCIC. You can ask your local law enforcement agency to enter the name of any missing child into the NCIC. If refused, go to the nearest FBI office with the request.

For More Info

Courts, U.S. District and Bankruptcy: The Definitive Guide to Searching for Case Information at the Local Level Within the Federal Court System, **2nd edition, (see appendix E or http://www.brbpub.com) is also an excellent guide for information.**

An index to nearly every bankruptcy filed in the U.S. since January 1992 (over five million records) is available on CD-ROM from Merlin Information Services, (800) 367-6646, http://www.merlindata.com. The CD-ROM, called "BANKO" National Bankruptcy Index, allows searches by personal or business name, address, Social Security number, file date and file number.

STATE COURT

For More Info

State courts—usually referred to as district court, superior court or state supreme court—conduct jury trials for larger monetary claims (usually over ten thousand dollars) and more serious criminal offenses. *The Sourcebook of State Public Records: The Definitive Guide to Searching for Public Record Information at the State Level* **(see appendix E or http://www.brbpub.com) describes the peculiarities of each state's laws or treatment of court records.** The guide gives addresses and telephone numbers for the state court administrators, location of state criminal records, plus details on the availability of the files, which differs greatly from state to state. For example,

- Indiana criminal records are only open to employers or the subject.
- Mississippi does not have a central state repository of criminal records. They suggest you obtain information at the county level.
- Montana criminal records are available from the 1950s on, with all felonies and misdemeanors for the past five years reported.
- North Carolina restricts access to criminal records to criminal justice and other government agencies authorized by law.

County and Municipal Courts

County and municipal courts usually handle

- felonies (crimes punishable by one year or more of jail time)
- misdemeanors (minor infractions with a fine or minimal jail time)
- civil actions
- small claims
- evictions
- probate (wills, estates, guardianships, conservatorships)
- juvenile matters
- domestic relations (divorce, child support, custody disputes)
- traffic offenses

For More Info

The court structure varies between states; therefore, the first step in searching modern court records is to determine the court jurisdiction for the state being researched. *County Court Records: A National Guide to Civil, Criminal and Probate Records at the County and Municipal Levels Within the State Court Systems, 4th edition (see appendix E or http://www.brbpub.com) is a guide to more than sixty-seven thousand county and city offices*, with addresses, telephone numbers and details regarding access. This guidebook summarizes each state's jurisdiction for civil, criminal, county, circuit, district, probate and municipal courts.

For example, DWI/DUI (driving while intoxicated/driving under the influence) is a criminal offense because it may involve a jail term of one year or more. But the court that hears a DWI/DUI case varies from state to state. In Michigan, for example, the record would be in recorder's court or municipal court. In New Mexico it would be in magistrate court or metropolitan court. In Kentucky, district court; in Florida, county court; and in Maine, superior or district court.

Court Indexes and Access

Indexes to court records also vary tremendously. Depending on the time period, the indexes may be in bound volumes, in a card file, on microfiche or microfilm, on printouts from outdated computers or in a current database maintained by the court. Policies and procedures also vary, for example,

- Some courts require a search fee; some do not.
- Some courts will allow the public to view the indexes; some will not.
- Some courts need twenty-four hours or more to retrieve files from storage.
- Some courts destroy files that are inactive for seven or more years.
- Some courts send files to the state archives for permanent storage.
- Some courts store old case files in the attic or basement where they are not easily accessible.

Indexes rarely include the name of every party to a case. For example, if the plaintiff sues the five owners of a restaurant, only the first name in the list of defendants will appear in the index. Maybe only the name of the restaurant will be in the index. The only way to locate cases such as this is to know the names of all parties from earlier research and to check those names in the index. If you do not, you may have to return to the index after discovering the group ownership.

PRISON POPULATION

Could it be that the person you seek is in prison? Do not discount the possibility.

According to Paula Mergenhagen's article "The Prison Population Bomb" (*American Demographics* magazine, February 1996), one million people lived in America's federal and state prisons in 1994. Another 3.7 million were on probation or parole, and half a million were confined to locally run jails. That comes to more than 5.1 million adults who were under some form of correctional supervision in 1994.

The photograph on page 118 came from the collection at the Colorado State Archives (CSA) in Denver, Colorado. Pictured is H.J. Lind, then thirty-nine years old, who was born in Pennsylvania and was residing in Conejos County,

Colorado, when he was convicted on 10 May 1882 of grand larceny and sentenced to fifteen years in the state penitentiary at Canon City, Colorado. The CSA has a state penitentiary prisoner's index covering 1871 to 1972, mug shots from 1877 to 1992, plus additional related records. See http://www.state.co.us/gov_dir/gss/archives/prison.html for a complete description.

Similar types of prisoner records may be located at other state archives or historical societies.

Telephone numbers and address for state penitentiaries will be listed in your local telephone directory within the government pages. You can also use the index provided by the National Association of State Information Resource Executives at http://www.nasire.org/ss/stcriminal.html. This organization serves as a topical clearinghouse to state government information on the Internet and has a category for links to state information on state departments of corrections. Some states do not have links.

The U.S. Government's National Bureau of Prison Inmate Locator Service will provide current and historical information on federal inmates; call (202) 307-3126.

COURT RECORDS RESEARCH TIPS

- For an extensive discussion of court records, see Arlene H. Eakle's chapter seven, "Research in Court Records," in *The Source: A Guidebook of American Genealogy*, rev. ed., edited by Loretto Dennis Szucs and Sandra Hargreaves Luebking (see appendix E). Although this chapter concentrates on earlier time periods, it does include twentieth-century information, including adoptions.
- *Unlocking the Files of the FBI: A Guide to Its Records and Classification System* by Gerald K. Haines and David A. Langbart (see appendix E) is a comprehensive guide to what to expect from FBI files, where to find them and how to obtain access. Under the Freedom of Information Act (FOIA), the FBI has begun releasing files on Americans dating from the 1920s to the present. But many files are also being destroyed under document retention guidelines developed by the FBI and the National Archives in the early 1980s. The FBI kept records of leaders in the fields of entertainment, journalism, business, publishing and writing, feminism, academia, the counterculture, politics, athletics, science, law enforcement, medicine and religion.

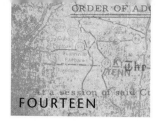

Voter Registration

V oter registrations provide the age and/or exact birth date and current address of the voter. In some cases the record gives a history of address changes and may indicate a date of death or a Social Security number. Information on citizenship, such as date of naturalization, is sometimes recorded and, of course, party affiliation.

The voter registration below gives the Social Security number, death information and date of birth for Alberta F. Acott. Her death is also listed in the Social

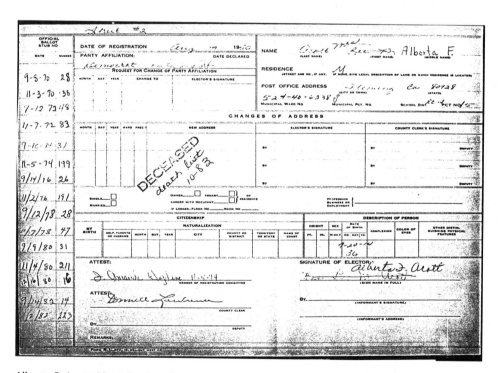

Alberta F. Acott, Voter Registration. Logan County, Colorado Clerk and Recorder, Alphabetical Voter Registration Records, 1932–1985, Colorado State Archives, Denver, Colorado.

The naturalization data (see chapter sixteen) is valuable to help locate the documents which may give the exact place of Amelia's birth or the date and port of her arrival into the U.S.

This voter registration indicates that Amelia is a homeowner. When the home is sold, the real estate records (see chapter ten) may indicate a change of address for the Adams family or information on the date of death of one or both persons.

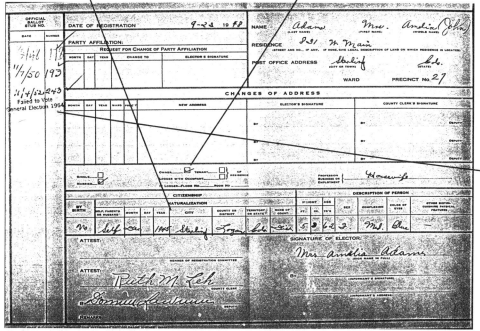

The "Failed to Vote General Election 1954" is a clue that could indicate an approximate date of death or that she moved to another city or state. Comparing the dates on this voter registration with those of her husband, John (see upper right corner), may help. If he continues to vote after 1954, it is likely that Amelia died between November 1952 (when she last voted) and November 1954 (when she did not vote).

Amelia Adams, Voter Registration. Logan County, Colorado Clerk and Recorder, Alphabetical Voter Registration Records, 1932–1985, Colorado State Archives, Denver, Colorado.

Security Death Index (see chapter seven); however, her date of death is reported in the SSDI as April 1983 rather than October. This demonstrates the importance of comparing data among documents and being certain that you have not misinterpreted something. In this case, October 1983 is the date of the death list that included Alberta Acott, not the date of her death.

The "Changes of Address" section on Amelia Adams's voter registration (shown above) is blank, but will be filled in for those to whom it applies. **When researching common surnames, the former and current addresses can help differentiate individuals with the same name.**

A "Cancellation of Previous Registration" is sometimes filed with voter registrations, such as the example on page 122. The cancellation indicates that Charles G. Bartsch moved from Logan County, Colorado, to Phelps County, Nebraska, in 1974.

Research Tip

ACCESSING VOTER REGISTRATION RECORDS

Most states maintain voter registration files at the county level; therefore, you must know the county of residence to access the records. A few states do have a statewide index to voters, usually found in the secretary of state's office. The

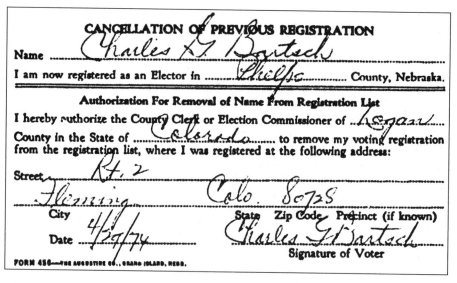

Charles G. Bartsch; Cancellation of Previous Registration. Logan County, Colorado Clerk and Recorder, Alphabetical Voter Registration Records, 1932–1985, Colorado State Archives, Denver, Colorado.

more detailed record, however, will be in the county offices.

Inactive voter registrations are often purged or destroyed by the county or state government. There are exceptions; some counties archive the records or transfer them to the state archives or historical society.

Information brokers purchase voter registration records and resell the data in compliance with state laws regarding use of voter data. The general public cannot access this information directly, but you can hire a private investigator who contracts with the information brokers.

CD Source

Voter Registrations on CD-Rom

Some recent (beginning about 1995) voter registrations are sold on CD-ROM and available through public record vendors Merlin Information Services ([800] 367-6646, http://www.merlindata.com) and QuickInfo Corporation (http://www.quickinformer.com/). Voter CD-ROMs are available for Alaska, Arkansas, Colorado, Connecticut, Delaware, District of Columbia, Georgia, Guam, Iowa, Kansas, Michigan, Missouri, Nevada, New Hampshire, New Jersey, New York, North Carolina, Ohio, Oklahoma, Texas and Utah. More states are added periodically.

Tip

VOTER REGISTRATION RESEARCH TIPS

- **Avoid requesting voter registration information sixty days before an election. The clerks are stressed and not as cooperative as other times.**
- Do not expect telephone service. Most counties require research requests to be made in writing or by personal visit.

FIFTEEN

Licenses and Registrations

Nearly everyone needs a license of some type, whether it be to drive a car, own a dog or sell real estate. Not only do you need a license to drive, but your car needs to be licensed, titled and registered. You need a license to go fishing, and if you paint houses for a living, you may need a license (as do most other businesses).

The public records created by this bureaucracy can be useful in locating an individual. A birth date, address, telephone number or other miscellaneous data may be just the item needed in your search. There are four types of licensing included in this chapter:

- Federal Aviation Administration—pilot and aircraft licensing/registration
- State Department of Motor Vehicles—driver's license and driver's history, and vehicle licensing and registration
- State Licensing and Business Registration Agencies—occupational, professional and business licenses
- State Game and Fish Department—hunting and fishing licenses

FEDERAL AVIATION ADMINISTRATION (FAA)

To obtain the address of an FAA licensed pilot, write to FAA Airmen's Certification Branch, AVN-460, P.O. Box 25082, Oklahoma City, OK 73125. **The Landings Web site (http://www.landings.com) contains a database of more than 600,000 pilots certified by the FAA.** You can search by surname only (if unique) or by surname and given name. Results include full name of the pilot, current address, date of last medical exam, type of pilot's certificate, rating and FAA region. If you have an aircraft's number, you can obtain the owner's name, address and details regarding the airplane.

Internet Source

STATE DEPARTMENT OF MOTOR VEHICLES

The Department of Motor Vehicles (DMV) in each state maintains driver's license records, vehicle registrations, accident records and related records that include identifying information on individuals. Depending upon the state's laws, you may find registrations for more than cars and trucks, including boats, jet skis, snowmobiles, motorcycles, trailers, motor homes (RVs) and trailers/mobile homes.

Access to these records varies according to state law. The Driver's Privacy Protection Act of 1994 protects the privacy of persons licensed to drive by prohibiting certain disclosures of information. The states are modifying their laws to comply with the federal law; therefore, access is currently in flux. *The MVR Book: Motor Services Guide* (see appendix E or http://www.brbpub.com) gives a summary of access and law for each state and is updated annually.

Tip

California closed their DMV records to the public in 1990 after the murder of actress Rebecca Schaeffer by an obsessive fan who had obtained her home address from the DMV. **But California offers a forwarding service to assist in contacting individuals.** Request their Message Forwarding Service Form (INF 1211B). The department reviews the message for content and rejects messages that, in the opinion of the department, appear to be harmful to the driver or contrary to public interest. If the DMV matches the information in their database with that on the form, they forward the message to the individual. Rejected messages are returned to the requester. There is, of course, a small fee for this service.

Some driver and vehicle registrations (beginning in about 1995) are sold on CD-ROM and available through public-record vendors such as Merlin Information Services ([800] 367-6646 http://www.merlindata.com) and QuickInfo Corporation (http://www.quickinformer.com/). Driver/vehicle CD-ROMs are available for Colorado, Florida, Iowa, Maine, New Hampshire, Maryland, Massachusetts, Minnesota, Mississippi, Oregon, South Carolina, Texas, Utah and Wisconsin. More states are added periodically.

The New England Historic Genealogical Society (http://www.nehgs.org/), has the following driver's license records:

Florida: 1993
Massachusetts: 1978, 1983, 1988, 1991, 1993, 1995
New Hampshire: 1993

STATE LICENSING AND BUSINESS REGISTRATION AGENCIES

Most occupations—including electrician, plumber, doctor, realtor, insurance agent, nurse and funeral director—require licensing. Licensing is most often regulated by the state, but the laws vary among states. For example, a dietitian is required to be licensed in Wisconsin, but not in Michigan or Missouri.

The Sourcebook of State Public Records: The Definitive Guide to Searching for Public Record Information at the State Level, 3d edition (see appendix E or http://www.brbpub.com) includes a list of each state's occupational licensing and business registration boards and agencies.

For More Info

These licensing or registration agencies will verify if a particular person is licensed, but may charge a fee to release such information as address, current or most recent employer, education or any disciplinary actions or complaints.

Membership directories of professional organizations can often provide an address or employer's name. These directories can be found in many public libraries, and some are now appearing on the Internet. Three common examples:

Attorneys

The Martindale-Hubbell Lawyer Locator (http://www.martindale.com/) covers the entire U.S. and foreign countries. The database includes year of birth, undergraduate school and law school attended, firm name, type of practice, business address, telephone and fax numbers and list of business partners.

Dentists

The Dental Directory Service (http://www.teeth.com) is designed to locate a dentist near your residence, but it can also be used for a general search. Not all states are represented, and you cannot search by name. Information includes the dentist's business address, telephone number and E-mail address. Some dentists maintain a Web page, which may provide additional information (such as education).

Physicians

The American Medical Association's Web site at http://www.ama-assn.org lists thousands of physicians licensed in the U.S. The directory will provide the physician's office location, office telephone number, gender, medical school, year of graduation, residency training and specialty.

The National Genealogical Society (http://www.ngsgenealogy.org) will search the American Medical Association's Deceased Physician File, 1878–1969, for a fee. The database usually includes date and place of birth and death, medical school attended, place of practice, hospital affiliation and citation to an obituary.

For directories of other professional organizations (as well as many other groups), consult the *Encyclopedia of Associations*, available in most libraries.

STATE GAME AND FISH DEPARTMENT

State hunting and fishing license information can provide an updated address or birth date for an individual. Currently, thirty-three states maintain a central repository of fishing and/or hunting licenses which can be accessed by the public.

The Sourcebook of State Public Records: The Definitive Guide to Searching for Public Record Information at the State Level, 3d edition (see appendix E or http://www.brbpub.com) gives information on the records available in each state. For example,

- California: Records are not available to the public.
- Massachusetts: Fishing license information is held by the Division of Fisheries and Wildlife in Boston for one year only. Older records are maintained at several locations off the premises. You must know the store where

Case Study

DRIVER'S HISTORY PROVIDES CLUES TO LOCATE INDIVIDUAL

The last known address of a man was invalid. He had rented a home, and telephone calls to the landlord and neighbors were answered with rude comments and slammed receivers. The man was not listed in the telephone directory, and every avenue of research kept giving us the same invalid address.

His driver's history did not provide a new address, but it did list several traffic tickets and a suspension of his license. Using the traffic ticket data on the driver's history, we examined the original traffic ticket. It told us he was a truck driver, and it named his employer.

The employer cooperated by giving a message and our telephone number to the gentleman. He returned our call and was pleased to learn that he was an heir to an estate.

the license was purchased and the month it was purchased. The licenses are filed by license number only. (In other words, fishing licenses in Massachusetts are nearly impossible to research.)

- Minnesota: The Fish and Wildlife Division in St. Paul has records dating from 1979 for doe and turkey (spring season) permits and for (fall season) permits from 1985 for moose, from 1982 for bear and from 1990 for turkey. The records are open to the public. All information is released.
- South Dakota: They have a central database, but do not release records to the public.
- Texas: The Parks and Wildlife Department will only confirm that an individual has a license. They will not provide any additional information.

SIXTEEN

Immigration and Naturalization

More than 40 percent of living Americans, or 100 million of them, can trace their roots to an ancestor who came through Ellis Island between its opening in 1892 and its closing in 1954. But immigration did not end with the closing of Ellis Island. Considering the millions of persons who have immigrated into the U.S. since 1954, it is conceivable that immigrant-related records will be useful in locating individuals.

Various records were created as a result of immigration. They include
- passenger arrival record
- border crossings
- alien registration
- passports
- naturalization/citizenship

Only the passenger arrival records and border crossings are open to the public. The remaining records of living persons are protected by the Privacy Act. If the person is deceased, you can obtain naturalization and immigration records by providing proof of death.

Notes

PASSENGER ARRIVAL RECORDS

Ellis Island (http://www.ellisisland.org/), the largest reception center for immigrants, processed more than over twelve million immigrants between 1892 and 1954. The peak immigration period in American history was between 1892 and 1924, when approximately seventeen million persons arrived through either New York Harbor or Ellis Island.

Ellis Island is developing an American Family Immigration History Center. The first phase of the project will be a database of those seventeen million arrivals. Information will include names of ships, dates of arrival, cities and countries of origin, marital status, relatives in America and destinations. The curators at Ellis Island hope to eventually expand the database to include data on arrival in other years and through other ports.

Immigration passenger lists include not only the names of immigrants, but they also list visitors and U.S. citizens returning from abroad. The list of citizens (vs. immigrants) gives the name; age; sex; marital status; date and place of birth, if born in the United States; date of naturalization and name and location of court, if applicable; and current address.

The following **twentieth-century passenger arrival records have been microfilmed by the National Archives** and are available to rent or purchase at the archives branches (see appendix B). The National Archives Web site (http://merrimack.nara.gov/genealogy/immigration/immigrat.html) has details on the following ports:

Microfilm Source

Alabama, Florida, Georgia and South Carolina ports: 1890–1924
Baltimore, Maryland: 1891–1957
Boston, Massachusetts: 1891–1943
Detroit, Michigan: 1906–1954
Galveston, Texas: 1896–1951
Gulfport, Mississippi: 1904–1954
Gloucester, Massachusetts: 1918–1943
Key West, Florida: 1898–1945
New Bedford, Massachusetts: 1902–1954
New Orleans, Louisiana: 1900–1952
New York, New York (also known as Castle Garden and Ellis Island): 1820–1957
Pascagoula, Mississippi: 1903–1935
Philadelphia, Pennsylvania: 1883–1948
Portland, Maine: 1893–1943
Providence, Rhode Island: 1911–1954
San Francisco, California: 1882–1957
Savannah, Georgia: 1906–1945
Seattle, Washington: 1890–1957
Zapata, Texas: 1923–1953 (includes applications for Nonresident Alien's Border Crossing Identification Cards, 29 April 1945 through 15 September 1953)

Technique

Immigration passenger lists are arranged first by port and then chronologically. To find information about a particular individual, you must know the port, exact date of arrival, and name of vessel.

Port of Galveston, Texas

The five major ports of arrival were Baltimore, Boston, New Orleans, New York and Philadelphia. Galveston, Texas, was also an important entry point for a large number of immigrants, primarily Germans and Eastern Europeans, between the 1840s and 1920. Scores of Eastern European and Russian Jews immigrated through the Galveston port, seeking resettlement in the Midwest and West.

The Texas Seaport Museum (http://www.phoenix.net/~tsm/default.html) in Galveston has the only computerized listing of immigrants who arrived through this port. Their database of more than 130,000 passengers from 1846 to 1948 includes each passenger's name, age, gender, occupation, country of origin, ship name, dates of departure and arrival and destination in the U.S.

You can access the Galveston Immigration Database at the musuem or send a written research request to the museum. Their staff will search the database for a fee. Send inquiries to Texas Seaport Museum, 2016 Strand, Galveston, TX 77550 (phone [409] 763-1877, fax [409] 763-3037).

BORDER CROSSING RECORDS
Canadian Border Crossings

Records were kept of individuals who crossed the border between Canada and the U.S. from 1895 to 1952. Approximately three million cards, known as the St. Albans Passenger Arrival Records, include passengers arriving by train or ports along the border from Washington to Maine. Each card typically includes name, age, exact place of birth, last residence, occupation, name and address of relative in former country, name and address of relative in the destination city, whether the person's first visit to the U.S., date and vessel of seaport arrival, date and place of border crossing and physical description. There are four indexes:

- Soundex Index to Canadian Border Entries Through the St. Albans, Vermont, District, 1895–1924 (M1461, 400 rolls)
- Alphabetical Index to Canadian Border Entries Through Small Ports in Vermont, 1895-1924 (M1462, 6 rolls)
- Soundex Index to Entries Into the St. Albans, Vermont, District Through Canadian Pacific and Atlantic Ports, 1924–1952 (M1463, 98 rolls)
- Card Manifests (alphabetical) of Individuals Entering Through the Port of Detroit, Michigan, 1906–1954 (M1478, 117 rolls)

The St. Albans Passenger Arrival Records are available at all National Archive branches.

Mexican Border Crossings

The National Archives plans to microfilm Mexican border crossings. Until they are filmed, and consequently more available to the public, they can only be examined at the National Archives in Washington, DC.

PASSPORTS

Passports were not required by law for U.S. citizens traveling overseas prior to World War I, except during the Civil War. Microfilmed passport records are available for research at the Family History Library, and its Family History Centers for the years 1795 to 1920, and indexes are available for the years 1830 to 1831, 1850 to 1852 and 1860 to 1925.

Applications after 1925 are in the custody of the Passport Office, Department of State, 1111 Nineteenth St., NW, Suite 200, Washington, DC 20524, (202) 955-0291. To access these, you must have permission of the individual who applied for the passport. If the person is deceased, you must send a copy of the death certificate and a statement of your relationship to the deceased.

Tip

IMMIGRATION RECORDS

Records related to immigration are rich in data and may include the following information:

- exact date and place of birth
- maiden name of woman
- marriage(s) date/place
- names and birth dates/ places of children
- aliases or name change information
- names and addresses of relatives in the U.S. and/or country of origin
- date of arrival into the U.S.
- name of ship and port of arrival into U.S.
- photograph

CD Source

PASSENGER AND IMMIGRATION LISTS INDEX, 1538–1940 ON CD-ROM

The Passenger and Immigration Lists Index, 1538–1940, on CD-ROM (http://www.familytreemaker.com/) lists approximately 2.75 million individuals and is based upon data provided by Gale Research, Inc. The information was collected from published passenger lists, naturalization records, church records, family and local histories, as well as voter and land registrations. Entries for twentieth-century immigrants are a small portion of this index; nevertheless, it is worth checking.

ALIEN REGISTRATION

Since the 1929 Alien Registration Act, aliens have been required to register their current residence and place of employment annually with the federal government. By law these records are restricted only to people or agencies designated by the Attorney General.

National Archives Record Group 118 (Attorneys and Marshals) includes a collection of World War I alien files at the National Archives, Central Plains Region in Kansas City, Missouri. This collection consists of alien applications for permits to continue residing within certain restricted zones.

Information on the applications includes the alien's residence, birth, employment and a certificate or affidavit in support of the application made by a friend or employer. A second file provides similar information on male and female aliens required to register, but it also includes their fingerprints, record of military service, and the names and birth dates of their children between ten and fourteen years of age. Both files include physical descriptions and photographs of the aliens.

The Minnesota Historical Society has registration forms completed by non-citizen adults in Minnesota in February 1918 as a result of the 1918 Alien Registration and Declaration of Holdings, under the auspices of the Minnesota Commission of Public Safety. Questions on the form include name, place of birth, years in the country, port of entry, date of arrival, occupation, name of spouse and names of children.

NATURALIZATION (CITIZENSHIP)

The Immigration and Naturalization Service (INS) has custody of citizenship-related records created after 27 September 1906. Requests for photocopies of these records must be submitted on INS Form G-639, the Freedom of Information/Privacy Act Request (see appendix F). This form can also be downloaded from the INS Web site at http://www.ins.usdoj.gov/. Again, privacy laws protect information on living people.

The laws regarding women and naturalization are somewhat confusing. Marian L. Smith's article, "Women and Naturalization, ca 1802–1940" in *Prologue: Quarterly of the National Archives and Records Administration* (Summer 1998, vol. 30, no. 2, on the Internet at http://www.nara.gov/publications/prologue/natural1.html) explains that after 1907, marriage determined a woman's nationality status completely. This changed nothing for immigrant women, but women born U.S. citizens could lose their citizenship by marrying an alien.

Congress passed the Married Women's Act, also known as the Cable Act, on 22 September 1922. This law gave each woman a nationality of her own. No marriage since that date has granted U.S. citizenship to any alien woman nor taken it from any woman who married an alien. Women were then eligible to apply for citizenship on the same terms as men.

IMMIGRATION AND NATURALIZATION RESEARCH TIPS

- Locating survivors of the Holocaust requires specialized sources and research strategies. Gary Mokotoff's how-to book on Holocaust research, *How to Document Victims and Locate Survivors of the Holocaust* (Teaneck, NJ: Avotaynu, 1995, http://www.avotaynu.com) is an excellent guide to major repositories and sources. It includes a list of more than four thousand towns for which there is documentation at Yad Vashem in Jerusalem, the principal repository of Holocaust information.
- ***They Became Americans: Finding Naturalization Records and Ethnic Origins*** by Loretto Dennis Szucs (see appendix E) is a detailed description of all types of naturalization records.
- *American Naturalization Records, 1790–1990: What They Are and How to Use Them* by John J. Newman (see appendix E) is another excellent guide to naturalization.

For More Info

Case Study

PETITION FOR NATURALIZATION PROVIDES INFORMATION ON POLISH IMMIGRANT

A Polish immigrant (with an exceptionally common Americanized given name and surname) died in 1993 with a sizeable estate. There were no known surviving relatives, and the exact place of his birth and the names of his parents were unknown. We were asked to locate his heirs to distribute the estate.

Interviews with relatives of his late wife indicated the man had filed for citizenship sometime in the 1950s. Using indexes to federal naturalization records in his city of residence, a match was made with the address we had found in the city directories. The index provided the information we needed to obtain his citizenship documents. Since we had proof of his death, the records were available for inspection.

The Petition for Naturalization gave his exact place of birth in Poland, his residence, his occupation, the date and place of his marriage in Italy and his spouse's name. It included the date of his arrival into the port of New York and the name of the ship, the names of his children, plus the date and place of birth of each child. The original variation of his name was also reported on the petition.

Unfortunately, the destruction of records in Poland prevented the location of heirs.

SEVENTEEN

Finding Assistance

Brick Wall Buster

I f after diligent searching you cannot find your military buddy, lost love, birth parent, classmate or whomever you are researching, **seek the advice or services of a professional**. They are experienced in public record searches and may be able to solve your case. An *ethical* professional will also tell you if your search has any promise of success. Some people just cannot be found. But many can, and sometimes you need the expertise of a professional genealogist, private investigator or adoption specialist.

BEFORE HIRING A PROFESSIONAL

1. **Summarize your case as succinctly as possible.**

   If you present information to a professional in bits and pieces, it will cost you extra to have him organize the data. Preparing a summary also forces you to gather *all* the facts you have collected. Sometimes the omission of a seemingly insignificant piece of information can make the difference between a successful search and an unsuccessful one.

2. **Prepare a list of sources you have already examined.**

   You do not want to pay the professional to repeat your research. It is also important to explain *exactly* what you did, because the professional may know of an updated source or a different way to ask questions.

   For example, you tell the professional that you telephoned the University of Kansas alumni office and asked if they had a current address for Linda Sue Taft, who attended the university in 1969. The university refused to cooperate, citing privacy laws. The professional will note that you did not ask if Linda had been a student or a graduate each of which may generate different results.

3. **Determine a budget.**

   Be prepared to discuss expenses and fees with the professional. Conducting searches can cost from twenty-five to one hundred dollars per hour, plus the expenses involved in retrieving documents and accessing databases. A clear understanding of financial limits is imperative for both the client and the professional.

FINDING A PROFESSIONAL GENEALOGIST

A professional genealogist is an expert in records that identify and locate family members. If your search involves family relationships, a genealogist can help you. Remember, however, that some genealogists specialize in Colonial research, for example, and would not be experienced in searching modern records. Genealogists who advertise as specialists in the twentieth century will be better suited for research in locating living persons.

Professional genealogists are not licensed; the only way consumers can protect themselves is to hire a genealogist who is a member of the Association of Professional Genealogists (APG), has been certified by the Board for Certification of Genealogists (BCG), or has been accredited by the Family History Department of the Church of Jesus Christ of Latter-day Saints (the Mormons).

APG, BCG and the Family History Library require their members or associates to sign a code of ethics and submit to arbitration services should there be a dispute between a client and professional. Below are addresses and additional information about each organization:

- Association of Professional Genealogists
  P.O. Box 40393
  Denver, CO 80204-0393
  http://www.apgen.org/
  A Directory of Professional Genealogists is available on-line, and at many libraries and archives. The directory can also be purchased; see the Web page for details. **Send a SASE for the free brochure** *So You're Going to Hire a Professional Genealogist.*

    APG is an organization of nearly twelve hundred members worldwide who promote genealogy as a profession and encourage professionalism in genealogy. All members must abide by a code of ethics. APG members conduct research or serve in related fields—librarians and archivists, writers and editors, consultants and indexers, instructors and lecturers, booksellers and publishers, computer specialists and geneticists. Many certified and accredited genealogists are members of APG.
- Board for Certification of Genealogists
  P.O. Box 14291
  Washington, DC 20044
  http://www.genealogy.org/~bcg
  A roster of certified researchers is available on-line or can be purchased. See the Web page for details.

    BCG tests and certifies researchers in the U.S., Canada and abroad. Genealogists certified by the BCG must renew their certification every five years and must agree to a code of ethics.

Money Saver

- Family History Library
  35 NW Temple St.
  Salt Lake City, UT 84150
  Send a SASE for a roster; specify geographic or topical specialization needed.

  The Family History Department (FHD) of the Church of Jesus Christ of Latter-day Saints tests and issues accreditation in specialized areas of research. Accredited genealogists are not necessarily members of the Mormon church nor do they limit themselves to Mormon clients. FHD-accredited genealogists go through a review process every five years and must agree to a code of ethics.

FINDING A PRIVATE INVESTIGATOR (PI)

Private investigators subscribe to a variety of databases not available to the general public. They can therefore assist with searches if you have a Social Security number, an exact date of birth or an address within the last five to ten years.

The yellow pages and the Internet are easy ways to find private investigators; however, always check out their credentials. Ask for the investigator's license number and verify that she is indeed currently licensed. Some states do not require PI licensing, but have a membership organization that monitors ethics. Confirm the investigator's membership before you hire.

ION, Inc., is a worldwide investigator referral service on the Internet (http://www.pihome.com/). Their Web site gives licensing information for each state, as well as names and addresses of PI associations.

Internet Source

FINDING AN ADOPTION SPECIALIST

Researchers who specialize in tracing adoptions have a network and resources that can sometimes be the only means for solving an adoption-related search. These specialists go by various titles, including Confidential Intermediary, Independent Search Consultant and Adoption Search Consultant. The best way to locate adoption specialists is to ask for recommendations from either of the following two national organizations:

Adoptees' Liberty Movement Association (ALMA)
P.O. Box 727, Radio City Station
New York, NY 10101-0727
(212) 581-1568
http://www.almanet.com/

Concerned United Birthparents, Inc. (CUB)
2000 Walker St.
Des Moines, IA 50317
(800) 822-2777
http://www.webnations.com/cub/

EIGHTEEN

Putting the Pieces Together

The major theme throughout this book is that research is unpredictable. The task of locating someone is similar to putting together a jigsaw puzzle. And no two puzzles are exactly the same.

A city directory may provide the essential information needed to find someone; whereas, a voter registration may solve another case. An interview with a former neighbor may break a case or provide absolutely no new information.

The focus of your research then becomes record types, rather than following exact research steps. For example, you know that the exact birth date of the person you want to find will help in using other records. So you ask yourself what types of records might provide a birth date? The answer would be voter registration, driver's records, military discharges, and divorce files. You then research the availability of those record types and examine them for the person you have targeted.

Below is a summary of information usually found in records. Not all record types will be accessible, depending upon privacy laws and record retention. Content within the records will vary from state to state and by time periods.

FULL NAME
birth certificate
city directory
telephone directory
tax assessor
voter registration
driver's records
military discharge
divorce files
civil and criminal files
bankruptcy
professional licensing

incorporations
DATE OF BIRTH
baptismal
voter registration
driver's records
military discharge
marriage license
divorce files
PLACE OF BIRTH
social security number
voter registration
residence of parents

NAMES OF SIBLINGS
city directories
marriage license
  (witnesses)
obituaries of parents
probate of parents
high school yearbook
NAMES OF PARENTS
city directories
newspaper report of
  marriage

NAME(S) OF SPOUSE
marriage records
divorce records
city directories
telephone directories
tax assessor
liens
bankruptcy
NAMES OF CHILDREN
divorce records
city directories
vehicle registrations
NEIGHBORS
householder directory

telephone directory
CURRENT ADDRESS
city directory
telephone directory
tax assessor
voter registration
driver's records
PRIOR ADDRESSES
city directories
telephone directories
tax assessor
voter registration
driver's records
civil and criminal files

SOCIAL SECURITY
 NUMBER
voter registration
real estate records
military discharge
liens
divorce records
UCC filings
Social Security Death
 Index (if deceased)

SUCCESS
When You Find the Person

Once you find the person you seek, the next step is contacting him. This can be a fragile situation, depending upon the reasons behind the search. A birth mother may rejoice at being found, or she may resent the intrusion into her life. A parent or child isolated for years from one another due to divorce may have similar reactions. In other words, the consequence of finding someone is totally unpredictable.

The majority of people, however, like being found. The re-connection with a lost family member or friend can be exhilarating. In the process, we learn to appreciate and cherish our friends and family.

Good luck with your search. And should you find the person you seek, stay in touch so you won't have to look for him again.

APPENDIX A

State Health Departments

Sources

F ollowing is a list of state health departments for ordering vital records—birth, death, marriage and divorce certificates. The accessibility of the records, time periods covered and fees vary greatly among states; verify policies by telephoning the appropriate office. The National Center for Health Statistics (http://www.cdc.gov/nchswww/howto/w2w/w2welcom .htm) and VitalChek (http://www.vitalchek.com/) give additional data for each state.

Alabama Department of Public Health
P.O. Box 5625, Montgomery, AL 36103-5625
Information: (334) 206-5418   *Fax:* (334) 262-9563

Alaska Vital Records
P.O. Box 110675, Juneau, AK 99811-0675
Information: (907) 465-3391   *Fax:* (907) 465-3618

Arizona Vital Records
2727 W. Glendale, Phoenix, AZ 85051
Information: (602) 255-3260   *Fax:* (602) 249-3040

Arkansas Vital Records
4815 W. Markham St., Little Rock, AR 72205
Information: (501) 661-2726   *Fax:* (501) 663-2832

California Vital Records
Department of Health Services, P.O. Box 730241,
Sacramento, CA 94244-0241
Information: (916) 445-2684   *Fax:* (800) 858-5553

Colorado Vital Records
Colorado Department of Health, 4300 Cherry Creek Dr. South,
Denver, CO 80222-1450
Information: (303) 692-2224   *Fax:* (800) 423-1108
http://www.cdphe.state.co.us/hs/cshom.html

Connecticut Department of Health

410 Capital Ave., Hartford, CT 06134-0308

Information: (860) 509-7897

Delaware Vital Statistics

P.O. Box 637, Dover, DE 19903

Information: (302) 739-4721   *Fax:* (302) 736-1862

District of Columbia Vital Records

800 Ninth St. SW, 1st Floor, Washington, DC 20024

Information: (202) 783-1809   *Fax:* (202) 783-0136

Florida Vital Statistics

P.O. Box 210, 1217 Pearl St., Jacksonville, FL 32231

Information: (904) 359-6911   *Fax:* (904) 359-6993

Georgia Department of Human Resources

47 Trinity Ave. SW, Vital Records Room #217-H, Atlanta, GA 30334

Information: (404) 657-7996

Phone: (404) 657-2062   *Fax:* (404) 524-4278

Hawaii Vital Records

1250 Punch Bowl Ave., Room #103, Honolulu, HI 96813-1865

Information: (808) 586-4539

http://www.hawaii.gov/health/sdohpg02.htm

Idaho Vital Statistics

P.O. Box 83720, Boise, ID 83720-0036

Information: (208) 334-5988   *Fax:* (208) 389-9096

Illinois Department of Public Health

Division of Vital Records, 605 W. Jefferson St., Springfield, IL 62702-5097

Information: (217) 782-6553   *Fax:* (217) 523-2648

http://www.idph.state.il.us/vital/home.htm

Indiana State Department of Health

2 N. Meridian St., Indianapolis, IN 46204

Information: (317) 233-2700   *Fax:* (317) 233-7210

http://www.state.in.us/doh/index.html

Iowa Department of Health

321 E. Twelfth, 4th Floor, Des Moines, IA 50319

Information: (515) 281-4944

http://www.idph.state.ia.us/pa/vr.htm

Kansas Vital Statistics

900 SW Jackson St., Room #151, Topeka, KS 66612-2221

Information: (785) 296-1400

Phone: (785) 296-3253   *Fax:* (785) 357-4332

Kentucky Vital Records

275 E. Main St., Frankfort, KY 40621

Information: (502) 564-4212   *Fax:* (502) 227-0032

Louisiana Vital Records Registry

Office of Public Health, 325 Loyola Ave., New Orleans, LA 70112

Information: (504) 568-5152

Maine Office of Vital Statistics
State House Station 11, Augusta, ME 04333-0011
Information: (207) 287-3184   *Fax:* (207) 287-1907

Maryland Vital Records
4201 Patterson Ave., Baltimore, MD 21215
Information: (410) 764-3038   *Fax:* (410) 358-7381

Massachusetts Vital Records
470 Atlantic Ave., 2nd Floor, Boston, MA 02210
Information: (617) 753-8600
Phone: (617) 753-8606   *Fax:* (617) 423-2038

Michigan Vital Records
P.O. Box 30195, Lansing, MI 48909
Information: (517) 335-8656   *Fax:* (517) 321-5884
http://www.mdch.state.mi.us/pha/osr/vitframe.htm

Minnesota Department of Health
717 Delaware St. SE, P.O. Box 9441, Minneapolis, MN 55410-9441
Information: (612) 676-5121   *Fax:* (612) 331-5776
http://www.health.state.mn.us

Mississippi Vital Records
2423 N. State St., Jackson, MS 39216
Information: (601) 960-7450
Phone: (601) 960-7981   *Fax:* (601) 352-0013

Missouri Department of Health
930 Wildwood, Jefferson City, MO 65109
Information: (573) 751-6400   *Phone:* (573) 751-6387
http://www.health.state.mo.us/cgi-bin/uncgi/birthanddeathrecords

Montana Vital Records
111 N. Sanders, Helena, MT 59604
Information: (406) 444-4228   *Fax:* (406) 444-1803
http://www.dphhs.mt.gov

Nebraska Vital Statistics
P.O. Box 95065, Lincoln, NE 68509
Information: (402) 471-2871

Nevada Vital Records
505 E. King St., Room #102, Carson City, NV 89710
Information: (702) 687-4481   *Fax:* (702) 687-6151

New Hampshire Vital Records
6 Hazen Dr., Concord, NH 03301
Information: (603) 271-4650

New Jersey Department of Health
Bureau of Vital Statistics, CN 370, Trenton, NJ 08625-0370
Information: (609) 633-2860   *Fax:* (609) 392-4292

New Mexico Vital Records
1190 Saint Francis Dr., Santa Fe, NM 87505
Information: (505) 827-2338   *Fax:* (505) 984-1048

New York City Department of Health

125 Worth St., Room #133, New York, NY 10013

Information: (212) 788-4520   *Fax:* (212) 962-6105

http://www.ci.nyc.ny.us/health

New York State Vital Records (except New York City)

P.O. Box 2602, Albany, NY 12220-2602

Information: (518) 474-3038

Phone: (518) 474-3077   *Fax:* (518) 432-6286

North Carolina Vital Records

225 N. McDowell St., Raleigh, NC 27603

Information: (919) 733-3526   *Fax:* (919) 829-1359

http://www.schs.state.nc.us/schs/

North Dakota Vital Records

State Capitol Building, Judicial Wing, Bismarck, ND 58505

Information: (701) 328-2360   *Fax:* (701) 328-1850

http://www.ehs.health.state.nd.us

Ohio Bureau of Vital Statistics

P.O. Box 15098, Columbus, OH 43215-0098

Information: (614) 466-2531   *Fax:* (614) 466-6604

Oklahoma State Department of Health

1000 NE Tenth St., Oklahoma City, OK 73117

Phone: (405) 271-4040

Oregon Vital Records

Center of Health Statistics

800 NE Oregon St., Suite #205, Portland, OR 97232

Information: (503) 731-4095

Phone: (503) 731-4108   *Fax:* (503) 234-8417

http://www.ohd.hr.state.or.us

Pennsylvania Vital Records

101 S. Mercer St., 4th Floor, New Castle, PA 16101

Information: (724) 656-3100   *Fax:* (724) 652-8951

Rhode Island Department of Health

3 Capitol Hill, Cannon Bldg., Providence, RI 02908-5097

Information: (401) 277-2811

South Carolina Vital Records

2600 Bull St., Columbia, SC 29201

Information: (803) 734-4830

Phone: (803) 734-6663   *Fax:* (803) 799-0301

South Dakota Vital Records

600 E. Capitol Ave., Pierre, SD 57501-2536

Information: (605) 773-3355

Phone: (605) 773-4961

http://www.state.sd.us/doh/vitalrec/vital.htm

Tennessee Vital Records

421 Fifth Ave. North, 1st Floor, Central Service Building
Nashville, TN 37247-0450

Information: (615) 741-0778   *Fax:* (615) 726-2559
http://www.state.tn.us/health/vr/index.html

Texas Bureau of Vital Statistics

Texas Department of Health, P.O. Box 12040, Austin, TX 78711-2040
Information: (512) 458-7111
http://www.tdh.state.tx.us/bvs

Utah Department of Health

288 N. 1460 West, P.O. Box 141012, Salt Lake City, UT 84114-1012
Information: (801) 538-6380   *Fax:* (801) 538-9467
http://hlunix.ex.state.ut.us/bvr/home.html

Vermont Department of Health

P.O. Box 70, 108 Cherry St., Burlington, VT 05402
Information: (802) 863-7275

Virginia State Department of Health

P.O. Box 1000, Richmond, VA 23218-1000
Information: (804) 225-5000

Washington Vital Statistics

Center for Health Statistics, P.O. Box 9709, Olympia, WA 98507-9709
Information: (360) 753-5936   *Fax:* (360) 352-2586
http://doh.wa.gov/topics/chs-cert.html

West Virginia Vital Registration

State Capitol Complex, Building #3, Charleston, WV 25305
Information: (304) 558-2931

Wisconsin Vital Statistics

1 W. Wilson St., P.O. Box 309, Madison, WI 53701
Information: (608) 266-1371   *Fax:* (608) 255-2035
http://www.dhfs.state.wi.us/vitalrecords/index.htm

Wyoming Vital Records

Hathaway Building, Cheyenne, WY 82002
Information: (307) 777-7591   *Fax:* (307) 635-4103
http://wdhfs.state.wy.us/vital_records/

National Archives and Regional Facilities

ARCHIVES I

National Archives and Records Administration (NARA)
Seventh St. and Pennsylvania Ave., NW, Washington, DC 20408

ARCHIVES II

National Archives at College Park
8601 Adelphi Rd., College Park, MD 20740-6001

Washington National Records Center
4205 Suitland Rd., Suitland, MD 20746-8001
Phone: (301) 457-7000   *Fax:* (301) 457-7117
E-mail: center@suitland.nara.gov
Area served: Washington, DC; Maryland; Virginia; West Virginia

NARA's National Personnel Records Center (NPRC),
Civilian Personnel Records
111 Winnebago St., St. Louis, MO 63118-4199
Fax: (314) 425-5719   *E-mail:* center@cpr.nara.gov

NARA's National Personnel Records Center, Military Personnel Records
9700 Page Ave., St. Louis, MO 63132-5100
Fax: (314) 538-4005   *E-mail:* center@stlouis.nara.gov

NARA REGIONAL FACILITIES
Central Plains Region

NARA's Central Plains Region (Kansas City)
2312 E. Bannister Rd., Kansas City, MO 64131-3011
Phone: (816) 926-6920
Fax: (816) 926-6982   *E-mail:* archives@kansascity.nara.gov
Area served: Iowa, Kansas, Missouri, Nebraska

NARA's Central Plains Region (Lee's Summit)
200 Space Center Dr., Lees Summit, MO 64064-1182
Phone: (816) 478-7079   *Fax:* (816) 478-7625
Area served: New Jersey, New York, Puerto Rico, the U.S. Virgin Islands
(temporary records)

Great Lakes Region
NARA's Great Lakes Region (Chicago)
7358 S. Pulaski Rd., Chicago, IL 60629-5898
Phone: (773) 581-7816   *Fax:* (312) 353-1294
E-mail: archives@chicago.nara.gov
Area served: Illinois, Indiana, Michigan, Minnesota, Ohio, Wisconsin
NARA's Great Lakes Region (Dayton)
3150 Springboro Rd., Dayton, OH 45439-1883
Phone: (937) 225-2852   *Fax:* (937) 225-7236
E-mail: center@dayton.nara.gov
Area served: Indiana, Michigan, Minnesota, Ohio

Mid-Atlantic Region
NARA's Mid-Atlantic Region (Center City/Philadelphia)
Ninth and Market Sts., Philadelphia, PA 19107-4292
Phone: (215) 597-3000   *Fax:* (215) 597-2303
E-mail: archives@philarch.nara.gov
Area served: Delaware, Maryland, Pennsylvania, Virginia,
West Virginia
NARA's Mid-Atlantic Region (Northeast Philadelphia)
14700 Townsend Rd., Philadelphia, PA 19154-1096
Phone: (215) 671-9027   *Fax:* (215) 671-8001
E-mail: center@philadelphia.nara.gov
Area served: Delaware, Pennsylvania; federal courts in Maryland,
Virginia, West Virginia

Northeast Region
NARA's Northeast Region (Boston)
380 Trapelo Rd., Waltham, MA 02154-6399
Phone: (781) 647-8100   *Fax:* (781) 647-8460
E-mail: archives@waltham.nara.gov
Area served: Connecticut, Maine, Massachusetts, New Hampshire, Rhode
Island, Vermont
NARA's Northeast Region (Pittsfield)
10 Conte Dr., Pittsfield, MA 01201-8230
Phone: (413) 445-6885   *Fax:* (413) 445-7599
E-mail: archives@pittsfield.gov
NARA's Northeast Region (New York City)
201 Varick St., New York, NY 10014-4811
Phone: (212) 337-1300   *Fax:* (212) 337-1306

E-mail: archives@newyork.nara.gov

Area served: New Jersey, New York, Puerto Rico, the U.S. Virgin Islands (permanent records)

Pacific Region

NARA's Pacific Region (Laguna Niguel)

24000 Avila Rd., 1st Floor, Laguna Niguel, CA 92677-3497

Phone: (949) 360-2644

Area served: Arizona, southern California, Clark County, Nevada

NARA's Pacific Region (San Francisco)

1000 Commodore Dr., San Bruno, CA 94066-2350

Phone: (650) 876-9009   *Fax:* (650) 876-9233

E-mail: center@sanbruno.nara.gov

Area served: Northern California, Guam, Hawaii, Nevada (except Clark County), American Samoa, Trust Territory of the Pacific Islands

Pacific Alaska Region

NARA's Pacific Alaska Region

654 W. Third Ave., Anchorage, AK 99501-2145

Phone: (907) 271-2443   *Fax:* (907) 271-2442

E-mail: archives@alaska.nara.gov

Area served: Alaska

NARA's Pacific Alaska Region (Seattle)

6125 Sand Point Way NE, Seattle, WA 98115-7999

Phone: (206) 526-6507   *Fax:* (206) 526-4344

E-mail: archives@seattle.nara.gov

Area served: Idaho, Oregon, Washington

Rocky Mountain Region

NARA's Rocky Mountain Region

Building 48, Denver Federal Center, P.O. Box 25307, Denver, CO 80225-0307

Phone: (303) 236-0804   *Fax:* (303) 236-9297

E-mail: center@denver.nara.gov

Area served: Colorado, Montana, New Mexico, North Dakota, South Dakota, Utah, Wyoming

Southeast Region

NARA's Southeast Region

1557 Saint Joseph Ave., East Point, GA 30344-2593

Phone: (404) 763-7477   *Fax:* (404) 763-7033

E-mail: archives@atlanta.nara.gov

Area served: Alabama, Florida, Georgia, Kentucky, Mississippi, North Carolina, South Carolina, Tennessee

Southwest Region

NARA's Southwest Region

501 W. Felix St., Building 1, Fort Worth, TX 76115-3405

or

P.O. Box 6216, Fort Worth, TX 76115-0216

Phone: (817) 334-5525 *Fax:* (817) 334-5621

E-mail: center@ftworth.nara.gov

Area served: Arkansas, Louisiana, Oklahoma, Texas

National Cemetery System

Sources

The Arlington National Cemetery in Virginia is managed by the Department of the Army. The other following national cemeteries are under the administration of the Department of Veterans Affairs (formerly the Veterans Administration). The Web address for the VA is http://www.va.gov/va.htm.

Alabama

Fort Mitchell National Cemetery
553 Highway 165, Seale, AL 36875   (334) 855-4731
Mobile National Cemetery
1202 Virginia St., Mobile, AL 36604   (334) 690-2858

Alaska

Ft. Richardson National Cemetery
P.O. Box 5-498, Building 997 Davis Highway
Fort Richardson, AK 99505   (907) 384-7075
Sitka National Cemetery
P.O. Box 1065, Sitka, AK 99835   (907) 747-8637

Arizona

National Memorial Cemetery of Arizona
23029 N. Cave Creek Rd., Phoenix, AZ 85024   (602) 379-4615
Prescott National Cemetery
VA Medical Center, 500 Highway 89 North, Prescott, AZ 86301
(520) 776-6028

Arkansas

Fayetteville National Cemetery
700 Government Ave., Fayetteville, AR 72701   (501) 444-5051
Fort Smith National Cemetery
522 Garland Ave., Fort Smith, AR 72901   (501) 783-5345

Little Rock National Cemetery
2523 Confederate Blvd, Little Rock, AR 72206   (501) 324-6401

California
Fort Rosecrans National Cemetery
92166 Point Loma, P.O. Box 6237, San Diego, CA 92106
(619) 553-2084
Golden Gate National Cemetery
1300 Sneath Lane, San Bruno, CA 94066   (650) 589-7737
Los Angeles National Cemetery
950 S. Sepulveda Blvd., Los Angeles, CA 90049   (310) 824-4311
Riverside National Cemetery
22495 Van Buren Blvd., Riverside, CA 92508   (909) 653-8417
San Francisco National Cemetery
P.O. Box 9012, Presidio of San Francisco, San Francisco, CA 94129
(415) 561-2008
San Joaquin Valley National Cemetery
32053 W. McCabe Rd., Gustine, CA 95322   (209) 854-1040

Colorado
Fort Logan National Cemetery
3698 S. Sheridan Blvd., Denver, CO 80235   (303) 761-0117
Fort Lyon National Cemetery
VA Medical Center, "C" St., Fort Lyon, CO 81038
(719) 384-3152 Ext. 231

Florida
Barrancas National Cemetery
Naval Air Station
80 Hovey Rd., Pensacola, FL 32508   (904) 452-3357
Bay Pines National Cemetery
P.O. Box 477, 10000 Bay Pines Blvd., Bay Pines, FL 33504
(813) 398-9426
Florida National Cemetery
P.O. Box 337, Bushnell, FL 33513   (352) 793-7740
St. Augustine National Cemetery
104 Marine St., St. Augustine, FL 32084   For information, contact
Florida National Cemetery: (352) 793-7740

Georgia
Marietta National Cemetery
500 Washington Ave., Marietta, GA 30060   (770) 428-5631

Hawaii
National Memorial Cemetery of the Pacific
2177 Puowaina Dr., Honolulu, HI 96813   (808) 566-1430

Illinois

Alton National Cemetery
600 Pearl St., Alton, IL 62003
For information, contact Jefferson Barracks National Cemetery
(St. Louis, Missouri): (314) 260-8691

Camp Butler National Cemetery
R.R. #1, Springfield, IL 62707   (217) 522-5764

Danville National Cemetery
VA Medical Center
1900 E. Main St., Danville, IL 61832   (217) 431-6550

Mound City National Cemetery
Junction—Highways 37 and 51, Mound City, IL 62963
For information, contact Jefferson Barracks National Cemetery
(St. Louis, Missouri): (314) 260-8691

Quincy National Cemetery
Thirty-sixth and Maine Sts., Quincy, IL 62301
For information, contact Keokuk National Cemetery (Keokuk, Iowa):
(319) 524-1304

Rock Island National Cemetery
P.O. Box 737, Rock Island Arsenal, Moline, IL 61265
(309) 782-2094

Indiana

Crown Hill National Cemetery
700 W. Thirty-eighth St., Indianapolis, IN 46208   (317) 925-8231

Marion National Cemetery
VA Medical Center
1700 E. Thirty-eighth St., Marion, IN 46952   (765) 674-0284

New Albany National Cemetery
1943 Ekin Ave., New Albany, IN 47150   (812) 948-5234

Iowa

Keokuk National Cemetery
1701 J St., Keokuk, IA 52632   (319) 524-1304

Kansas

Fort Leavenworth National Cemetery
Fort Leavenworth, KS 66027
For information contact Leavenworth National Cemetery:
(913) 758-4105

Fort Scott National Cemetery
P.O. Box 917, Fort Scott, KS 66701   (316) 223-2840

Leavenworth National Cemetery
P.O. Box 1694, Leavenworth, KS 66048   (913) 758-4105

Kentucky

Camp Nelson National Cemetery
6980 Danville Rd., Nicholasville, KY 40356   (606) 885-5727

Cave Hill National Cemetery
701 Baxter Ave., Louisville, KY 40204
For information, contact Zachary Taylor National Cemetery:
(502) 893-3852

Danville National Cemetery
377 N. First St., Danville, KY 40442
For information, contact Camp Nelson National Cemetery:
(606) 885-5727

Lebanon National Cemetery
R.R. #1, P.O. Box 616, Lebanon, KY 40033   (502) 692-3390

Lexington National Cemetery
833 W. Main St., Lexington, KY 40508
For information, contact Camp Nelson National Cemetery:
(606) 885-5727

Mill Springs National Cemetery
Nancy, KY 42544
For information, contact Camp Nelson National Cemetery:
(606) 885-5727

Zachary Taylor National Cemetery
4701 Brownsboro Rd., Louisville, KY 40207   (502) 893-3852

Louisiana

Alexandria National Cemetery
209 Shamrock Ave., Pineville, LA 71360   (318) 473-7588

Baton Rouge National Cemetery
220 N. Nineteenth St., Baton Rouge, LA 70806
For information, contact Port Hudson National Cemetery:
(504) 389-0788

Port Hudson National Cemetery
20978 Port Hickey Rd., Zachary, LA 70791   (504) 389-0788

Maine

Togus National Cemetery
VA Regional Office Center, Togus, ME 04330   (207) 623-8411

Maryland

Annapolis National Cemetery
800 West St., Annapolis, MD 21401
For information, contact Baltimore National Cemetery:
(410) 644-9696

Baltimore National Cemetery
5501 Frederick Ave., Baltimore, MD 21228   (410) 644-9696

Loudon Park National Cemetery
3445 Frederick Ave., Baltimore, MD 21229
For information, contact Baltimore National Cemetery:
(410) 644-9696

Massachusetts

Massachusetts National Cemetery
Bourne, MA 02532, (508) 563-7113

Michigan

Fort Custer National Cemetery
15501 Dickman Rd., Augusta, MI 49012   (616) 731-4164

Minnesota

Fort Snelling National Cemetery
7601 Thirty-fourth Ave. South, Minneapolis, MN 55450
(612) 726-1127

Mississippi

Biloxi National Cemetery
400 Veterans Ave., P.O. Box 4968, Biloxi, MS 39535-4968
(228) 388-6668
Corinth National Cemetery
1551 Horton St., Corinth, MS 38834
For information, contact Memphis National Cemetery (Memphis, Tennessee): (901) 386-8311
Natchez National Cemetery
41 Cemetery Rd., Natchez, MS 39120   (601) 445-4981

Missouri

Jefferson Barracks National Cemetery
2900 Sheridan Rd., St. Louis, MO 63125   (314) 260-8691
Jefferson City National Cemetery
1024 E. McCarty St., Jefferson City, MO 65101
For information, contact Jefferson Barracks National Cemetery: (314) 260-8691
Springfield National Cemetery
1702 E. Seminole St., Springfield, MO 65804   (417) 881-9499

Nebraska

Fort McPherson National Cemetery
HCO 1, P.O. Box 67, Maxwell, NE 69151   (308) 582-4433

New Jersey

Beverly National Cemetery
916 Bridgeboro Rd., Beverly, NJ 08010   (609) 877-5460
Finn's Point National Cemetery
RFD No. 3, Fort Mott Rd., Salem, NJ 08079
For information, contact Beverly National Cemetery: (609) 877-5460

New Mexico
  Fort Bayard National Cemetery
    P.O. Box 189, Fort Bayard, NM 88036
    For information, contact Fort Bliss National Cemetery (Fort Bliss, Texas): (915) 564-0201
  Santa Fe National Cemetery
    501 N. Guadalupe St., P.O. Box 88, Santa Fe, NM 87501
    (505) 988-6400

New York
  Bath National Cemetery
    VA Medical Center, Bath, NY 14810   (607) 776-5480
  Calverton National Cemetery
    210 Princeton Blvd. Calverton, NY 11933   (516) 727-5410
  Cypress Hills National Cemetery
    625 Jamaica Ave., Brooklyn, NY 11208
    For information, contact Long Island National Cemetery:
    (516) 454-4949
  Long Island National Cemetery
    2040 Wellwood Ave., Farmingdale, NY 11735-1211
    (516) 454-4949
  Woodlawn National Cemetery
    1825 Davis St., Elmira, NY 14901
    For information, contact Bath National Cemetery: (607) 732-5411

North Carolina
  New Bern National Cemetery
    1711 National Ave., New Bern, NC 28560   (919) 637-2912
  Raleigh National Cemetery
    501 Rock Quarry Rd., Raleigh, NC 27610   (919) 832-0144
  Salisbury National Cemetery
    202 Government Rd., Salisbury, NC 28144   (704) 636-2661
  Wilmington National Cemetery
    2011 Market St., Wilmington, NC 28403   (910) 343-4877

Ohio
  Dayton National Cemetery
    VA Medical Center, 4100 W. Third St., Dayton, OH 45428
    (937) 268-6511

Oklahoma
  Fort Gibson National Cemetery
    1423 Cemetery Rd., Fort Gibson, OK 74434   (918) 478-2334

Oregon
  Eagle Point National Cemetery
    2763 Riley Rd., Eagle Point, OR 97524   (503) 826-2511

Roseburg National Cemetery
VA Medical Center, Roseburg, OR 97470   (541) 440-1000
Willamette National Cemetery
11800 SE Mount Scott Blvd., Portland, OR 97266   (503) 273-5250

Pennsylvania
Indiantown Gap National Cemetery
R.R. #2, P.O. Box 484, Indiantown Gap Rd., Annville, PA 17003-9618   (717) 865-5254
Philadelphia National Cemetery
Haines St & Limekiln Pike, Philadelphia, PA 19138
For information, contact Beverly National Cemetery (Beverly, New Jersey): (609) 877-5460

Puerto Rico
Puerto Rico National Cemetery
P.O. Box 1298, 168 National Cemetery Ave., Bayamon, PR 00960   (787) 798-8400

South Carolina
Beaufort National Cemetery
1601 Boundary St., Beaufort, SC 29902-3947   (803) 524-3925
Florence National Cemetery
803 E. National Cemetery Rd., Florence, SC 29501 (803) 669-8783

South Dakota
Black Hills National Cemetery
P.O. Box 640, Sturgis, SD 57785   (605) 347-3830
Fort Meade National Cemetery
VA Medical Center, Fort Meade, SD 57785
For information, contact Black Hills National Cemetery: (605) 347-3830
Hot Springs National Cemetery
VA Medical Center, Hot Springs, SD 57747
For information, contact VAMC Engineering Service: (605) 745-4101

Tennessee
Chattanooga National Cemetery
1200 Bailey Ave., Chattanooga, TN 37404   (423) 855-6590
Knoxville National Cemetery
939 Tyson St. NW, Knoxville, TN 37917
For information, contact Mountain Home National Cemetery: (423) 461-7935
Memphis National Cemetery
3568 Townes Ave., Memphis, TN 38122   (901) 386-8311

Mountain Home National Cemetery
VA Medical Center, P.O. Box 8, Mountain Home, TN 37684
(423) 461-7935
Nashville National Cemetery
1420 Gallatin Rd. South, Madison, TN 37115   (615) 327-5360

Texas
Fort Bliss National Cemetery
5200 Fred Wilson St., Fort Bliss, TX 79906   (915) 564-0201
Fort Sam Houston National Cemetery
1520 Harry Wurzbach Rd., San Antonio, TX 78209   (210) 820-3891
Houston National Cemetery
10410 Veterans Memorial Dr., Houston, TX 77038   (713) 447-8686
Kerrville National Cemetery
VA Medical Center, 3600 Memorial Blvd., Kerrville, TX 78028
For information, contact Fort Sam Houston National Cemetery:
(210) 820-3891
San Antonio National Cemetery
517 Paso Hondo St., San Antonio, TX 78202
For information, contact Fort Sam Houston National Cemetery:
(210) 820-3891

Virginia
Alexandria National Cemetery
1450 Wilkes St., Alexandria, VA 22314
For information, contact Quantico National Cemetery:
(703) 690-2217
Arlington National Cemetery
Arlington, VA 22211   (703) 697-2131
Balls Bluff National Cemetery
305 U.S. Ave., Leesburg, VA 22075
For information, contact Culpeper National Cemetery:
(703) 825-0027
City Point National Cemetery
Tenth Ave. and Davis St., Hopewell, VA 23860
For information, contact Richmond National Cemetery:
(804) 222-1490
Cold Harbor National Cemetery
Route 156 North, Mechanicsville, VA 23111
For information, contact Richmond National Cemetery:
(804) 222-1490
Culpeper National Cemetery
305 U.S. Ave., Culpeper, VA 22701   (703) 825-0027
Danville National Cemetery
721 Lee St., Danville, VA 24541

For information, contact Salisbury National Cemetery (Salisbury, North Carolina): (704) 636-2661

Fort Harrison National Cemetery

8620 Varina Rd., Richmond, VA 23231

For information, contact Richmond National Cemetery: (804) 222-1490

Glendale National Cemetery

8301 Willis Church Rd., Richmond, VA 23231

For information, contact Richmond National Cemetery: (804) 222-1490

Hampton National Cemetery

Veterans Medical Center, Hampton, VA 23667   (804) 723-7104

Quantico National Cemetery

P.O. Box 10, 18424 Joplin Rd., Triangle, VA 22172   (703) 690-2217

Richmond National Cemetery

1701 Williamsburg Rd., Richmond, VA 23231   (804) 222-1490

Seven Pines National Cemetery

400 E. Williamsburg Rd., Sandston, VA 23150

For information, contact Richmond National Cemetery: (804) 222-1490

Staunton National Cemetery

901 Richmond Ave., Staunton, VA 24401

For information, contact Culpeper National Cemetery: (703) 825-0027

Winchester National Cemetery

401 National Ave. Winchester, VA 22601

For information, contact Culpeper National Cemetery: (703) 825-0027

Washington

Tahoma National Cemetery

18600 SE 240th St., Kent, WA 98042-4868   (206) 768-5263

West Virginia

Grafton National Cemetery

Route 2, P.O. Box 127, Grafton, WV 26354

For information, contact West Virginia National Cemetery: (304) 265-2044

West Virginia National Cemetery

Route 2, P.O. Box 127, Grafton, WV 26354   (304) 265-2044

Wisconsin

Wood National Cemetery

5000 W. National Ave., Building 1301, Milwaukee, WI 53295 (414) 383-5300

Repositories With Major Genealogical Collections

Library/Archive Source

Allen County Public Library
Genealogy Department, 900 Webster St., P.O. Box 2270
Fort Wayne, IN 46801-2270   (219) 424-7241   http://www.acpl.lib.in.us/

American Antiquarian Society
185 Salisbury St., Worcester, MA 01605   (508) 755-5221

Dallas Public Library
1515 Young St., Dallas, TX 75201   (214) 670-1433
http://www.lib.ci.dallas.tx.us/home.htm

Denver Public Library
10 W. Fourteenth Ave. Parkway, Denver, CO 80204-2731   (303) 640-6200
http://www.denver.lib.co.us/

Detroit Public Library
Burton Historical Collection, 5201 Woodward Ave., Detroit, MI 48202
(313) 833-1480   http://www.detroit.lib.mi.us/

Enoch Pratt Library
400 Cathedral St., Baltimore, MD 21201   (410) 396-5430
http://pac.pratt.lib.md.us/

Family History Library
35 NW Temple St., Salt Lake City, UT 84150   (801) 240-2331

Houston Public Library
Clayton Library Center for Genealogical Research
5300 Caroline, Houston, TX 77004-6896   (713) 524-0101
http://www.hpl.lib.tx.us:1080/

Library of Congress
Local History and Genealogy Reading Room
Jefferson Building, 10 First St. SE, Washington, DC 20540   (202) 707-5537
http://lcweb.loc.gov/catalog

Los Angeles Public Library

History and Genealogy Department

630 W. Fifth St., Los Angeles, CA 90071   (213) 228-7000

http://www.lapl.org/

Mid-Continent Public Library

North Independence Branch

317 W. Highway 24, Independence, MO 64050   (816) 252-0950

http://www.mcpl.lib.mo.us/

National Genealogical Society

4527 Seventeenth St. North, Arlington, VA 22207-2399   (703) 525-0050

http://www.ngsgenealogy.org/

New England Historic Genealogical Society

101 Newbury St., Boston, MA 02116   (617) 536-5740

http://www.nehgs.org/

New York Public Library

U.S. History, Local History and Genealogy Division

Fifth Ave. and Forty-second St., New York, NY 10018-2788

(212) 340-0849 http://www.nypl.org/

Newberry Library

60 W. Walton St., Chicago, IL 60610   (312) 943-9090

http://www.newberry.org/

St. Louis Public Library

History and Genealogy Department

1301 Olive St., St. Louis, MO 63103   (314) 241-2288

http://www.slpl.lib.mo.us/

Samford University

AGS Depository and Headquarters

Harwell Goodwin Davis Library

800 Lakeshore Dr., Birmingham, AL 35229   (205) 870-2749

http://davisweb.samford.edu/

Seattle Public Library

1000 Fourth Ave., Seattle, WA 98104   (206) 386-4629

http://www.spl.lib.wa.us/

State Historical Society of Wisconsin

(see Wisconsin, State Historical Society of)

Sutro Library

480 Winston Dr., San Francisco, CA 94132   (415) 731-4477

http://sfpl.lib.ca.us/gencoll/gencolsu.htm

Western Reserve Historical Society

10825 East Blvd., Cleveland, OH 44106   (216) 721-5722

http://www.wrhs.org/

Wisconsin, State Historical Society of

816 State St., Madison, WI 53706   (608) 264-6535

http://www.shsw.wisc.edu/

Reading List

Adoption

Askin, Jayne and Molly Davis. *Search: A Handbook for Adoptees and Birthparents*. 2d ed. Phoenix: Oryx Press, 1992.

Carangelo, Lori. *The Ultimate Search Book: Worldwide Adoption and Vital Records*. Bountiful, UT: Heritage Quest, 1998.

Klunder, Virgil L. *Lifeline: The Action Guide to Adoption Search*. Cape Coral, FL: Caradium Publishing, 1991.

Rillera, Mary Jo. *Search and Support Directory*. Westminster, CA: Triadoption Publication, n.d.

Printed Source

Reference Books

Bentley, Elizabeth Petty. *The County Courthouse Book*. 2d ed. Baltimore: Genealogical Publishing Co., 1995.

————. *The Genealogist's Address Book*. 3d ed. Baltimore: Genealogical Publishing Company, 1995.

Colletta, John Philip. *They Came in Ships: A Guide to Finding Your Immigrant Ancestor's Arrival Record*. Rev. ed. Salt Lake City: Ancestry, Inc., 1993.

County Court Records: A National Guide to Civil, Criminal and Probate Records at the County and Municipal Levels Within the State Court Systems. 4th ed. Tempe, AZ: BRB Publications, Inc., 1998.

Eichholz, Alice, ed. *Ancestry's Red Book: American State, County and Town Sources*. Rev. ed. Salt Lake City: Ancestry Publishing Co., 1992.

Haines, Gerald K. and David A. Langbart. *Unlocking the Files of the FBI: A Guide to Its Records and Classification System*. Wilmington, DE: Scholarly Resources, Inc., 1993.

The Handybook for Genealogists. 9th ed. Logan, UT: Everton Publishers, 1998.

Hone, E. Wade. *Land and Property Research in the United States*. Salt Lake City: Ancestry, Inc., 1997.

Humling, Virginia. *U.S. Catholic Sources: A Diocesan Research Guide*. Salt Lake City: Ancestry, 1995

Johnson, Lt. Col. Richard S. *How to Locate Anyone Who Is or Has Been in the Military: Armed Forces Locator Directory*. 7th ed. Spartenburg, SC: MIE Publishing, 1995.

Kemp, Thomas J. *International Vital Records Handbook*. 3d ed. Baltimore: Genealogical Publishing Co., Inc., 1994.

Meyerink, Kory L., ed. *Printed Sources: A Guide to Published Genealogical Records*. Salt Lake City: Ancestry, Inc., 1998.

Mills, Elizabeth Shown. *Evidence! Citation & Analysis for the Family Historian*. Baltimore: Genealogical Publishing Co., 1997.

The MVR Book: Motor Services Guide. Tempe, AZ: BRB Publications, Inc., 1998.

Neagles, James C. *U.S. Military Records: A Guide to Federal and State Sources, Colonial American to the Present*. Salt Lake City: Ancestry, Inc., 1994.

Newman, John J. *American Naturalization Records, 1790–1990: What They Are and How to Use Them*. Bountiful, UT: Heritage Quest, 1998.

Public Record Research Library. *The Librarian's Guide to Public Records: The Complete State, County, and Courthouse Locator*. Tempe, AZ: BRB Publications, Inc., 1998.

Rose, Christine. *Nicknames: Past and Present*. 3d ed. San Jose: privately printed, 1998.

Rose, Christine, and Kay Germain Ingalls. *The Complete Idiot's Guide to Genealogy*. New York: Alpha Books, 1997.

Schaefer, Christina K. *Guide to Naturalization Records of the United States*. Baltimore: Genealogical Publishing Co., 1997.

Smith, Juliana Szucs. *The Ancestry Family Historian's Address Book*. Salt Lake City: Ancestry, Inc., 1997.

The Sourcebook of County Court Records, 4th ed. Tempe, AZ: BRB Publications, Inc., 1998.

The Sourcebook of Federal Courts, U.S. District and Bankruptcy: The Definitive Guide to Searching for Case Information at the Local Level Within the Federal Court System. 2d ed. Tempe, AZ: BRB Publications, Inc., 1996.

The Sourcebook of State Public Records: The Definitive Guide to Searching for Public Record Information at the State Level. 3d ed. Tempe, AZ: BRB Publications, Inc., 1997.

Szucs, Loretto Dennis. *They Became Americans: Finding Naturalization Records and Ethnic Origins*. Salt Lake City: Ancestry, Inc., 1998.

Szucs, Loretto Dennis, and Sandra Hargreaves Luebking, eds. *The Source: A Guidebook of American Genealogy*. Rev. ed. Salt Lake City: Ancestry, Inc., 1997.

APPENDIX F

Internet Sites

 he following Internet sites are referenced in this book. Web addresses change often; if you are unable to connect to a site, use an Internet search engine and enter keywords to find the new URL.

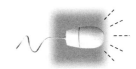

Internet Source

Adoption

http://www.almanet.com/

http://www.webnations.com/cub/

Allen County Public Library

http://www.acpl.lib.in.us/Genealogy/genealogy.html

American Legion

http://www.legion.org/index.htm

Association of Professional Genealogists

http://www.apgen.org/

Attorneys

http://www.martindale.com

Bankruptcy

http://www.brbpub.com

http://www.merlindata.com

Board for Certification of Genealogists

http://www.genealogy.org/~bcg

Census

http://www.nara.gov

http://www.census.gov/genealogy/www/agesearch.html

http://www.usgenweb.org/census/

http://www.rootsweb.com/~usgenweb

Census Rental Program

http://www.nara.gov/publications/microfilm/micrent.html

City Directories

http://www.kinquest.com/genealogy/citydir.html

http://www.acpl.lib.in.us/genealogy/genealogy.html

http://www.newberry.org/
http://www.nehgs.org/
http://www.heritagequest.com/genealogy/microfilm/
http://www.cyndilist.com/finding.htm

College/University
http://www.mit.edu:8001/people/cdemello/univ.html
http://www.uiuc.edu/cgi-bin/ph/lookup
http://www.lynxu.com/brats/index.html

Colorado Marriage and Divorce Records
http://www.quickinfo.net/madi/comadi.html

Colorado Prison Records
http://www.state.co.us/gov_dir/gss/archives/prison.html

Colorado Vital Records
http://www.cdphe.state.co.us/hs/cshom.html

Court Records
http://www.brbpub.com

Courthouse Addresses
http://www.everton.com
http://www.brbpub.com

Criminal Records
http://www.nasire.org/ss/stcriminal.html

Dallas Public Library
http://www.lib.ci.dallas.tx.us/home.htm

Dentists
http://www.teeth.com

Denver Public Library
http://www.denver.lib.co.us/

Detroit Public Library
http://www.detroit.lib.mi.us/

Disabled American Veterans
http://www.dav.org

Ellis Island
http://www.ellisisland.org

Enoch Pratt Library
http://pac.pratt.lib.md.us/

Family Group Sheets
http://www.everton.com/charts/freeform.html
http://www.familytreemaker.com/fgs.html

FBI
http://www.fbi.gov

Genealogical Forms and Supplies
http://www.ancestry.com
http://www.everton.com/
http://www.ngsgenealogy.org/

Genealogical Search Engines
http://www.cyndislist.com

http://www.usgenweb.com/
Genealogical Societies
http://www.fgs.org/
http://www.ngsgenealogy.org/
http://www.nehgs.org/
Genealogical Software
http://www.familytreemaker.com
http://www.uftree.com/uft/uft.html
http://www.whollygenes.com
http://www.genealogy.org/~paf/
http://www.leisterpro.com/
http://www.sierra.com/titles/genealogy/bot.html
Harvard University
http://www.harvard-magazine.com
Hawaii Vital Records
http://www.hawaii.gov/health/sdohpg02.htm
Holocaust
http://www.avotaynu.com
Houston Public Library
http://www.hpl.lib.tx.us:1080/
Hunting and Fishing Licenses
http://www.brbpub.com
Illinois Vital Records
http://www.idph.state.il.us/vital/home.htm
Immigration and Naturalization
http://www.ellisisland.org
http://www.phoenix.net/~tsm/default.html
http://www.ins.usdoj.gov
http://merrimack.nara.gov/genealogy/immigration/immigrat.html
http://www.nara.gov/publications/prologue/natural1.html
Indiana Vital Records
http://www.state.in.us/doh/index.html
Information Broker
http://www.merlindata.com
http://www.quickinformer.com
http://kadima.com
Iowa Vital Records
http://www.idph.state.ia.us/pa/vr.htm
Jewish Research
http://www.avotaynu.com
Kansas Telephone Books
http://history.cc.ukans.edu/heritage/kshs/library/tele-a.htm
Kentucky Marriage, Divorce and Death Records
http://ukcc.uky.edu/~vitalrec/
Libraries
http://www.acpl.lib.in.us/genealogy/genealogy.html

http://www.lib.ci.dallas.tx.us/home.htm
http://www.denver.lib.co.us/
http://www.detroit.lib.mi.us/
http://pac.pratt.lib.md.us/
http://www.hpl.lib.tx.us:1080/
http://lcweb.loc.gov/catalog/
http://www.lapl.org/
http://www.mcpl.lib.mo.us/
http://www.nypl.org/
http://www.newberry.org/
http://www.slpl.lib.mo.us/
http://davisweb.samford.edu/
http://www.spl.lib.wa.us/
http://sfpl.lib.ca.us/gencoll/gencolsu.htm
http://www.wrhs.org/
http://www.shsw.wisc.edu/

Library of Congress

http://lcweb.loc.gov/catalog

Los Angeles Public Library

http://www.lapl.org/

Maine Marriage Records

http://www.state.me.us/sos/arc/archives/genealogy/marriage.htm

Michigan Vital Records

http://www.mdch.state.mi.us/pha/osr/vitframe.htm

Mid-Continent Library

http://www.mcpl.lib.mo.us/

Military

http://www.nara.gov/regional/mprsf180.html
http://www.militarycity.com

Military Associations/Organizations

http://vets.com/inside/assoc.htm
http://www.vets.org
http://militarywoman.org/homepage.htm
http://www.dav.org
http://www.legion.org/index.htm

Military Brats

http://www.lynxu.com/brats/index.html

Military: Korea and Vietnam Casualty Lists

http://www.nara.gov/nara/electronic/korvnsta.html

Military: WWI Draft

http://www.ancestry.com

Minnesota Death Records (Wadena County)

http://www.rootsweb.com/~mnwadena/deathpage.htm

Minnesota Obituaries

http://www.pconline.com/~mnobits/

Minnesota Vital Records
http://www.health.state.mn.us
Missouri Vital Records
http://www.health.state.mo.us/cgi-bin/uncgi/birthanddeathrecords
Montana Vital Records
http://www.dphhs.mt.gov
Motor Vehicles
http://www.brbpub.com
http://www.merlindata.com
http://www.quickinformer.com
http://kadima.com
National Archives
http://www.nara.gov
http://merrimack.nara.gov/genealogy/immigration/immigrat.html
National Association of State Information Resource Executives
http://www.nasire.org/ss/stcriminal.html
National Center for Health Statistics
http://www.cdc.gov/nchswww/howto/w2w/w2welcom.htm
National Genealogical Society
http://www.ngsgenealogy.org/
National Union Catalog of Manuscript Collections
http://www.lcweb.loc.gov/coll/nucmc/nucmctxt.html
New England Historic Genealogical Society
http://www.nehgs.org/
New York City Vital Records
http://www.ci.nyc.ny.us/health
New York City: WWI Draft
http://www.italiangen.org/igg011.htm
New York Public Library
http://www.nypl.org/
Newberry Library
http://www.newberry.org/
North Carolina Vital Records
http://www.schs.state.nc.us/schs/
North Dakota Vital Records
http://www.ehs.health.state.nd.us
Obituaries
http://www.cyndislist.com/obits.htm/
http://www.polaris.net/~legend/gateway5.htm
Ohio Death Records
http://www.ohiohistory.org/textonly/resource/archlib/brthdth1.html
Oregon Vital Records
http://www.ohd.hr.state.or.us
Physicians
http://www.ama-assn.org

Pilots
http://www.landings.com
Private Investigators
http://www.pihome.com/
Professional Genealogists
http://www.apgen.org/
http://www.genealogy.org/~bcg
Real Estate Records
http://www.hamiltoncountyauditor.org
http://www.iaao.org/hub1.htm
Reunions
http://www.reunionsmag.com
St. Louis Public Library
http://www.slpl.lib.mo.us/
Samford University
http://davisweb.samford.edu/
Seattle Public Library
http://www.spl.lib.wa.us/
Selective Service System
http://www.sss.gov/records.htm
Social Security Administration
http://www.ssa.gov/faq_services.html
Social Security Death Index
http://www.ancestry.com
http://www.familytreemaker.com
http://kadima.com/
http://kindredkonnections.com
http://www.uftree.com/
Social Security Death Index—Errors
http://www.familydetective.com
Soundex
http://www.nara.gov/genealogy/soundex/soundex.html
South Dakota Vital Records
http://www.state.sd.us/doh/vitalrec/vital.htm
Subscription Databases
http://www.ancestry.com
http://kadima.com/
http://www.genealogylibrary.com
Sutro Public Library
http://sfpl.lib.ca.us/gencoll/gencolsu.htm
Telephone Directories
http://teldir.com/
http://www.anywho.com/
http://www.bigfoot.com/
http://four11.com/
http://www.infospace.com/

http://www.lookupusa.com/
http://pc411.com/
http://www.switchboard.com/
http://whowhere.com/
http://infousa.com
http://www.hallogram.com/mailers/fonedisc/pro.html

Tennessee Death
http://www.state.tn.us/sos/statelib/pubsvs/death.htm

Tennessee Vital Records
http://www.state.tn.us/health/vr/index.html

Texas Seaport Museum
http://www.phoenix.net/~tsm/default.html

Texas Vital Records
http://www.tdh.state.tx.us/bvs

US GenWeb
http://www.usgenweb.org/

Utah Vital Records
http://hlunix.ex.state.ut.us/bvr/home.html

Vital Records
http://www.vitalchek.com/
http://www.cdc.gov/nchswww/howto/w2w/w2welcom.htm
http://travel.state.gov/vital_records_services.html

Voter Registrations
http://www.merlindata.com
http://www.quickinformer.com
http://kadima.com

Washington Vital Records
http://doh.wa.gov/topics/chs-cert.html

Western Reserve Historical Society
http://www.wrhs.org/

Wisconsin, State Historical Society of
http://www.shsw.wisc.edu/

Wisconsin Vital Records
http://www.dhfs.state.wi.us/vitalrecords/index.htm

Wyoming Vital Records
http://wdhfs.state.wy.us/vital_records/

Yearbooks
http://www.highschool.com

APPENDIX G

Research Work Sheet

Sources

Following is a blank copy of the form referred to in chapter one of *Locating Lost Family Members & Friends*. For information on how to complete this form and its importance to a successful search, see pages 4 and 5.

The form is copyright 1999 by Kathleen W. Hinckley, but you are free to photocopy it for your *personal* use. No use in a printed work is permitted without permission.

How to complete this form and its importance to a successful search is covered in chapter one.

RESEARCH WORK SHEET

Full Name _____
First, middle, last, nickname, maiden name

Spelling Variants of Surname _____

Social Security Number _____

Date and Place of Birth _____
If exact date of birth is unknown; give approximate five-year range

Physical Description _____

Marital Status _____
Name of spouse(s) or ex-spouse(s) and date of marriage(s) and divorce(s), if applicable

Occupations _____

Employers _____
Include dates and addresses if known

Last Known Address _____

_____
As many as possible. If exact address unknown, list city and/or state. Include dates of former addresses.

Prior telephone number(s) _____

Education _____
High school, occupational, college. Include years attended and whether graduated.

Military Service _____
Branch, rank, dates, place of discharge, serial number

Religion _____

Hobbies _____

Financial Status _____

Children: Names, Birth Dates and Birthplaces _____

_____

_____

_____

_____

Name/Address/Telephone of Friends _____

_____

_____

_____

Research Work Sheet (Page 2)

Family Information

For each sibling: name, birth date, last known address, marital status (marriage[s], names of spouse[s], ex-spouse[s]), date and place of death

For parents/setpparents: names, birth dates, last known address(es),marriage (s), dates and places of death
For children: marriages

_____

_____

_____

_____

_____

Signature _____
(Photocopy from marriage record, deeds or court documents)

Index

More Great Books Full of Great Ideas!

The Unpuzzling Your Past Workbook: Essential Forms and Letters for All Genealogists—Now unpuzzling your past is easier than ever using forty-two genealogical forms designed to make organizing, searching, record-keeping and presenting information effortless. *#70327/$15.99/320 pages/paperback*

Unpuzzling Your Past: A Basic Guide to Genealogy—140,000 copies sold! Make uncovering your roots easy with this complete genealogical research guide. You'll find everything you need—handy forms, sample letters and worksheets, census extraction forms, a comprehensive resource section, bibliographies and case studies. Plus, updated information on researching courthouse records, federal government resources and computers on genealogy. *#70301/$14.99/180 pages/paperback*

The Handybook for Genealogists, Ninth Edition—More than 750,000 copies sold! Since 1947, the Handybook has proven itself as the most popular and comprehensive research aid available for tracking down major state and county records essential to genealogists. Save countless hours of your research time by consulting its up-to-date listings of archives, genealogical libraries and societies. State profiles cover history and list sources for maps, census and church records. The county profiles tell you where to find custody records, property records and key addresses. Color maps are included of each state and their counties. *#70411/$34.99/380 pages/60 color maps/hardcover*

First Steps in Genealogy—If you're just stepping into the fascinating field of genealogy, this book will get you off to a successful start. Desmond Walls Allen, a recognized genealogical expert, will teach you step-by-step how to define your goals and uncover facts about the people behind the names and dates. Learn to organize your research with pedigree charts, group sheets and filing systems. Discover what sources are available for research, starting with

your family scrapbook or attic. Also included are sample forms, a resource directory and glossary. *#70400/$14.99/128 pages/paperback*

Organizing Your Family History Search—Few hobbies generate more paperwork than genealogy. Sharon DeBartolo Carmack shows you how to successfully tackle the arduous process of organizing family research, from filing piles of paper to streamlining the process as a whole. With her flexible filing system and special research notebook, she reveals how you can free up time, conduct better research and become a more effective genealogist. *#70425/$16.99/176 pages/paperback*

The Genealogist's Companion & Sourcebook—115,000 copies sold! Uncover promising new sources of information about your family history. This hands-on guide shows you how to get past common obstacles—such as lost public records—and discover new information sources like church and funeral home records, government documents, newspapers and maps. *#70235/$16.99/256 pages/paperback*

A Genealogist's Guide to Discovering Your Female Ancestors—Discover special strategies for overcoming the unique challenges of tracing female genealogy. This comprehensive guide shows you methods for determining maiden names and parental lineage: how to access official documents; plus where to find information unique to women of ethnic origins. Also included is a glossary of terms specific to female genealogy, a detailed bibliography with more than 200 resources, plus and extensive source checklist. *#70386/$17.99/144 pages/paperback*

A Genealogist's Guide to Discovering Your Italian Ancestors—This easy-to-use reference guides you step-by-step through researching your Italian ancestors—as far back as the 1700s! You'll learn how to find—and read—Italian vital records; write letters requesting data from Italian officials; and use American records like census and naturalization records, and family letteres and church records. You'll also find information on

how to read foreign handwriting, and much more. *#70370/$16.99/128 pages/ 42 b&w illus./paperback*

How to Tape Instant Oral Biographies, Second Edition—With fun interviewing techniques and exercises, family members of all ages will learn how to spark memories, recall treasured stories, and relate old family anecdotes, sayings, recipes and more. Comes complete with blank family history sheets and work pages. *#70448/$12.99/144 pages/paperback*

How to Write the Story of Your Life—This friendly guide makes memoir writing an enjoyable undertaking—even if you're a nonwriter. Five hundred "memory sparkers" will help you recall forgotten events in each stage of your life and 100 topic ideas help add variety to your story. Includes excerpts from actual memoirs and plenty of encouragement to keep you moving your story towards completion. *#10132/$14.99/230 pages/paperback*

Writing Family Histories and Memoirs—Your family history and personal stories are too vital to lose. Turn them into a lively record for the next generation with this handy writing reference. You'll find helpful how-to advice on working from memories and interviewing family members, using public records, writing and publishing. *#70295/$14.99/272 pages/paperback*

Writing Life Stories—Creative writing instructor Bill Roorbach explains how you can turn your life's untold stories into vivid personal essays and riveting memoirs. His advice and exercises will open up your memories, help you shape life events into plot lines and craft finely-wrought stories worthy of publication. *#48035/$17.99/224 pages/ hardcover*

Reaching Back—Record life's most meaningful moments to share with future generations. This easy-to-use keepsake edition includes space for family stories, photos, heirlooms, family trees, and helps you research and record you family's unique history. *#70360/$14.99/160 pages/paperback*

Family History Logbook—Weave your personal history into the colorful web of national events. You'll find an extensive list of historical events spanning the years 1900 to 2000, along with a special section to record your own milestones. *#70345/$16.99/224 pages/ paperback*

The Everyday Life Series

You've tracked down vital statistics for your great-great-grandparents, but do you know what their everyday lives were like? These titles will give you a vivid and detailed picture of life in their own time. Learn what your relatives likely wore, what they ate, and how they talked. Social and religious customs, major occupations and family life are all covered. These "slice-of-life" facts will readily round out any family history.

The Writer's Guide to Everyday Life . . .

. . . from Prohibition to World War II
#10450/$18.99/272 pages/hardcover

. . . in Renaissance England
#10484/$18.99/272 pages/hardcover

. . . in Regency and Victorian England
#10545/$18.99/240 pages/hardcover

. . . in the 1800's
#10353/$18.99/320 pages/hardcover

. . . in the Wild West
#10600/$18.99/336 pages/hardcover

. . . in Colonial America
#10640/$14.99/288 pages/paperback

Creating Family Newsletters—This idea-packed book shows you how to write and design family newsletters that will bring "mail box cheer" to your friends and relatives the world over. More than 100 full-color examples—from hand-crafted to computer generated—offer great ideas for creating your own unique newsletters for every occasion. *#10558/$19.99/120 color illus./128 pages/paperback*

Scrapbook Storytelling, Step by Step—Go beyond typical scrapbooking techniques! Here is how to recall your favorite family stories and combine them with cherished photos, collages and illustrations to create unique booklets, albums, gift items and more. *#70450/$19.99/120 color illus./128 pages/paperback*

Publishing Your Family History on the Internet—With this first-ever guide, even if you're a beginning computer user, you can design and publish your own genealogical Web sites. Learn how to display your family history data—including pictures, sounds and video—onto the Web. *#70447/ $19.99/320 pages/140 b&w illus./paperback*

The Internet for Genealogists, Fourth Edition—This completely revised and updated guide to the latest genealogy websites will give you quick access to the resources you need. Includes more than 200 addresses to genealogy sites, libraries, catalogs, maps, gazetteers, bookstores, on-line databases and living persons directories. *#70415/$16.99/192 pages/paperback*

Charting Your Family History: The Legacy Family Tree Software Solution—Now you can organize your genealogical records with ease, thanks to the Legacy Family Tree software on CD-ROM—the most comprehensive and easy-to-use genealogy software on the market today. Legacy allows unlimited data input, viewing of up to seven Family or Pedigree views at one time, over twenty customized reports plus the linking of pictures and sounds to any member of your family tree. System requirements: IBM 486 or faster compatibles, minimum 8MB memory, 20MB hard drive space, Windows 3.1 or Windows 95, VGA or higher. *#70420/$49.95/270 page book with PC compatible CD-ROM*

Families Writing—Here is a book that details why and how to record words that go straight to the heart—the simple, vital words that will speak to those you care most about and to their descendants many years from now. *10294/$14.99/198 pages/paperback*

Turning Life into Fiction—Learn how to turn your life, those of friends and family members, and newspaper accounts into fictional novels and short stories. Through insightful commentary and hands-on exercises, you'll hone the essential skills of creating fiction from journal entries, identifying the memories ripest for development, ethically fictionalizing other people's stories, gaining distance from personal experience and much more. *#48029/$14.99/208 pages/paperback*

How to Have a 48-Hour Day—Get more done and have more fun as you double what you can do in a day! Aslett reveals reasons to be more productive everywhere—and what "production" actually is. You'll learn how to keep accomplishing despite setbacks, ways to boost effectiveness, the things that help your productivity and much more. *#70339/$12.99/160 pages/120 illus./ paperback*

Make Your House Do the Housework, Revised Edition—Take advantage of new work-saving products, materials and approaches to make your house keep itself in order. You'll discover page after page of practical, environmentally-friendly new ideas and methods for minimizing home cleaning and maintenance. *#70293/$14.99/208 pages/215 b&w illus./paperback*

Stephanie Culp's 12-Month Organizer and Project Planner—The projects you're burning to start or yearning to finish will zoom toward accomplishment by using these forms, "To-Do" lists, checklists and calendars. Culp helps you break any project into manageable segments, set deadlines, establish plans and follow them—step by attainable step. *#70274/$12.99/192 pages/paperback*

Don Aslett's Clutter-Free! Finally and Forever—Free yourself of unnecessary stuff that chokes your home and clogs your life! If you feel owned by your belongings, you'll discover incredible excuses people use for allowing clutter, how to beat the "no-time" excuse, how to determine what's junk, how to prevent recluttering and much more! *#70306/$12.99/224 pages/50 illus./paperback*

Confessions of a Happily Organized Family—Learn how to make your mornings peaceful, chores more fun and mealtime more relaxing by getting the whole family organized. *#70338/$11.99/240 pages/paperback*

Clutter's Last Stand—You think you're organized, yet closets bulge around you. Get out of clutter denial with loads of practical advice. *#01122/$12.99/280 pages/paperback*

Office Clutter Cure—Discover how to clear out office clutter—overflowing "in" boxes, messy desks and bulging filing cabinets. Don Aslett offers a cure for every kind of office clutter that hinders productivity—even mental clutter like gossip and office politics. *#70296/$10.99/192 pages/175 b&w illus./paperback*

It's Here . . . Somewhere—Need help getting and keeping your busy household in order? This book provides step-by-step instruction on how to get more places out of spaces with a room-by-room approach to organization. *#10214/$10.99/192 pages/50 b&w illus./paperback*

How to Get Organized When You Don't Have the Time—You keep meaning to organize the closet and clean out the garage, but who has the time? Culp combines proven time-management principles with practical ideas to help you clean up key trouble spots in a hurry. *#01354/$14.99/216 pages/paperback*

How to Conquer Clutter—Think of this book as a "first aide guide" for when you wake up and find that clutter has once again taken over every inch of available space you have. You'll get insightful hints from A to Z on how to free yourself from clutter's grasp. *#10119/$12.99/184 pages/paperback*